Time It Was

with ✦ · ♡ · hope

Leonard

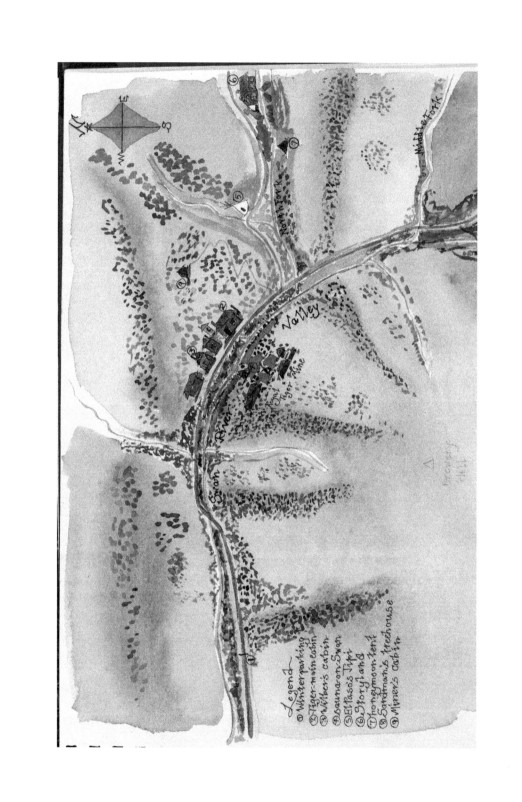

Legend
① Winter parking
② Tiger-main cabin
③ Wither's cabin
④ Sauna-on-Swan
⑤ El Paseo's Tipi
⑥ Storyland
⑦ Honeymoon Tent
⑧ Sandmouth treehouse
⑨ Miner's cabin

TIME IT WAS

MEMOIR OF A MODERN PIONEER

NONNIE THOMPSON

BAY TREE PUBLISHING, LLC
PT. RICHMOND, CALIFORNIA

© 2017 Nonnie Thompson

This is a work of creative nonfiction. Events are portrayed to the best of the author's memory. Some names have been changed to protect the privacy of the people involved.

Library of Congress Cataloging-in-Publication Data

Names: Thompson, Nonnie, author.
Title: Time it was : memoir of a modern pioneer / Nonnie Thompson.
Other titles: Memoir of a modern pioneer
Description: Pt. Richmond, California : Bay Tree Publishing, LLC, [2017]
Identifiers: LCCN 2017034375 | ISBN 9780996676557 (pbk.)
Subjects: LCSH: Thompson, Nonnie. | Breckinridge Region (Co.)--Social life and customs--20th century. | Hippies--West (U.S.)--Biography. | Neumann, Wilber. | Mountain life--Colorado. | Hippies--West (U.S.)--Social life and customs--20th century. | Country life--West (U.S.) | Americans--British Columbia--Biography. | Nineteen seventies. | Women--West (U.S.)--Biography.
Classification: LCC F784.B7 T66 2017 | DDC 978.8/45--dc23
LC record available at https://lccn.loc.gov/2017034375

Dedicated to love:
To David, whose patience and support allowed this catharsis.
To Wyatt, whose passion and knowing encouraged the telling.

It should not be denied... that being footloose has always exhilarated us. It is associated in our minds... with absolute freedom, and the road has always led West.
—Wallace Stegner

CHAPTER ONE

For the first time since running away from home, I was completely alone. Standing on the snowy mountain highway where
the bus from Denver had dropped me off, I watched the February
sun set behind the western peaks. Its shadow cast an icy gray across
the valley. Behind the sign announcing the entrance to "Frisco,
Colorado—Elevation 9,254 feet," a café glowed invitingly. I had
spent almost all of my cash on the bus ride; I couldn't afford a
hot meal and didn't dare waste the waning daylight. My destination was Breckenridge, a ski town of rumored possibilities, just a
few miles south. Hitchhiking was my only option, but the traffic
was sparse on Route 9. The cars, pickups, and delivery trucks only

accelerated as they left Frisco and passed me, without a glance. I assessed my situation. The trappings of my life slumped in an army knapsack and three brown paper bags in the gravelly snowdrift at my feet. I mentally reviewed my warmer clothing: Fair Isle sweaters, a rainbow of turtlenecks, ragg wool socks, and waffle-weave long johns. I was sure I'd brought the wool socks my mom had knit for me. (Or had I?) My high-heeled boots and sky-blue ski parka kept me warm, for now, but that would change quickly with the dropping temperature.

Hitching my way to a fresh start, I was determined yet ill equipped. For three months, I had bounced from family to friends, moving ever west. I'd slept on floors, bummed meals, and taken little responsibility for my eager escape from home. I'd been a slacker, until I awoke curled up next to the furnace in a Denver flophouse and realized I had betrayed my dream. My dream of pursuing my passion. Now, in my quest for freedom, I was blazing a clean trail. For the first time in my seventeen years, no comfort of friend or contact awaited me. Not for the first time, I began to feel afraid.

On cue with my fears, a stranger approached, walking with the swagger of youthful confidence and the weight of the lumpy duffle on his back. Ice-stiffened bell-bottoms and a stained Mexican shirt showed under his long Army Surplus coat. Black ringlets tumbled onto his shoulders and swayed to cover his face, his downcast eyes picking a path through the jumble of filthy snow. As he closed the gap between us, I could see he was road-worn. My gaze lowered to his feet as he ambled onto my snowdrift.

"Hey there, headin' to Breckenridge?" he stammered, sounding frozen or stoned, or both.

I nodded, hesitant and unsure in my response. It was 1971. Free love and psychos ran wild in these parts. A young woman on a dark and lonely road could conjure myriad scenarios of danger (Charlie Manson, for one) and they all shot through my mind in vivid detail.

"My friends say it's bitchin'," he continued. "I'm Matthew, just rolled in from New York."

"I'm Nonnie, from Jackson Hole," I offered. Nothing more.

"Let's hitch together," he said. "You can crash with my friends, for sure."

When I looked up, his youth surprised me. His face was nice-looking, almost pretty. Brown eyes twinkled under dense lashes, rosy putty-soft cheeks widened to make way for an electric grin. I wondered: If it came to it, would I have to protect him?

"Yeah, right on," I conceded, remembering that my instincts had gotten me this far.

Matthew seemed harmless, and his apparent connections in Breckenridge made him my new best friend. As the evening deepened along with a biting cold, I was glad to have the company. While we waited, we shared the adventures of our oh-so-young lives. We stood like ice sculptures, our mittened hands crammed securely into warm armpits.

"Man, what a trip it was, getting here!" He wove his tale. "I hitched, and met some freaks!" He hesitated in the gloaming, as if in the grip of a flashback. "Yeah, *really fuckin' freaky* freaks! There's some weird shit going on in the Midwest, lemme tell ya. I tried to stay clear of the pigs. But they're *everywhere*. Ya know?"

"Yeah," I offered. "Last spring, we did a road trip to see the Jefferson Airplane. We dropped acid before the concert. It was bitchin'," until the pigs stopped our van. Totally freaked us out." These were our war stories, the shared past through which we formed our kinships.

"Martin and Tommy, they're my bros in Breckenridge," Matthew said, his cool confidence giving me hope. "Well, they're kinda older than me, but we hung out back in Pelham, in New York. Anyway, all those guys did Woodstock, man. It was a total groove. Saw Hendrix, Joplin, and *everybody*. Now they've scored an old mining cabin near Breckenridge. Put visqueen over the windows, scored an old cook stove, furniture, the whole shit. They've got it all together!" As he described the scene, I began to believe. "Yeah, you can crash with us, for sure."

His metered, mellow style made him seem somehow trustworthy, and his youthful bravado made me grin. I liked him. He could be the little brother I'd never had but always wanted. He was following the promise of nirvana from the eastern seaboard to the Rocky Mountains. He had fairytale plans built on stories he'd heard: a mountain cottage, a toasty hearth, a gathering of drug-addled youth. His Alice's Wonderland of colorful and mysterious characters drew me too. As another hippie on a quest, I welcomed his version of the vision. *"I am he as you are he as you are me and we are all together…"*

"We'd better get serious about catching a ride," I said. A dank night had replaced the winter sun's weak but cheery glow, and I shivered anew. "You're just gonna hafta hide." Without a word, he bounded over the snow bank like a sprite, landing in the snowplow scree with a thud and a moan. We laughed.

As I kept an eye on the traffic, my nose filled up with piny coolness and my ears with forest scamperings. A certain comfort. Before long an old pickup slowed and a door swung open, creaking with ice. I jumped into the cab, sending bags and packs before me. Matthew chucked his duffle in the bed and slid in beside me as the unwitting cowboy continued his evening drive. No need for more than basic pleasantries. *Hey, colder than a witch's tit, ain't it?* And *Fer sure, man, thanks for the ride.* He knew we'd all be going to Breckenridge, pretty much the end of the road.

I was glad to be in the warm truck, and moving again. Hot air blasted from unseen vents and I massaged my tingling fingers. Laying my head back on the seat, I gazed up through the rear window. Above us, a zillion starlights punctured the black sky. Even as I contemplated the mysteries ahead, I was glad to be back in the country, away from the city lights and the peopled crush of Denver. Through the windshield, the old two-lane highway dipped and swayed in the headlights. As we bounced ahead, the glow from houses on the valley floor made me wonder about my next home. And the home I'd left behind with such urgency.

My mind tumbled across two thousand miles; to late fall on

Cape Cod. The watercolor brilliance of summer had been washed from the marsh, blown out by a relentless cold rain whose pummeling served to equalize the pressure raging inside our once-vibrant summerhouse. My earsplitting anger at my parents was amplified for impact over R&B on the stereo and wind through the seams. It burst through the glass walls and sailed over the blue inlet, over the golden sea grass, was lost in the breakers of the Atlantic Ocean. Still they didn't seem to hear. I was frustrated and defeated, explosive and cruel, but not for the usual adolescent reasons. At a time when American youth were supposedly pushing back from authority, I was desperately seeking it. My friends were finishing prep school, heading for prestigious colleges, tracked by ambitious parents. But I was being encouraged to take my annoying sixteen-year-old self on the road.

This shouldn't have been a surprise, given our family history. From age eleven to fourteen, my friends and I had been sent into New York City alone, our borrowed handbags stuffed with parental credit cards, our only instructions: "Stay on Fifth Ave." When I was fourteen, Daddy dragged us from our home, friends, and schools to travel the farthest reaches of the world for a year. He courted danger and distraction on a whim, with four girls and our mother in tow. Sometimes I even wondered if he was actually trying to lose us.

My two older sisters had since fled to their own futures, while my little sister hid in the shadow of my outrageous behavior. But no matter what I tried, I could not get my parents to care. They had given up on me, but I threw one last challenge at them. I told them I was going to quit school. No response. I said I could take care of myself. Nothing. I told them that, as a minor, I needed parental permission to drop out. Daddy looked up, got up, and drove straight to the school to sign my release. Then he gave me fifty bucks and an army rucksack. Just like that, he eliminated, or liberated, another daughter.

So, on a dull November morning, instead of heading to Nauset Regional High School, I packed my belongings like a child with a bandanna-on-a-stick. With the full torment of my young soul, I went to my parents to announce that I didn't need them, that I was leaving. I knew they would be sitting comfortably in the living room with their morning coffee. As my footfalls echoed on the spiral staircase and my cumbersome pack bumped narrow walls, my heart and brain raced ahead. Was I really ready? Was leaving the only answer? But as I entered the room, the familiar scene steeled my resolve. Beyond my parents and through the fragile glass walls, winter grays scudded over green marsh. I saw geese fighting headwinds, water-whipping white in the ebb tide, and felt the lure of my own survival. The chance for conciliation was past. I was on my way.

"SCREW YOU, I'm leaving!!" I crowed. Clearly annoyed by the interruption, they reacted as expected.

"Well, you know you'll to have to face the consequences of your choices." Daddy's monotone proved his apathy, and his calm turned my conflict into unbridled fury. This was his mind-game now, his win. I staggered at the weight of it.

"It'll be better out there." I recovered the full force of my emotions. I couldn't give in.

"Life is fraught," Mommy whispered, her standard retort, as she stood and left the room, her classic reaction.

"So, where'll you go?" Daddy asked, standing his ground.

"Back to Wyoming," I told him, my original plan. I had seen the freedom movement on TV, in the nightly news. I'd tasted, ingested, and craved the western frontiers since our past year living in Jackson Hole. I knew I could be myself out there.

"Go, then..." he said, his stoic apathy betraying a twinkle of envy. I gasped at his dismissal, but pride fueled my departure. I knew he dreamed of shaking off his children, following his own wanderlust over the far horizon. He knew I was following my heart. I would do what he couldn't. I resolved to go.

As I strode down our dirt drive, away from the discomfort of home, I turned to see Daddy, frozen on the walk. Mommy was nowhere in sight. I hefted my burden and increased my pace. The

Atlantic Ocean was at my back. Ahead and to the west, I knew, a new home with a caring "family" of like-minded misfits awaited. I was sure I was doing the right thing, yet I wondered. What if Daddy had called me back, or Mommy had reached out? But they hadn't. My only option, I felt, was to get away. Far away.

Of course, foremost among my baggage, flung headlong into the pickup that now hurtled toward Breckenridge, were traits granted to me by the parents I was fleeing: my father's resilience and impulsive exploring, my mother's puritan sensibility. And in my resolve was the fantasy of their regret—I hoped they'd despaired at my leaving. (Mommy *did* cry some nights in private, I later learned, but Daddy maintained the steely conviction that consequences would serve to punish my brazen independence.)

With my surviving dignity and meager possessions, I'd set off for Wyoming. Somewhere along the way, I'd veered to Colorado, to Denver, and now this. Even as I faced the unknowns at the end of this lonely highway, I believed they held my better future. And with Matthew, my new brother, the first of my new family, by my side, I welcomed it eagerly.

Breckenridge was already asleep, put to bed on a winter's weeknight, when the cowboy dropped us off. By the dimly lit outlines of false-fronted stores, Matthew squinted at the faded map he clutched in a sodden mitten. I double-checked his landmarks over his shoulder as we trudged out of town on a trail, knee deep in crusty snow. We moved in silent focus. Soon the trail disappeared, the forest thickened and progress became slow and hard. Matthew tracked a faint rift in the snow, barely visible by pale starlight. His mumblings and our crunching footfalls produced the only sounds. The trail was unused and steep, and my bags were cumbersome, the paper now damp. Between the shadows and my imagination, the trees morphed into bears or untoward men, sounds drifted, amplified and distorted. I began to question Matthew's judgment—and mine. But when we saw a dim glow in the trees, my clammy skin stopped crawling and my hyper-breathing eased.

Suddenly, the forest was thick with smoke, and a hazy veil eventually gave way to a log cabin. The familiar rhythm of rock 'n' roll drew us in. Matthew and I increased our pace, tripping over a junk-littered snowfield toward the rough-hewn and tiny cabin. Our bumbling approach cued a small pack of dogs, soon barking and running at us rambunctiously. As we lurched onto a cluttered landing, the door cracked open, and then swung wide with the force of jubilation. I paused in the shadows as Matthew was greeted by a motley clutch. It was a joyous reunion, lots of laughing, hair and beads flying.

Martin, Tommy, and Cheryl looked me over cautiously. Maybe it was my uptown rags: the fancy ski parka, the dainty boots. Matthew introduced me as "Nonnie, from Wyoming, we hitched in together." I was welcomed inside, but as the heavy door swung closed, the group's attention immediately returned to their Pelham pal, a long-lost link to home. A buzzing swarm of gossip, news, and hugs took hold until they remembered their dinner, already set on the cable spool table.

We gathered around it on tree stumps, wooden chairs, and five-gallon buckets. Settling in, I watched the group who were all about my age. They were dressed colorfully like gypsies adorned with embroidery, stained by use, and worn in comfort. In the dim light, their serene faces and languid movements betrayed the effects of a pre-dinner joint. The scent of irregular hygiene, wood and pot smoke, incense and kerosene was pungent, as if it had drenched the tattered furniture and Indian spreads hanging about. Dinner, brown rice and overcooked vegetables drowned in Tamari, was served in bowls with chopsticks. The water in my mug was fresh clear nectar, skimmed from a hole chopped into the frozen stream—at great effort, I was told.

My fellow diners ate with speed and yummy sounds. Barely speaking, they chortled into their bowls. I examined the group. Tommy's jet-black hair hung tight past his shoulders, resting on a salvaged Tyrolean sweater that clung like a cape at his neck. His dark and patchy beard had a silken sheen that reflected the lamplight.

Cheryl's bright eyes and ruddy cheeks animated her face perched atop a carrot-orange turtleneck. She eyed the diners, especially Martin, assessing their pleasure at her meal. Martin – taller, older, and haughtier – appeared to be the leader, if there was one, and Cheryl's old man. His brown hair was wispy and thick, pulled back from his long forehead and tied with a flowered ribbon. His banter was quick and sharp. A chopstick novice, I stared at my bowl. My stomach rumbled and my hand quivered. Just as I hesitated, Martin threw down his chopsticks and went after his grains with a trowel-like hand. Instantly I was liberated and did the same.

With my hands in my rice and a self-satisfied grunt rising from my throat, I wondered if for the first time I was experiencing real freedom from my past, from the family I hadn't chosen. This meal was a workshop for me—an unexpected introduction to what my new life could be—and I found an accepting comfort in the loving, chaotic scene. In the midst of strangers, as the potbelly stove warmed the room and dried my heavy socks, I began to relax. It felt like those times in high school hanging out at home when your parents weren't around, stoned and relaxed. Yet these hippies were on their own, far from parents and rules, living a life they'd created and owned. I drifted, deeper into the moment and farther from my past. Music pulsed from speakers somewhere and, with a toke and a thread of vague conversation, we sank into the evening.

Chapter Two

Awakening to the alpenglow and the noisy slumber of my new friends, I was cold again. The cook stove had lost the fire in its belly. The air in the cabin was crisp, too cold for my light-cotton sleeping bag, now frozen to the hard plank floor. I spent a few minutes blowing impressive smoke rings with my frosty breath, then scanned the floor for kindling. I gradually became aware of strangers sleeping here and there. Groovy freaks, yes, but strangers nonetheless. From one of the lofts came the sound of a faint but still screaming guitar. The tape player was hooked up to a car battery, and it sounded like Zeppelin had been performing all night in endless 8-track limbo.

"You been learnin', baby, I been learnin',
All them good times, baby, baby, I been yearnin'...
Wanna whole lotta love, wanna whole lotta love, ..."

Drifting to the familiar tune, I thought of Daddy's radio stations, WICC-AM Top 40 and WJZZ-FM Jazz, which kept us stocked with music on LP and reel-to-reel. Music formed the backbeat of my childhood memories. Between my parents, my three sisters, and me, the turntable rarely stopped spinning. Brubeck, Supremes, Mozart, and Simon & Garfunkel wafted through the rafters of our 1725 Connecticut saltbox. At Mommy's knee, we memorized every word of Broadway hits like *Gigi, My Fair Lady,* along with Fred Astaire classics like "The Way You Look Tonight" and "Cheek to Cheek." AM radio played during carpool in the Country Squire. On longer road trips, we'd rouse a chorus of Yale Glee Club songs, or Joan Baez and Beatles hits. Music bound us together and gave us the joy of soulful expression.

I thought of my sisters, each now adrift on her own sea. How were they, and did they think of me? Dede was away at college. Betsy was in love with a bad boyfriend in Wyoming. Both were officially adults, and officially on their own. The last time I'd seen Sarah, my younger sister, she was a freshman at Nauset Regional. What would they think of my new life? It might be months before we reconnected again, but they were still my kindred spirits. In that moment I missed our childhood, the fantastic lie we lived while our world fell apart.

If you need me, call me. No matter where you are, no matter how far.
Don't worry, baby, Just call my name, I'll be there in a hurry, You
don't have to worry...

When I peeled my bag off the frozen floor and sat up in my corner, raw sunlight streamed through the visqueen and I could see that last night's soft kerosene light had been kind to the general ambiance. The cabin wasn't quite as charming as my first impressions had indicated. Stained cardboard boxes filled one corner. In another, wooden crates held 8-tracks and LPs, and a road-worn guitar leaned in dusty abandon. Another crate held mittens, hats, and gaiters, and a lidded crock near dog bowls held dog food, I guessed. On the windows, old blankets hung from roofing nails and, pulled aside with a length of twine, did give the room a certain coziness. The cast-iron cook stove stood in central importance. I saw wooden spoons and panhandles, the remnants of last night's dinner making. I looked around for the sink and thought about getting to work.

But first, I had to pee. It was early, and the uncoolness of waking anyone was a genuine concern. Eventually, the urge overcame me and I hopped up, pulled my boots over my long johns, and grabbed my flimsy jacket. A mêlée of anxious dogs rose up with me and together we tumbled through the door, down the trail to the rickety old outhouse. I hated outhouses, the stench and the unknown, but Mother Nature called. Tearing open the thin door, I climbed onto the seat and squatted to my great relief. The dogs milled about doing their own business, then raced me back to the cabin's relative warmth. We were ready for the day to begin.

Back inside, Cheryl emerged from the loft. Disheveled and groggy, she looked younger and smaller than she had the night before. Her hair hung greasy to her shoulders, her waffle-weave long johns and ragg socks stiff with dirt, and she was pale. She stared back at me, probably seeing a mirror image. As she found kindling, wadded up paper, grabbed the Diamond matches, and lit the cook stove, she seemed annoyed. She grunted and sighed as she dug out glass jars of granola and dried apricots from makeshift shelves behind exotic cloths. Was she pissed off about something? Suddenly, she turned and gave me a big, broken-toothed grin.

"Oh, fuck it," she said. "Let's go on down to the Gold Pan for coffee." I wasn't much of a coffee drinker, but it sounded like a warm and active plan. She motioned at my little nest. "You're gonna wanna get your shit off the floor, before the dogs decide to bed down in it." I gathered my paltry possessions on my yellow sleeping bag, rolled it up and propped it on a shelf. We both pulled on pants: hers patched overalls, mine bell-bottom jeans, and boots: hers hiking, mine heeled. And our coats: hers warm, mine... what? Cheryl laughed and threw me a big down Army jacket. She stoked the stove, barked at the dogs to stay, and threw open the door to the day.

The trail was short, unlike the one from the night before, and opened onto Ski Hill Road. Bounding over the snow bank and onto the hard-packed road, Cheryl and I came face-to-face with ski-racked station wagons, crawling to their alpine destination and the resort at Peak 8. Clean Midwestern families peered at us from under fur caps. They reminded me of my past, and the fact of not being confined in a wagon with my family put an extra spring in my step. I threw back my shoulders and breathed in the fresh morning freedom. We walked downhill against the traffic – figuratively and literally moving in opposing directions.

Breckenridge's Main Street appeared to be gearing up for a rich man's boom. Weathered wood offset by glossy, rainbow-hued Victorian trim showed the extent of the renovations and the money invested. A real estate office, ski shop, and the visitor's center wrapped the first corner. Empty lots along Main Street had crisp Sold stickers plastered over tired For Sale signs, and glossy hotel and condo posters decorated their lot lines. As soon as the ground thawed, backhoes and carpenters would invade. Cheryl babbled a running commentary on our surroundings.

"This is a real fucking tourist trap," she proclaimed. "They hate us hippies, so we try to ignore them," she continued. "But the ski boom, building boom, keeps all the freaks that want to work in money, so we don't complain and keep to ourselves. They leave us alone, we build their fantasies!"

We turned left at Main Street, hopped onto the boardwalk and into the Gold Pan Saloon. We were barely through the door, my eyes still adjusting to the dark, when a woman perched on a barstool accosted us. The crusty owner of the Gold Pan, Nikki knew Cheryl was only nineteen and yelled a husky-voiced reminder of Colorado's drinking law. We scooted through, Cheryl snickering and mumbling a retort. She, apparently, was my kind of rabble-rouser, bucking rules without breaking them. I snickered along with her and tried to keep up. The stale scent of beer and cigarettes hung in the air. Heavy oak tables and chairs were pushed aside for mopping. Wagon wheel chandeliers hung from high ceilings. We turned past the bar, a temple of carved oak and beveled mirrors, pushing through the saloon doors and into the café.

I saw at once that this was the local hangout. Besides a few tourists loading up on bacon and eggs before hitting the slopes, the tables were encircled with young longhairs. Large men lounged on skinny diner chairs, legs and arms akimbo, winter layers shed and hats removed from matted hair. The tables were littered with their bottomless cups of coffee and the plated remnants of breakfast, golden yolk and rosy ketchup smears. As they bandied county news, the small dining room echoed with their stoned amusement.

Cheryl stepped to a central spot and commanded their attention. "This is Nonnie from Jackson Hole," she pronounced, and I met everyone, gathering a list of nicknames and squatting spots in the county. The scent of wood, coal, and pot smoke was pervasive, and familiar. I learned that Bien, Lucky, El Paso, Tinker, Tipi Chuck, and Boogie Paul lived in cabins and tipis in old mine towns called Blue River, Wakefield, Muggins, and Brown's Gulch. Apparently, I was staying in the Peak 8 Cabin with Cheryl and the Pelham boys. Some settlements included women. All had dogs. A few of the men lived discreetly in the unfinished high-class condos they were building, though it was hard to imagine anyone in this funky clan being discreet. We sat among them, horned in on their ramblings. They were enthused, passionate, and embracing life, wild but sincere. This was the community I'd yearned for. I soaked it in, trying to associate names and faces.

Waitresses and sisters Janet Planet and Patty Day worked the room and nodded hello, smiling from behind lip-locked Camels. Nikki and her husband, kindly old Vern, may have owned the Gold Pan, but Janet and Patty ran the place, two hard-drinkin' and smokin' gals from Texas. You didn't cross or question them.

When my new friends headed off to jobs and whatnot, Cheryl and I grabbed a table in the back. We ordered coffees and fries from Janet, her gravelly voice and pencil-studded braid marking her seniority. When our coats were off, Cheryl fixed us coffees that tasted like melted coffee ice cream, heated to a warming elixir. Then she began her saga: where she was from, why she was here, and mostly what she wanted. Irreverent and funny, she had an easy style, a blunt honesty and an unconscious lisp. I liked her, and as it turned out, she was more like me than I'd imagined.

"I came here from Oakland. My folks threw me out so they wouldn't have to pay for college. I ended up in Oklahoma with my grandparents, didn't know what else to do. But that place was creepy, small town paranoia and all." Cheryl paused her forlorn tale, looking me over. "Hey, we gotta get you some new threads," she said. "*You* look like a fucking narc."

I knew she was right. With my fashion jeans, slick skiwear, and bright Indian tops, I did have a too-slick look, more "Hippie Chic." I didn't want it to be obvious that my parents had money, that I'd had privileges, or that I'd shunned them all to live free and poor. But the truth was: My clothes were new, from head shops in Provincetown and ski shops in Jackson Hole, bought with my parents' credit cards. I needed to get some new, old clothes right away.

"So I split from Okie and hitched to Vermont," she continued. "That's where I met Martin and Tommy. . . Man, *that* place was full of cool space cadets. They had driven their van up from New York, but Martin had the bitchin' idea to go hang out in Jamaica and get Rasta. So we went back to New York and hung out at Idlewild looking for a flight to the islands. Man what a trip. We ended up hitching a ride on a private plane, probably a drug dealer's, right into Negril. We lived on the beach for months, smoked the best ganja, until we were thrown out.

"Breckenridge has been bitchin'." But I'm a California girl, not really into this endless cold and kind of over the whole dirty cabin thing. I'm ready to throw open the windows and bring in buckets of wildflowers. I hear that's still a few months off." As Cheryl loosened up, I was having fun, learning lots and feeling welcome. She was excited to have a new girl in town—there were just a few, it seemed—and it'd been a long winter already taking care of the men. Like the boomtowns of the old west, Breckenridge had a short-timers' boom 'n' bust mentality that sat well with single guys. They'd flocked here for fast money, hard drinking, and good drugs, but, she assured me, they were starting to settle down.

We finished up, paid Planet, and headed out into the chill. Cheryl suggested we head back to Peak 8 and smoke a fatty.

As we walked back up the hill and across the trail, I took in the peaks, the foothills, and the town, the aura of my new home. The false-fronts from last night were enlivened by the light of day. The spirits and hope of gold-miners revived. This time it was in the simple expectations of this new brand of squatters: Pay dirt meant freedom. Rather than rushing for gold and building a fortune, these folks were restoring the past and growing a community. A young community, one that received newcomers gratefully, had welcomed me. Their generosity fed my faith that I would be okay. Any fear for my safety had disappeared. By midday on my first day in Breckenridge, I knew that I had found a home and that, barring any dramatic disappointments, this was a place I would come to know intimately.

Chapter Three

Winter held Breckenridge in its bitter grip, even as lower elevations along Colorado's Front Range erupted in sunset-mauve crocuses and sunrise-yellow daffodils. At 9,600 feet, grays and browns dominated. The only red emanated from the woodstove embers; the only blue filled the mountain sky. The short days were cold and dry. Storms rolled through, pushing wind through cracks in the hastily winterized Peak 8 cabin. Powdery snow sifted through chinks and settled lightly in whorls on the cold floor. Some mornings we'd wake to find the cabin's exterior buried in drifts that reached towards the eaves, the path to the outhouse filled in and the trail to the road disappeared in the night.

The Peak 8 men, now including Matthew, clomped out to work early, when there was work they were willing to do. They had proved to be lazy and discriminating, in a funny and endearing way. So Cheryl and I would dig ourselves out, throwing fresh snow ever higher over growing trash piles. To stay warm and feed the hungry crew, we would bake, making a dozen loaves of hearty bread in an afternoon. Covered in flour up to our elbows, we'd knead and roll and knead again. We spent those long quiet days gossiping and laughing, sharing intimate high school stories. If we were flush with stash, we'd bake psychedelic brownies and laugh all the harder.

My muscles hardened from the kneading, skiing, and shoveling. My shoulders grew broader from chopping wood and picking holes in the icy stream for fresh water, and I found great satisfaction in the accumulated results of my hard work. I hoped I was maturing into the pioneer woman of my ancestors' days. I savored stories of the way people had survived in these mountains for centuries. Back before snowplows cleared the roads, before electricity lit and gas warmed the homes.

Fortunes had been made and lost by intrepid squatters in these parts since the summer of 1859, when gold was discovered along the Blue River. A base camp was established, and that year the Gold Pan Saloon was built, a rough-and-ready miners' bar. The first white settlement on Colorado's Western Slope, Breckenridge boomed with a prospectors' and speculators' community that swelled to 1,657 by 1880. By the early 1900s, the mining boom was going bust, a decline that continued until the Blue and Swan Rivers finally shut down their mining operations during World War II. Deserted and forgotten, Summit County was a ghost of its former self, with hundreds of historic buildings sitting vacant, mostly simple mining shanties and log cabins. When I arrived in 1971, the Breckenridge population stood at 548, not counting the scores of hippies now squatting in its hills.

Like the miners of yore, we toiled by day, drank hard, and rose hell late into the night. None of which prevented me from getting an early start on the day. When the sun rose, the scent of running pinesap and the trickle of melting snow made me restless to explore. As weather allowed, I'd grab a pair of cross-country skis and head out. Sometimes Matthew would come along—he wasn't one for a regular job, but he loved an adventure—sometimes Cheryl or Tommy would accompany me. I knew better than to ski alone into the wilderness. Unfamiliar with long, thin wooden skis, bamboo poles, and small leather boots, I tromped and skittered around. My new sport had me spending plenty of time hauling my butt off the snow and hanging around in wet jeans before I got any good at it. For weeks, we roamed the hills, slipping deep into the woods as we hunted for squatters' cabins.

One weekend morning, Matthew and I followed the Blue River to a bend where the scents and sounds signaled the presence of a nearby settlement. Wood smoke blanketed the trees and the howling of dogs, echoing in the dense forest, announced our arrival. A pile of rusting mechanical parts rose from the receding snowdrifts, proof of the coming spring. Finally a cabin appeared, patched with tarpaper and corrugated tin. Layers of visqueen covered window openings where glass had busted out or never been. A stovepipe pushed through the roof sheeted with tin. Fatheaded roofing nails and strips of cedar held it all in place. A recent renovation, we knew, the patching would last until spring thaw could sort things out.

The door opened on the Wakefield Mine cabin and Brother Paul welcomed us like long lost brethren. Visiting was a pastime in the county. Folks valued a day spent sitting a spell with friends, new and old. Tasks were shared, the work made light by many hands, along with fat fingers of pot.

Bertie Ray, Roger, Andi, and Paul were mid-project, so we tucked in to an afternoon of cooking, chopping, crafting, and improving. Matthew helped Roger finish sealing their tiny sauna, a makeshift cleansing unit. We all dreamed of the luxurious times ahead. Bert was filling the woodpile, so I chopped kindling for morning starters. The tools were always sharp and stout in these self-surviving homes, and the larders were always stocked, as stores were far away and travel often dicey. It wouldn't do to run out of honey in a blizzard.

The Wakefield folks were from Denton, Texas, college pals who'd made a break to the north. They'd started a drywall business in the burgeoning ski area and had finished their cabin with a lightening sheen of sheet rock. High-energy and productive, they were spirited, warm, and welcoming. The day ended with an early dinner of brown rice and veggies. Roger and Paul picked up a guitar and harmonica, and the lot of us sang Texan tunes. We found our way home in the dark, dragging skis and happy highs back to town.

Personalities and goals fit uniquely into each cabin, I discovered, and each supplied a special skill to the boomtown growth. At Brown's Gulch, New Jersey roofers Bernie, Tipi Chuck, Lionel, and Boogie Paul settled around beautiful Annie. They were a little rough, but mellow and very funny, and they always had a fatty and a story of high adventure. Jim and Kathy lived at the Muggins Mine in a school bus, with Janet Planet. Theirs was a peaceful and nurtured home. In Jumbo, there was a girls' club comprised of Sandra, her toddler daughter, Vala, and Joyce.

Hailing from disparate regions and backgrounds, my new friends in and around the valley had blown off family, education, and traditional society for a culture of their own making. They didn't talk of home. Like frontiersmen, they were miles and months removed from their pasts. Their tales centered on the unique journeys that had brought them to Breckenridge. On mishaps and miracles, hilarious or tragic, all spoke with passion, and I felt safe in the easy rapport. My place in their midst was accepted, my story not unlike theirs.

Music was central to our lives. News flowed of bands coming to town, to Keystone, Aspen, Boulder. The Allman Brothers and The Youngbloods would be rockin' the Mile High Raceway, Jethro Tull at Red Rocks, and Dan Hicks and His Hot Licks at Tulagi's in Boulder, for starters. Road trips were brainstormed, plans laid. Latest rock and country releases were played and critiqued. The Temptations, Cat Stevens, Little Feat, Carole King, and Marvin Gaye all had new albums, and Joplin's postmortem LP *Pearl* had just been released. The sounds of Buffalo Springfield, The Rolling Stones, Grateful Dead, Ten Years After, and Steve Miller were in constant stream. We had no TV or radio, and no need for them. We played the tunes we owned over and over again. Selection was pivotal, as were lyrics. Some were our battle cries, or our poetry, our meditation, or just the words that could "blow your mind, turn your head around." Music defined us. Our angst and our passion, along with the power of our freedom, came through in words we would have written, if we could. The artists were living the same lives and trucking the same torturous, fantastic trail as we were. And they were expanding and exploring their feelings with the same drugs.

Hot gossip was urgent and relevant: who was bedding whom, who was evading the sheriff, where folks were working. News of ski area jobs were good, but low priority. Men and women worked together on the ski area or nearby hotel project. Building by building, project by project, they were transforming the mountain from an old mining site into a modern ski resort. Working for the Man, the Establishment Man, was their vocation but their hearts were in the hills and plans for spring. The bright colors and fragrant thawing would be on us soon. Reticent snow was thin and crunchy, storms were infrequent, and the earth burst forth in patches.

The women intrigued me, calling up the centuries' old craft of wilderness pioneers and working tirelessly to carve out and sustain their rough-hewn lives. I found something to admire and glean from each and every one. Bound by the hardship of a lingering storm or lay-off, the pleasures of a peyote shipment or a sweet mountain ascent, we clung together like a school clique or a minority sect. Ours was a harsh life not suited to most women of the time: tough and sweet, nurturing and resilient. We took on all that the men would, and could equally be counted on for a jump-start, a birthday cake, a roaring fire, or an embroidered patch on a jean jacket. There were few of us that first winter, mostly unattached and curious. We were a team, experimenting with and sharing the new rules of homesteading. We were goddesses and we wanted for nothing.

In the meantime, Cheryl and I waited tables at the Gold Pan when Planet or Patty needed a break. In the back near the kitchen was a long table, littered with ashtrays and French fry or sundae dishes. When our friends weren't working, that's where they'd hang out. Our half-smoked Camels burned in the tray, awaiting our breaks between customers. It was an easy job: part hanging out, part yelling orders to the grumpy chef, and part hustling to keep up. We served the skiers, tourists, and hippies with equal aplomb.

Evenings at the Gold Pan Saloon, we partied (when Nikki was off duty) with our friends as they passed through town on their way from work to their cabins. Paydays were always an occasion for irreverent yet innocent fun. Warm and loose, we drifted from table to dance floor. With guys outnumbering the girls by ten-to-one, we were novelties and reveled in it. Working hard by day, we were princesses by night, held in reverence by the men. We never paid for a drink, meal, or anything for that matter. Where love was free, it was never assumed. If we felt threatened by horny drifters or drunken strangers, our mountain men friends stepped up, defending and rescuing us. If we wanted to drink legally, Cheryl and I could head uptown to the Greenhorn, a 3.2 beer bar for the eighteen to twenty-one crowds. No one we knew ever went near it. We ventured in once and found a pinball and pizza hall, stinking with sloppy, obnoxious frat boys on a ski bender. No need to return—we preferred illegal, sneaky drinking anyway.

One Sunday night in late February, Cheryl and I headed to our other hangout, the All American Bar. Its purple Victorian false-front, orderly interior, and live music drew the devoted and the tourists. Owned by a member of our clan who happened to have money, the AA Bar could always be counted on for a special night. As we swung through the double doors, all heads turned and, as usual, we were caught like wild game in a hunter's sights. After a series of catcalls and laughs, however, the locals returned to their billiards and beers. Cheryl surveyed the room.

"Ooooh, look," she whispered. "The Tiger Boys." She made a beeline for four haggard men, unfamiliar to me, hunched over a pitcher of beer and foamy glasses. I hurried to follow, leaving the murmur of desperate men in my wake. The Tiger Boys were deep in discussion and hardly noticed us. We slid in and listened. They were engrossed in the business of their commune: debts, moves, changes, and dogs. When Cheryl finally got their attention, she repeated her standard introduction: "Hey, guys, this is Nonnie, just rolled in from Jackson Hole."

Eight steady eyes checked me out. I blinked.

"Nonnie, from Jackson Hole" still worked. Jackson Hole was an elite ski area, in neighboring Wyoming that touted the best powder and greatest vertical drop in the country. I had lived there long enough to adopt the identity and evoke a certain mystique. No one had to know that I was an Easterner, not just yet, anyway. The east held the drama of a bad soap opera to these Westerners. It was an association I couldn't argue with, so I avoided it.

The Tiger Boys were sparing with their words. Joe and John had just returned from southern Colorado, retrieving Frank after his Outward Bound adventure. Bruce had been keeping the ghost town fires burning with Murray, who hadn't come to town tonight. John, Joe, and Frank, college buddies, had found the abandoned cabins. Murray and Bruce had fallen in. Dogs and chicks had followed, though none of the women had stayed.

This is how I met the boys of the Royal Tiger Mine, a ghost town up the Swan Valley, nine miles outside of Breckenridge. They were all in their mid-twenties, and mountain men: dark and rough. In the do-you-know-so-and-so banter, it came out that Frank and I knew the same guy in Jackson, and suddenly I felt a connection. Just like that, familiarity opened a door.

"Yeah, so we're just talkin' about Isabel, our cook. She split, and now we need another," Joe mumbled through his dark, sudsy moustache. His eyes were hooded under dense brows; his look was intense.

"Whaddaya think?" They all nodded. Frank looked at me. John

and Bruce watched Cheryl, waiting for an answer.

"I would but, ya know, Tiger is just too far out there for me," she said, finally. Listening carefully, I thought, I like *far out there.*

"I'll do it?" I spoke, shifting in my chair, my voice steady. I glanced at Cheryl. She looked surprised, but nodded approval. The Tiger Boys appeared surprised, too, but relieved.

"Can ya cook?" Frank tested me.

"Sure," I lied, and my deception became my conviction. My cooking skills were restricted to scrambled eggs and watching my dad flip burgers on the grill. No need for them to know. For a cook in these communes, there would be no pay. There was no need for money. The commune would supply all necessities, and even some niceties. So simple and symbiotic. I welcomed it.

"OK, then, cool," all agreed. And with that "job interview" my career, and my life, took an unexpected turn. I didn't have to impress anyone or prove my skills, better that I hadn't tried. Simple enthusiasm had done the trick. Tiger was home to five men, these four and Murray, and five mountain dogs. Soon, it would be my home too. Exactly, or even generally, what that meant I had no clue. It wouldn't take long to find out: The job began immediately.

We sat for a round of beers, and I took a closer look at my new employers. Bruce asked the polite getting-to-know-you questions. We laughed with friendly ease. As my eyes lifted from my beer glass, I caught Frank smiling at me, and for the first time I noticed the warmth in his dark eyes and the square white teeth under his thick moustache. Heat rose on my teenaged face and I instantly resumed the study of my vanishing beer on the barn-wood table. My knees tingled and I was glad to be firmly seated.

CHAPTER FOUR

I awoke in the Peak 8 cabin the next morning ready to begin my new life. As my commitment sank in, Cheryl and others warned that once I got out to Tiger I'd feel isolated. The cabins were over a mile past the end of the plowed road, a long, cold walk or cross-country ski from the car parking. Trips to town had to be planned, never undertaken on a whim. I'd be alone most of the day while my employers worked construction jobs around the county. Didn't I want to stay in town, close to the party, stores, and friends?

Nope. I'd had my fill of town. Far from intimidated, I was eager to get to my new home, to get to know my boys. Already I was thinking of them as "my" boys. What if they changed their minds and got someone else? I didn't want to take the chance. I wanted to be the cook at Tiger, ready or not. I'd been raised to be that way, ready to get on with it.

"Whaddaya waitin' for?" my father loved to say. Whether hesitating in the car at a school dance, or failing to kick my horse to a trot, I never had a good retort. I'd learned to push myself, ready or not.

It had only been six months since I'd gone AWOL during an American Youth Hostel bike trip. The journey began in Halifax, where twelve inexperienced teens mounted new bikes for thirty days of riding and camping. Nova Scotia was charming, its green hills dotted with brightly painted seaports and farms, and I loved riding fast and free through the countryside. Never the typical teenager, I was up at seven o'clock every morning, ready to pedal through the cool morning hours in search of new sights. The leaders' languid morning routine—slow cooking, packing, and starting off at noon—drove me nuts. One morning, while the band of bikers slept, I slipped away: AWOL.

In three days I was home, facing unfazed parents who'd heard from AYH and were more annoyed than worried by the disruption. Both sighed and shook their heads as I rode up the drive; somehow they'd figured I'd survive. It wasn't the first time I'd seen them embarrassed or put out by my shenanigans, but I wondered why they weren't scared for me. In my twelve-hundred-mile, round-the-clock escape to home, I'd been plenty scared, camping alone through rural Maine, biking through urban Boston.

Now, I was on the road again, this time determined *never* to go home. Ready or not!

"Hey, Nonnie, sorry for the short notice, but tonight'd be a good time for us to pick you up. Is that cool?" Joe called at the Gold Pan just a few days after I'd signed on for the gig. His voice, almost monotone, had a casual Western cadence. At the end of each sentence was a snicker and curl of the lip I would come to count on.

"Tonight?" I said, trying to stay cool, my pulse quickening. "No problem. I'm packed."

It didn't take me long to get my stuff together. Cheryl and I spent the afternoon monopolizing the Laundromat, every washer churning the grime out of my clothes. In my travels around the county over the past month, I'd picked up a plethora of authentic mountain gear: an old pair of overalls, a man-sized dungaree jacket, seasoned leather boots, old sweaters, hand-knit scarves, and mittens. My rainbow of turtlenecks was reduced to a pale prism. Everything I owned went back into my backpack and three new grocery bags. Cheryl moped about my moving out of the cabin and her daily life. Sure we'd see each other on town trips, but we'd been inseparable since I'd come to Breckenridge. Our parting was bittersweet. She was struggling with Martin and with her own path, questioning her lifestyle and mostly bored to tears. Though she almost wished she were going along to Tiger, she encouraged me, and shed no tears at my leaving. For my part, I was ready to move on from Peak 8. The stoner pace was going nowhere. I was going to hike into an old ghost town and cook for five guys I'd known for less than an hour. At the time, this seemed no crazier than leaving from home at sixteen or sleeping with a furnace or hitching into town with Matthew or staying with his Pelham buddies in a one-room cabin. It was an adventure and, ready or not, I planned to jump into it with the same commitment.

When Joe's rusty yellow '65 Volvo wagon pulled up in front of the Laundromat that evening, Cheryl and I were standing by the door. It was about six o'clock and already dark. Frank was riding shotgun. They got out to load my gear and stopped in their tracks, dumbfounded by my pile. I couldn't deny that I came with baggage. I'd carried it a long way.

"This all ya got?" Frank said, poking fun at my paraphernalia. I hugged Cheryl hard and crawled into the back seat.

Halfway down the valley, we turned east onto a wide snow-scraped road. At the corner was High Tor Lodge, snowmobiling resort and nemesis of the Tiger Boys. They spat complaints as we passed. I asked for details, to fill the silence. Apparently, the resort sent snowmobiles roaring through their peaceful hinterland, leaving dogs howling and a ragged noise ricocheting across the river basin. When those unreliable scrap-metal monsters would inevitably break down, the Tiger residents, full of heart, had to help the stranded urbanites. Their generosity was repaid by more snowmobilers raping their world with a blatant disregard for the natural wonders of the mountains. It was a first-hand lesson in the animosities of hippies versus townies, locals versus tourists.

Past the bright lights of High Tor, my new landscape began. We wound through short turns and long flats, past cabins and telephone poles, driving deeper and deeper into the wilderness. Slowly gaining elevation, we drove into the dark night. Houses thinned, power poles stopped, steep trees thickened. The road went on. From the back seat, I strained to follow our headlights, reflecting off a distant snow bank, then bouncing into the trees and back onto a long straightaway. The sparse conversation in the front seat slowed and then quieted. The further we drove, the lonelier I felt. A few minutes past the final cabin, the last sign of civilization, we came to a stop at a giant snow bank—the end of the plowed road. Joe nosed the car into the white wall, between a few other old battered vehicles, and cut the engine. In the silence, I scanned the landscape through my window: black trees, charcoal sky, and insignificant starlight. Joe and Frank groaned as they opened their doors and climbed out. Snow squeaked under boots as they headed for the back. A feeble glow from the car's interior dome light flooded the darkness, and I clung to it. I was terrified of true, complete darkness.

It was in the blackest of my childhood nights that the buildup to my father's breakdown could be heard. My tiny bedroom was tucked under the eaves at the end of a long hall, in a house that had been a Revolutionary War hospital. The floorboards creaked and shuddered as Daddy made his way down the hall, moaning, crying, mumbling, pacing. Sometimes, in the flash of a bathroom light, his stooped shoulders and knobby legs came alive under the outline of his nightshirt. To a scared eight-year-old, the tunnel of a hallway seemed to amplify his pain. With a flick of a light switch darkness descended, shadows dissipated, and the pacing resumed.

Though I never feared that my father would harm me, his moods swung precipitously, and I didn't feel safe. I couldn't identify the fear, but the chance of the unknown kept me in nightmares and dark-phobia. From a tender age, I'd been undone by unintelligible sounds in the night. Human mutterings, heavy breathing, and crying in the dark could leave me wracked in an uncontrollable panic. As a little girl, I would often wake in such a state of terror that I'd crawl out of bed and creep toward the safety of my parents' room. Sometimes their door would be locked and I'd have to curl up on their stoop until deepening fear drove me back to the corner of my room. Or their door would be open and I'd rush to my mother's side of their bed, to whimper my gruesome imaginings.

"I dreamed a man came into my room, Mommy, with a knife..." my tiny voice would stammer.

"And then what?" came my father's irritated voice from across the bed, passing over my mother, who lay silent and immobile.

"And then he was gonna stab me!" I voiced my dread, making it more real.

"And then what? You'd be dead? SO, what?" Daddy spoke. His flat words were his final. My mother pretended to sleep. My father's dismissal and my mother's denial did nothing to quell the scary darkness, which haunted me still. Later I learned that all of my sisters had struggled with night terrors, sought consolation, and been met with the chilling "So what?" or the locked door.

Suddenly the car's interior light went out. I crawled out of the back seat and forced myself into the night. As my eyes began to adjust, I found touchstones in the darkness. Frank was hauling a sled out of a nearby bank; Joe was sorting priority household items from my mighty pile of junk. The bags and boxes of food and supplies filled the sled. My bags sat on the ground. The boys turned into the black evening. We were heading home for dinner. I felt afraid and lost, but my father's goading voice—"Whaddaya waitin' for?"—echoed in my mind.

I slid my pack on, gathered my bags, and followed my new employers up over the bank. They hauled the sled onto a wide trail that had been packed down, for good or bad, by the snowmobiles. The trees were thick on either side, defining the thruway. I was glad for them, and my expanding night vision. Joe and Frank kept a brisk pace. After a long day of work and city errands—and hiring a new cook—they were headin' for the barn. They glanced briefly over their shoulders, a certain comfort, but they were not my keepers. I understood that I was expected to keep up or walk alone. They would not wait. Determined to be a partner and not a burden, I hustled to keep up.

The dark was total, the silence broken only by the rhythmic crunching of our footfalls. After what seemed an eternity, we emerged from the trees and onto a mine-tailing bank, a rough jumble of rocks left by the mining process. The openness seemed bright compared to the blackness of the forest. The trail continued up and over, and we trucked along. A little further on, I became aware of the hard shapes of buildings in the distance. Long, clustered, and ramshackle, a commercial mining endeavor clung to the hill. As we entered "town," I made out structures of varying sizes—cabins, storefronts, and warehouses, vacant and creepy, no windows, broken doors and a breeze blowing eerily through them. Their ghostly presence made me shiver. My new employers trudged on, undaunted by any hint of ghostly miners' spirits. I smelled wood smoke, drawn down the valley on a faint breeze. Finally, a flicker of light appeared in the distance. The light, from a window in the very last cabin, appeared to be coming from a kerosene lamp.

Another dark night, another dark squatter's cabin, and another flood of light as the door creaked open. Yet again we were greeted by a pack of barking dogs, ever alert to approaching danger. But it was just us: Joe, Frank, and the new "cook." Unlike my first night in Breckenridge, there was no jolly reunion. John, Bruce, and the guy who turned out to be Murray were huddled around a cable spool table against a background of Indian throws and rough furnishings—a scene similar to the one I'd just left—and they gave us a toned-down but friendly greeting. Yet, unlike the scene I'd left, this cabin was warm, clean, and homey. We added our boots to a pile by the door and quickly dispensed with the unloading and storing of groceries.

After serving dinner to us travelers, they got down to news and plans. Jobs, opportunities, and who-the-hell-is-this-chick took center stage as we slurped the usual rice 'n' veggies. I was casual about my past, how I got there. They asked little of me.

Avoiding eye contact, I took the opportunity to assess my decision and my new home. The first room was small but cozy. A thick plank door shut out the night freeze, an iron bar clipping it to its frame. The room's two windows were both distorted by the now familiar layers of visqueen, which transformed the black of night into a fuzzy reflection of the glowing barn-wood interior. Under one window was a couch, long and low, greenish, nubby, and functional. A potbelly stove filled one corner, a bookcase the other. The stove radiated a slow burn and a pot on its lid steamed a refreshing vapor. Elegant glass oil lamps gave the cabin a dignified feel. There was one on the table, one in the next room—the kitchen. All I could see of my new workplace were the objects illuminated in the small circle of light made by that kerosene flame. A grinder gripping a low counter, a jumble of plastic food storage tubs, a cookbook, another reflection of visqueen.

When my attention turned back to the boys, John was telling me the general house rules.

"So, there's an outhouse out back, kinda up the hill, you'll find it, and hot water in the reservoir on the cook stove. You can brush your teeth in the sink, but empty the slop bucket before it gets full. And don't dump it near the front steps or it'll be an ice rink in the morning. You'll sleep in this loft," and he motioned straight up to a plank ceiling over rafters. "Frank and I are in here too. Joe, Bruce, and Murray sleep in the second cabin, next door. We'll be up and gone to work early. You'll figure the rest out as you go."

"I'll just go to bed then," I stammered, uneasy still and hoping to find a dose of comfort in sleep. I climbed the ladder, pushing most of my junk ahead of me, imagining ten eyes scrutinizing my every move. I crawled on hands and knees to the planks that formed my new bedroom, quietly rolled out my thin foam pad and my thin cotton bag, and slid fully clothed into my bunk.

From my perch, I could see my housemates as I listened. All hairy, dingy, and thick with plaid flannel, wool, and jeans, they seemed a clutch of mature mellow hippies, easily lumped together into a simple class of "Tiger Boys," which they were, but weren't. Already I could see them as different. John was quiet, short, and slight with dancing happy blue eyes. Joe was the driver; his dark hair hung thick, almost reaching his hunched shoulders. Frank was taller, more refined, dark and handsome. Bruce was mellow, almost monk-like, with wisps of a goatee and a mild voice. Murray was the wild card, with nervous eyes and flat dirty-blond hair, a quick and angry tongue. As I tried to relax, my new employers discussed my situation and their unintended part in it.

"Where the fuck did you find this jailbait?" demanded Murray. "She's a fucking child! We could be in a world of shit."

"She's cool, man! Mellow out. She's a fellow voyager, you'll see," Joe said, subduing a panicked Murray. The conversation turned back to news and plans. I turned back to my sweater-pillow. Sleep couldn't come soon enough…Tomorrow in the light of day, I thought, I'll find my way back to town. Strains of Buffalo Springfield drifted through the cabin and into my loft, swaddling me like an old blanket.

"There's something happening here, what it is, ain't exactly clear…
I think it's time we stop, children, what's that sound. Everybody looks what's going down…."

CHAPTER FIVE

D ay began dark and busy in the cabin. Curled up in my little loft, hesitant and cold, I could hear the business of men.
Frank, who slept in the kitchen, had been up early stoking the fire
and frying eggs. I could smell the rich scent of browning butter.
John, who'd crept out of the loft next to mine, was in the kitchen
with Joe and Bruce, who'd arrived from next door. They were ex-
citedly discussing their projects for spring as they slurped eggs
and tea—cold frames, veggie gardens, and a sauna to be built by
the creek. After last night's hike over miles of deep snow, I could
scarcely imagine spring, but I liked the sound of it. I liked these
guys. They were a team, embracing the burden of winter while

running for the end goal of spring, summer, and the rewards of hands-in-dirt. This was their home, and they were comfortable and proud in it. Their spirited voices began to thaw my fear. I felt safety in their strength.

Apparently forgetting that I was there, and much to my relief, they soon took off. The door swung, dogs whimpered, and snow crunched at their departure. I waited in my hideaway until their voices faded away, wondering whether I was now alone. Where was that odd Murray? I had to pee, so I ventured down the rough log ladder and into the domestic scene. A kettle of still-hot water steamed on the warm cook stove. A well-used cast-iron skillet showed remnants of eggs and butter. Dirty enamel camping plates and assorted mugs were stacked in the sink, my first chore.

Still dressed, I pulled on my boots and went to find the outhouse, stumbling through the heavy door and into the frozen Colorado dawn. Hardly looking around, I hustled to the tiny hut perched behind the cabin, up off the valley floor. Dogs bounded behind me, rambunctious but friendly. I slid open the barn-wood door, worn thin by ages of use, and climbed into the outhouse. Sitting for the first of my regular visits to the privy, the stories I'd heard of raccoons, porcupines, and snakes hiding in the outhouse holes filled my lurid imagination. Rural legends or not, I believed them all, but was too disgusted to inspect the hole before sitting. I sat in silent fear.

When I opened the door and stepped back into the snowy landscape, I was struck by a sense memory so familiar I issued an audible sigh. Here in perfect tableau before me was the glad and peaceful West that had stolen my heart. Across the wide Swan River Valley was a rough and rugged hill. Scooped and beaten by mining, riddled with shacks and roads, it lay abandoned, as serene as the coming dawn. My eyes were drawn from the deep green of the forest to the pink of the hillcrest, the pale blue of a Rocky Mountain morning. My ears were keen to the whisper of fresh wind in the treetops, broken only by the screech of hawks. But the most powerful sensation was the smell. A fresh pine scent rose from the boughs around me, and the algae-pink snow gave off a sweet odor of its own. A shiver ran through me: the elation of nature or a simple morning chill.

Just as I started down to my empty and toasty cabin, a creaking and cracking sounded from the second cabin. The door swung open and Murray emerged, churning crusty snow with steel-shanked boots and lunging past me toward the outhouse, followed by the two skulking German shepherds, Rex and Ky. As they passed, Ky curled her lip in my direction. She was a protective bitch, trained that way by Murray. Both of his dogs were mean, unlike Lady, John's shepherd, or White Cloud, Frank's shepherd /Samoyed mix. Dog personalities mimicked their owners'; I'd found that to be true, as I'd acquainted myself with the mountain people. Everyone had a dog, and meeting the dog often alerted me to the human personality behind the pet. Very telling.

Back in the cabin, I stopped at the potbelly stove, whistling, and glowing red with a good stoke. It was set for a while, thanks to my roommates. As I poked around the kitchen for firewood to keep the cook stove going, Murray burst through the door, grumbling about food.

"Can I make you some breakfast?" I backed away as I spoke. He looked like a hardened druggie; deep circles ringed his bloodshot eyes. Even with my limited knowledge of the other four, I wished they were here, now!

"Nope, I'm going to work." His gravelly voice startled, but his words relieved me. He looked no older than me, but aged by angst. Not really the commune type, I thought. Kind of a jerk. I was glad he was leaving and that I wouldn't have to serve him, not for the moment anyway.

"See ya later, then." I turned and tried to look busy as he left with his dogs, off down the trail, a mile and a half to the cars. Where was he going? I wondered. Where had the rest of them gone, and when would they return? As soon as he left, I realized that I'd blown my last chance of a ride into town and chosen to stay in this ghost town alone for what could be many, many hours. Stuffing a few larger sticks in the cook stove firebox, I crawled back up to my loft and gathered more layers. It was toasty in my little nest and I curled up for a good think. How had I ended up here, in this moment?

It all began, I realized, like a cheap dark-and-stormy thriller. When the black menace inside my once-happy Daddy emerged. When his hallway wanderings and sobbing became excessive. When he disappeared. He went (we later learned) to a mental ward. He had a nervous breakdown. He reappeared for short visits as a for-lorn, distant man we didn't recognize.

For my sisters and me, this was the moment our innocent sub-urban youth came to an abrupt end. Several years later, when I was twelve, Daddy came home to stay. Whether he was cured of his madness or had given up on the system, I'll never know, but he was a new and different Daddy. He talked little, confusing and unnerving us with a creepy silence. When he did talk, his bru-tal honesty was hurtful and we longed for that silence. When he hugged, it was too close, too desperate. My childhood hopes that I could make him happy were dashed, forever. What I didn't know was that the thin shell over Daddy's anxiety had finally and irrepa-rably shattered. What I knew was that his illness weighed heavily on our spirits, betraying our trust and humiliating our fragile egos. Frankly, I didn't care why. I was angry and scared. I wanted my old Daddy back.

Many years of unpredictable behavior followed. My friends got a kick out of Crazy Daddy, an edgy thrill they did not have at home. I was ashamed—of his childish ways, his creepy stares—and never sure what lurked in his quiet anger. One morning, he silently greeted me with a swift and hard slap across the face. His response to my shocked and teary expression was, "That's for not feeding your horse this morning!" I never knew what was coming, but it rarely felt loving.

When I was fourteen, Daddy announced that he was selling his successful radio stations and our home, wrenching us from our lives and packing us up for that trip around the world. Apparently his doctors had encouraged him to live his dream. In 1968, he saw the imminent breakdown of American society as an opportunity to escape his own mental breakdown. We fought the decision; we were four teenaged girls with BIG lives of our own. But he insisted on sharing "the experience of a lifetime." So from the social confines and certain comforts of suburbia, we went on an impulsive adventure. For an entire school year, we circled the globe, searching for his sanity and avoiding all questions. On cargo ships, local ferries, rented VW vans, and river pangas, we visited thirty-six countries and six continents, all under one supreme ruler. We had no choice. On the last leg, the decision was made to move us to Jackson Hole, Wyoming, a world-class ski resort. The logic was still unclear. In 1969, Jackson—the town, the high school, and the locals—was a backwater mystery to our teen senses. So isolated was Jackson, the "hole" was its literal geographic limits and few townies breached its boundaries. Their provincial attitudes and fear were unsettling. We'd been around, our minds and hearts definitely broad and open. We were instant outcasts. Marked and shunned.

But it was there—in a rented ranch house 20 miles from town—that Daddy fully abdicated his throne as family leader. He was tired, he was done. Four teenaged girls had pushed his fragile psyche to its limit, made his life too complicated. In that quiet western hideaway, he'd chosen freedom—his own. He had removed the nest, forcing us all to fly. The adventure, I got. The move, I accepted. Leaving my friends and any thread of normalcy, I bore. But the refusal to provide any guidance whatsoever, I couldn't handle. At sixteen, I was abandoned and pissed. So when we moved back to Cape Cod that summer and the situation failed to improve, I left. I ran. There was no doubt that if I failed at this, my own adventure, I'd reignite my father's judgment and humiliation. I'd allow him access to my spirit again, my fragile self-worth and insecurities.

My future was here. I was writing my own script now. And I was alone, eight snowy miles from Breckenridge. My choices had brought me this far, and my brave heart would keep me going. I had a new home, and a job to do, and for the first time people who were counting on me to do that job well. That felt good. Belonging was my goal, and trust was the key. The boys trusted me to have dinner ready when they got home, whenever that was. The day lay before me. I climbed down from the loft.

I was glad for my short time with Cheryl and the lessons I'd garnered from her. Stoking a fire, making a good brown rice in a pressure cooker (necessary at these altitudes) without an explosion, cleaning without running water, chopping wood, and fetching water from a hole in an ice-covered creek had become second nature to me. I surveyed the cabin, looking for basics. There was plenty of wood stacked by the stoves, and five-gallon jugs full of water. There were 8-track tapes and a stereo, possibly from a car and plugged into batteries, but I didn't dare touch it. Besides I was enjoying the quiet. The books stacked on barn-wood shelves were how-to mountain guides and true-life pioneer adventures. Kahlil Gibran, J. I. Rodale, Buckminster Fuller, Jack London, Baba Ram Dass, and Rachel Carson made good shelf mates for the *Whole Earth Catalog, Mother Earth News,* and *The Environmental Handbook.* The intent of serious research was promising. The rugs and couch showed the grime of wood smoke and the presence of dogs, so I dragged the rugs and the couch blankets outside and gave them a good shake. And swept the floor clean before letting Lady and White Cloud in off the bare and icy porch. They curled up quietly by the potbelly stove.

Next, I checked the kitchen. Bins of grains, jars of beans, dried fruit, flours, and honeys filled the tiny room. A cooler stuffed with veggies of all kinds and colors kept them fresh without freezing. The stove took up most of the space, a cast-iron behemoth with a water reservoir, a warming bin, a good-sized oven, and six burners. I checked the fire—gingerly, at first, and then regularly. There were a few cookbooks, a wide variety of cast-iron pans, a good-sized pressure cooker, and earthenware bowls. I saw chopsticks, wooden spoons, and muffin tins. The cabin was well stocked, Isabel had left it so, I gathered, and I thanked her for it. Obviously food was important to these bachelors, so I made it the priority of my day. Lucky I did, as the meal preparation took most of the day. Between stoking, chopping, cleaning, prepping veggies, steaming brown rice, and reading cookbooks, I was busy. I scurried about picking up papers, books, clothes, and the general accumulation of five busy lives. It was good to feel needed and useful, so productive that I even had time to go out for a hike.

Keeping Lady and White Cloud close, I followed the snowmobile road farther up the Swan River. It was a stunning early spring day, the sun warm, but a chill rose from the shadows. The forest felt at once familiar and mysterious. The sounds of the valley reminded me of winter in Jackson Hole: creaking of branches, rustling of wind, trickling of water under snow. Each view held the wide-open space and the resonance of fresh and healthy living that I'd been craving. But there were unfamiliar tracks, human or animal, and sounds that spooked the dogs. As the valley narrowed, I turned toward home and the setting sun.

The insulated windows were too thick for a clear view, and wanting a few minutes' warning of my bosses' return, I regularly peeked out the door for a sign of them—or anyone. I needn't have wondered. They came home in the dark and the dogs heard them long before I did. They trudged up the trail, their beards icy, their backpacks heavy with tools and goods. Was I Snow White awaiting my dwarves? It was a hard and satisfying life they had chosen, and I hoped that the smells of hot rice, sautéed veggies, soy and miso sauce, and tea might offer some sense of reward. I thought they seemed pleased by my work—the rugs and Indian throws aired and straightened, the kitchen clean and warm, the dogs happy and, most importantly, dinner ready. They brought beer.

"Looks pretty good," one of them commented as they sat down to eat.

"I wasn't sure…" I began, but the activity was brisk, no explanation necessary. They had moved on. They talked long and hard amongst themselves, about their work. They were building the Eisenhower Tunnel, taking I-70 under Loveland Pass, a speedway for skiers to the resorts of Vail, Breckenridge, and Keystone. Making good money, working on the highest car tunnel in the world. They were torn by the implications.

"Shouldn't those fucking rich city people have to work harder—like slogging over the pass—to get to their fun? Why should we make it easier for them?"

"Because we're making big bucks and it was gonna happen anyway."

This was a debate I'd heard all over the valley. These guys were not landowners, had no say in the boom going on in the area. Choosing to live near 10,000 feet meant definite compromises. For the isolation and uncrowded vistas, we gave up long, hot growing seasons, so there was little hope of self-sufficiency. Gathering our own firewood, scavenging other cabins and old mines for materials, and doing without worked to a certain degree. But we depended on the grocery stores, hardware stores, and gas outlets for our warmth and lighting. We needed that paycheck from The Man to complete the circle. Frustrating but fact: To stay in these mountains, we had to build the conduit and comfort for the "rapists" who stood against everything we believed. The evening ended early. No point in wasting kerosene. Work would begin again early tomorrow.

Chapter Six

My first true test as a cook came on Saturday morning when the boys requested pancakes. The batter was easy, whole-wheat flour, honey, baking powder, eggs, and milk—that much I knew—and we had plenty of butter and maple syrup. I pulled out the biggest iron skillet. The stovetop had already revealed the secrets of its cooking balance. I knew the exact locations of hot, warm, and cool spots. The oven had them too. It was worth the effort to move skillets and baking pans around regularly to ensure even cooking. Undercooked or burned meals were a waste and a disappointment. I placed the skillet far left over the fire for optimum heating.

It warmed quickly on the hot stove. I poured in a bit of oil and began. Frank was lazing in his bed, watching me and commenting, helping or maybe even flirting. Acting the cook, I nodded agreement to his asides. Yup, I already know, but thanks for the support. The first batch began to bubble. I remembered Mommy's Bisquick pancakes: When the top is covered with bubbles, carefully flip the cakes with a stiff spatula. Okay. Then, as I turned, I remembered Daddy's burgers: When you turn 'em, press 'em down with the back of the spatula to squeeze off the fat. Okay. But as my spatula settled on the rising cake, Frank shouted from his perch.

"What the hell're ya doin? Don't flatten the pancakes!" I flinched and looked at him, hopping half-naked out of his bunk to rescue breakfast. I stepped back, dropping the spatula in his waiting hand. Suddenly, I stood naked too, stripped of my lie, disrobed of my ruse. But as I searched Frank's face for disapproval, on this my judgment day, I saw that he was smiling as he hovered over the stove. He flipped the cakes, then turned and handed the spatula back to me with a nod. This would be our little secret. As I watched his strong back and rippled biceps pulling on his long johns, I felt my knees weaken again.

As Tiger's only cook, my tasks were grueling, physically demanding—and unimaginably satisfying. Fresh Tassajara bread, the staff of our lives, came from grinding wheat berries into flour, seven times through the grain mill, then mixing with water, honey, and yeast. Beating, kneading, rising, kneading, rising, shaping, and baking could take all day. But the resulting four hot fragrant loaves, set out with a tub of butter and a jar of honey, were a comfort worthy of the effort. Homegrown greens came from a jar of beans or seeds that had been soaked, rinsed over several days, and urged into delicate stringy sprouts. In their final day of growth, the jar was set in a window, or on the deck if it was warm, to turn bright green with life. When I needed to bathe, water hauled from the creek could be heated on the well-stoked stove, and in the midday lull a private sponge bath in the kitchen was divine. I was glad for my recently developed muscles. Grown brawny and tough, my arms and shoulders made possible the labor of baking, chopping wood, and hefting water jugs from creek to cabin. My legs and eyes were toned and tuned on daily mountain hikes, exploring the hills and the mining remnants with the dogs. My fear of wildlife, darkness, and my unknown future eased as my confidence grew. I had never felt so strong and resilient.

In April, as the winter weather began to soften, friends would wander up the trail to sit a spell, like we had in the early days, and I always welcomed the visit. But they couldn't be counted on: A surprise blizzard or an offer of daily work might turn them back. Cheryl loved to visit, motivated by the quiet, the adventure, and a break from Martin and her own chores. We spent many lazy afternoons watching bread rise and hashing out our personal demons. We were on the whole hopeful dreamers, but recollections of the difficult parts of our childhoods—the forces that had driven us way up into these mountains—could summon anger we weren't proud of. Matthew was mostly a no-show, seemingly always on the move, leaving Breckenridge or adjusting his lifestyle. I was never clear if the hardships and isolation were right for him. He was more heady, a philosopher, requiring an audience and, if possible, the company of hot women.

For my part, I thrived on the needs of my employers, who were quickly becoming my best friends. This was the family of my choosing, where expectations settled into mutual respect. We all worked hard, and each of our contributions was appreciated. I was the cook, cleaner, and planner of the household, bringing a sister/mother/feminine touch to the rough, shabby life. They had rescued the cabins from demise, but cozy as they were, life inside and out was a constant push. Finding wood was never-ending. A drink of fresh water could mean hours of chopping ice to get to the clear stream. Sometimes when a hard freeze was expected, we'd plug the icy hole just to keep from having to start over in the morning. We all contributed and, as the only girl, I was glad to be treated equally, gently but fairly and without condescension or judgment. I was expected to pull my weight, to be a helpful partner and not a burden.

Laundry, groceries, mail, phone calls, work-for-pay, beer, and new friends could always be found in town. I went occasionally, with the boys and especially on weekends, to visit or waitress at the Gold Pan. When a day trip to Boulder was needed—in equal parts for the city, the market, and the hustle—I'd go with them. Piling into Joe's yellow Volvo or Frank's 1954 aqua Chevy pick-up (as old as me), we'd truck up Loveland Pass, where the snow held far longer than in the valley. Descending onto the plains, we felt the city's excitement and tension before we even got out of the car.

When we pulled into Boulder's tree-lined, flower-filled neighborhoods and opened our windows to the scent of spring, the ripening of new life was intoxicating. We literally leapt for joy at the energy of it. Layers of waffle-weave long johns, down-filled nylon, and woolen socks gave way to thrift store cottons and Mexican gauze. We were liberated from the weight of winter. The fresh breeze on bare skin was sensuous and made me giddy. We'd rummage around the Green Mountain Granary, where oak barrels held whole, ground, and rolled grains and beans, and gallon glass jars of herbs, teas, and seeds lined the shelves. We were kids in the candy store and our short hippie dollars went a long way. The boys deferred to me for supplies and ideas, and we'd fill the bed of the truck with food for a month.

The scene on The Hill lured us to explore the people and the social condition. If there was a good band in town or a time-burning errand afoot, we'd spend the night with Frank's sister, Margaret, who lived on The Hill in a pretty little Victorian. Dan Hicks and His Hot Licks, Magic Music, spiritual be-ins, and street music kept us late that spring, but we were always relieved to get home to the cleansing quiet of Tiger.

The days flew by and I was digging my new life. I loved getting to know my boys, each super cool, smart, nice, and funny in his own way. Even Murray had backed down. Joe, John, and Frank had been best friends at University of Wisconsin, Madison, '64 to '68 (while I was in grade school). The school was good, one of the best, while radically hot and wintry cold. Joe and Frank were from

Denver, John from Milwaukee, so they were not strangers to cold. But the radical was new and exciting. They had stories of sit-ins and run-ins with law and more. Free love, drugs, and new ideals had turned them away from their parents' dreams toward their own.

After graduation, John had joined Vista (JFK's plan to challenge poverty's root causes) to avoid the draft and see the world; he'd ended up in a community of migrant workers in central California. Frank and Joe had gone home to Colorado, both draft-deferred courtesy of minor health concerns. They spent their first post-college summer as fire lookouts for the National Forest, Joe in the Bitterroot of Montana, and Frank in the Salmon-Challis of Idaho. In the tradition of Jack Kerouac, Gary Snyder, and Edward Abbey, they spent a contemplative season filling notebooks with ideas, ideals, and the scratchings of solitude, hiking with bears and snakes while watching for smoke. To the other extreme, they worked the winter in Aspen, waiting tables by night, skiing by day, an indulgent vacation of many months.

It was during that winter's bacchanal that Frank had been hit in the face by the plastic seat of an airborne Poma lift. On his end-of-day run to the après ski bar, he'd been skiing fast down the bunny slopes. He scared a woman ascending on the lift. She panicked and let go of the seat, which flailed wildly, eventually smashing his face with bone-shattering force. It had impacted all the delicate tissues and bones of his face, bloodied his nose, and blackened his eyes. Instead of going straight to the ER, in the infinite wisdom of the ski bum he'd dropped acid and gone to a party. There, Joe took one look at him, bloody and caved in, and urged him to the clinic. Before leaving, Frank had gone to a mirror to see what all the fuss was about. Through the magic of hallucinations, the horror magnified and distorted a thousand times, he freaked out. An air flight to Denver, parents, surgeons, admonitions ensued, and he'd been fitted with a new plastic cheekbone. That area of his face was still sensitive to the touch, and just the tiniest bit lopsided when he smiled, a constant reminder of that stupid woman on the Poma.

In the fall of '70, Joe, John, and Frank had found this ghost town, tracked down the Royal Tiger Mine owners, and asked for permission to secure, improve, and inhabit a few of the cabins. Permission granted, and here we were. Bruce and Murray had moved in, though I was never clear how or why. The five seemed like a good working team, for the most part, and were the only squatters in the area who actually had the owners' blessings. That added to my pride and made the Tiger Boys hipper than the rest.

Of course, I saw each of my employers as a potential old man, my old man, except Murray, and they all seemed interested in me. So I flirted with each in turn, testing the chemistry in four men with four distinct personalities. Bruce was quiet and withdrawn. With his liquid eyes, limber voice, lanky frame, measured speech, and a distracted tug of his trim goatee, Bruce held the respect and love of all who knew him. Yoga and meditation gave him a natural high, and he stood tall, a little aside of the rest. He was too reticent for me. Joe was smart, solid, and kind, wise even. He was good-looking, with a mass of dark hair, a thick moustache, and dark, furtive eyes. He and Frank were about the same size and coloring and folks often thought they were brothers. Joe was funny, endearing, and cynical, but he was moody, too moody for me. John was small and dear and solemn, with a smile that lit you from within. He was sensitive and artistic. He wrote to his parents, missed his sister, and had a passion for life. John was never cynical, never angry, and he burned with hope and trust. His vivid blue eyes pierced through his John Lennon glasses, auburn tresses and beard framing his cherry cheeks, and an easy smile waited on his lips. He was too gentle for me.

It wasn't long before I realized my connection with Frank went deeper than our shared friend in far-off Wyoming and my weak-kneed reaction to his smile. I guess I knew it instantly. He was a proper gentleman, a thoughtful resident. Unlike many in the greater community, Frank cared about people, his people and others. He never passed another without a word or smile or advice, or a connecting nod. He was appropriate and humble, and friends clung to his generosity. His humor was addictive, clever; I loved it and waited for it. Born to a family of wordy wit, I appreciated his thorough tumbling of words. And he was gorgeous. Thick, dark, and soft hair hung just to his neck, and filled across his chin and upper lip with a dense and sexy beard. His velvet brown eyes were set deep, under expressive brows, beside a strong, slightly crooked nose. His cheeks and lips formed a kissable surface, always soft and alluring. He was strong, mind and body, not tall or boastful. He was broad and stable. He knew what he wanted and he wanted me. Frank had to be the one. He was Jewish to my Christian, he was Summa Cum Laude to my high school dropout, he was middle class to my upper class, he was 25 to my 17, he was solid and I wanted him… We watched each other for a month before he finally reached out for me, and I melted in his hands.

On an otherwise unremarkable night as we all hung around the cabin, Frank and I slumped together on the old green couch. Our roommates read, music played, dogs lolled, and suddenly our hands touched. A palpable force held the touch even as we tried to move. The touch became a caress. The heat of the moment flushed my face. Our world closed in around us. Frank took my hand and kneaded it carefully. He slid a finger up my sleeve. I gasped. I twitched. I didn't know what to do, but I needn't have worried. His confidence engulfed my innocence. We squirmed in silence until the others went to bed, then he led me to his kitchen bunk. In the dark, by the warmth of the stove, layers of fabric fell away as he undressed me. My body responded to his able hands. His makeshift bed was small, and the rope weaving creaked and stretched with our weight. He was uninhibited, fluid. I was tense and modest. He wanted to free me, and he did, then and there, in the silence and the dark. By morning, if not before, I was head-over-heels in love.

No one was shocked when they came to breakfast in the morning and found us together—least of all John, who slept right above Frank. But they were all discreet. Luckily, Frank had gotten up early to flip eggs, but I was there, hiding under the blue rip-stop nylon of his well-worn camping bag. It smelled of wood smoke, incense, and his seductive scent, a hint of his Dr. Bronner's soap and my Skin Trip lotion. I wrapped myself in the nylon and essence and felt completely right. He glanced up from his iron skillet and winked.

Watching him with newly opened eyes, I realized that his easy rapport made him a natural leader. He may have been the first truly self-assured man I'd known. A mature man in a short list of males I'd dated. Of course, there'd been the boys of my youth, Matt, Limie, Sambo, Jimmy, and Greg, then Keith, my first true boyfriend in Jackson Hole. But he wasn't a man, just a narrow-minded, gorgeous boy with a taste for fame (after a single shot in *Glamour Magazine)*, a local fan club, and the ego to make me feel lucky to have him. He treated me like a lady-in-waiting, took my virginity without even knowing it, and bragged about his conquest. He was a small, unchallenged, unchanneled boy of nineteen and ours was a short, rough romance. I had no real idea how a man should treat his woman, but I knew I wanted to be special, not royalty, just thoroughly, truly, and respectfully adored. And I knew that a man of confident maturity could handle that. Frank had that, and I was ready to thoroughly adore him back. Loving Frank was the most natural thing to me.

Our Tiger family dynamic changed instantly. The last cook, Isabel, had remained unattached to the boys, though some free loving could be assumed. Frank and I were writing a new chapter and, in a tiny cabin, it was tough to ignore. Naturally, Joe and John worried over the sanctity of their boys club. But I was already an integral member of the family and of Tiger. We had grown so close, struggling with the harsh wilderness and establishing civilized and sacred mores. Mutual respect and acceptance and genuine care had kept Tiger conflict-free and strong. For the five guys, just the idea of a new girlfriend wanting to move in would have required scrutiny, yet here I was, already on the inside. Now, as Frank's old lady, they knew at least that I was going to stay, cooking, cleaning, and brightening all their lives. My new attraction and attention to one would not usurp my commitment to all.

CHAPTER SEVEN

Spring of '71 was a time of change and unrest all over the country. Tired of wars and the lies used to justify them, young adults had grown distrustful and rebellious toward The Establishment. Seeking peace, they were leaving the comfort and conformity of home in droves, running to the bosom of a brand-new reality: the counter-culture. In the company of strangers, they found the lifestyle they'd dreamed of, a utopia of free ideas and no rules. There were loosely ordered communes cropping up everywhere. Passing through a town or city, seekers had only to find the food co-op, coffee house, or long-hair on the street to be directed to free lodging or commune nearby. Some communes were closed; some free flowing and open to the transient. When it worked, an isolated enclave of like-minded people drew hippies toward the nirvana they sought. It was beautiful, it was a happening, and it was happening to us.

Easterners were heading west, everyone was. The West, it seemed, was not so much a place as a way, an adventure, a rite of passage. It tended to make humans as migratory as animals, embarking on the long journey west driven by dreams of possibility and the scent of freedom. The arid mountains and the high, thin air gave way to hallucinations of limitless potential. The sense of unknown and danger was the tonic that sent the brave onward and kept the fearful at home.

It shouldn't have surprised me that my parents had themselves chosen to explore the West, with its new horizons and attitudes. Nor that our concerned New England friends had gathered as we left, like colonists around a departing wagon train. What settlements would we discover? What way stations of refreshment? What civilizations? Grossly uninformed and oblivious, we had arrived in the west hardy and hopeful. We were at once swept up in it, easily sloughing off the preppy and stodgy East. I knew my parents' return to Cape Cod would be temporary; they had swallowed the western dream and would be back.

The Ozark, Appalachian, Sierra, and Rocky Mountains were all in the sights of folks trying to lose their way and begin anew. From our mountaintop, we saw them coming, converging on the open spaces. It was a good place to get lost. We saw them in Boulder, the city hippies who filled its parks and sidewalks. They were hanging loose; waiting for a change, spare change. It was circuslike, vivid and noisy with colors, characters, and moods. We'd laugh and pass. Not all hippies were cool. Some were just plain crazy. Bad drugs, latent anger, and general hysteria led some to the crime and violence you'd find in any culture. Sometimes they'd hit us up for a place to crash, but no, no, they weren't coming home with us. Our Tiger was sacred and special, no room for riff-raff. Sure we loved all our brothers and sisters, but if we didn't protect our tiny utopia, we'd end up with a little city of our own. At Tiger, we lived in a delicate balance of space and personalities.

Change was afoot, however, and as it turned out, we could not stem the flood.

With the warming of spring, our little ghost town expanded. College buddies, Stuart and Susan, arrived from Madison. Stuart carried a sense of knowing atop his tall shoulders, and he had the free mouth to share it. His loud and judgmental style irritated me, but Frankie tolerated him, so I did too. Joe and John were his good friends, and we respected that bond. His wife, Susan, regarded me warily and treated me like a distant cousin she didn't like but had to sit next to at family functions. She was uptight and fragile, and she let us all know it. Their matrimonial demand for privacy and privileges threatened to upset Tiger's balance. They never seemed to fit, bringing city culture to our quiet domain.

Then John fell for a girl. Maxine was a big, bawdy, funny Jew from New Jersey who seemed to be the antithesis of sweet John. Her humor was wry and took some getting used to, but he adored her and she pampered him like a puppy. They were blissful and tender toward one another, and she acted as a big sister to me, granting the advice, critiques, and fondness that I missed. Maxine's giant black 'fro preceded her into the rooms she entered headlong; whether intruding or joining, she pulled it all off without apology. After a period of cautious observing, I grew to find her laugh infectious and her heart true. One morning she descended from John's loft as I was getting out of Frank's kitchen crib. I was wearing a full-length Lanz flannel nightgown, as I had since childhood. It wrapped me up cozily from neck to toes, and I'd added wool socks for those first steps on the frosty cabin floor. Maxine inspected me squarely, and frowned.

"How the hell do you fuck Frank in that thing?" she shouted out. "That's a helluva sexy thing to wear to bed! You need a new nightie, honey…" I shrank back under the covers, laughing, knowing she was right and glad we were alone in the cabin.

"Oh, it comes off *real* easy," I said as I crawled out of hiding. That was Max! You could agree or disagree, but she was as honest as could be, and I loved her for it. She may have been the first person in my life who was that bold, blunt, and funny. Being with her was a healthy workshop for me in speaking frankness and trusting acceptance.

Frankie and I explored our love, new and intense. We were caught up in passion, laughter, and obvious longing. Whenever we were near, we closed the physical distance like two magnets. We made love in the dark of the cabin, in the afternoon quiet of the spring-warmed hills, and anywhere else we could find a little bit of privacy. Discretion was not a requirement of the free-loving life, but we preferred it. Ours was a dynamic that didn't need to be shouted out into the world. In a secret tongue, we made promises and talked of the future, a topic few were broaching.

New personalities made it interesting and, being hippies, we saw growth and change as positives. But when Bruce disappeared, we were saddened and confused. We knew he was going—Tiger had just become too crowded for him—but where and why he went were mysteries. One day he and his mellow aura were gone. Then Murray left, skulking away with Rex and Ky in tow. Good-bye. The change had begun.

As the snow retreated, the woods and trails became more boot-friendly, and Frank and I took the opportunity to further explore our valley. When the mud dried in the spring sun, we hiked up the ridge into the Royal Tiger mine, discovering tunnels and railways only hinted at from our cabin. The forlorn mine view we had memorized as we went about life in Tiger gave way on closer inspection to an infrastructure full of the mystery of a long-gone era. The evidence of hard labor gave us the sense of miners in pursuit. Without the aid of a flashlight, the details of the mine were vague and creepy. But an icy draft from the tunnel depths blasted us with the scent of decay, of iron and rich dirt.

On the plateaus and tailings below, machine shops, offices, and barns housed the rusted remainders of a vibrant pursuit. Skeleton sluices, trolleys, and elaborate infrastructures teased our imaginations with a sense of the dangerous edge in the miners' life. They did the grunt and bidding for silver barons in far-off Denver, and it had been a rough existence for their families, who carved homesteads in the very cabins where we now lived. These ghost-town glimpses filled us with a sense that we were carrying the mantle, and that we had a kindred responsibility to do it right. As I followed Frank through the tangle of creaking iron and timbers, charged by his exuberance and curiosity, I had the feeling that his steady hand could lead me through the rest of my life.

Back on terra firma, John, Joe, Frank, and Stuart—and just about all the hippies—were busy with work on the condo projects, making bright vacation bedrooms for New Yorkers and Texans, or on the tunnel. In a sense, the growing ski industry was a byproduct of our lives. We were paving the way for the rich by building their dream homes. Cheryl was right: We paid them little mind, and their money paid our bills. Only occasionally did their consumerism irritate us, when too many cars, strangers in the Laundromat, or idiots at the post office got in our way. High prices at the grocery store were a particular irritant. At one dollar a pound, button mushrooms cost more than hamburger. Being vegetarian in the mountains was proving expensive.

The Tiger crew began planning for a future in which self-sufficiency was the main goal. On sunny days, we'd drag chairs and pillows onto the deck and thumb through *Mother Earth News,* with its photos and stories of people perfecting the art of life in the wild. Images of rough-hewn homes and hands-in-the-dirt gardens looked like Shangri-La to us. The *Whole Earth Catalog* sold every manner of book, tool, and machine needed to make our dreams come true—organic gardening, composting, and animal husbandry. Blueprints and photos of crafting cabins, tipis, domes, and yurts made from stone, foam, wood, and concrete gave flight to a future of creative communities. Four hundred pages of ideas and plans, the whys and how-tos, fueled eager dialogues on the nature of true independence. We ordered plans for the lodgings that spoke to us, everything from Buckminster Fuller's geodesic domes to the Laubin's tipis.

Our reading motivated us to scour the land, the original garden, for edibles. Even at 9,000 feet, dry hillsides yielded the first green shoots in May. Max, Cheryl, and I scavenged and gathered from roadsides and meadows. It was a new and purposeful reason for expanded hiking and wandering, a treasure hunt. We searched Euell Gibbons' *Stalking the Wild Asparagus* and H.D. Harrington's *Edible Native Plants of the Rocky Mountains* for the safe bets. Chamomile grew between the tire ruts, fragrant and delicate. We'd pluck and dry it for teas. Young dandelion greens, miner's lettuce, and pigweed leaves tasted of the earth and freshened any sandwich or salad. Tender clover, rose, and yarrow flowers appeared for munching. Wild carrots, mustard greens, and nodding onions added spice to our soups. We were pretty pleased with ourselves—eating for free! Eventually, as the summer wore on, everybody was doing it, stalking the delectable mountain offerings.

Further inspiration called us to a tiny mining shack on the banks of Swan Creek that begged to be transformed into a rugged little sauna. Fortified with massive insulation, no windows, and a found door, the sauna added luxury to our everyday. With a little salvaged iron stove glowing fiery amber and a spritz of eucalyptus water, we began a morning ritual of cleansing and heightened consciousness. The hot steam brought naked bodies to drippy, fiery elation. With a sprint and a leap into the just-thawed creek, soulful howls resonated across the valley. It was magical, the perfect addition to our home.

As alpine spring turned to alpine summer, and snow still fell regularly, the Tiger Boys decided that true living off the land would require a move to warmer climes. Exotic locales were bandied about. New hippies blew through town with wonder-filled tales of budding communities in British Columbia, California, the southeast, the southwest. Someone knew someone in torrid Central America and showed up with a U.S. Mail package of peyote to prove it. In a moment of stoned clarity, Carlos Castaneda spoke to us: "A man of knowledge lives by acting, not by thinking about acting." And South America beckoned. Papayas, mangoes, avocados, and pot trees as well as abundant gardens and minimal clothing seemed like good intentions. *National Geographic* magazines, library books, and dreams filled our nights as a brightening sun and melting meadows filled our days.

When the boys homed in on Arkansas, we started hearing names like Leroy, Clyde, Billy-Bob, and Floyd. In anticipation of a new attitude, they decided to change their names. John became Abner, Joe became Elmer, and Frank became Wilber (his name stuck). We were motivated by the imaginings. Between work, chores, and long evenings by the still-robust fire, we dreamt and planned of farms, rivers, mild winters, and sizzling summers. Frank—now Wilber—and I planned together. In our vision, we worked side-by-side: building gardens, domes, greenhouses, ponds, and barns full of animals. We were in love, madly and publicly. I was his old lady, he was my old man. The coupling fit.

In May, Wilber traveled back to southern Colorado to train as an Outward Bound leader in the San Juan Mountains. It was cool with me, a great place for his talents. Besides, the changing dynamics of Tiger had put a strain on his private nature. A break to the wilderness was good. I was busy with new friends and becoming a regular hippie-chick waitress at the Gold Pan. The snow had melted and travel to town was easy.

Wilber returned tanned, rippled, and exhausted after two weeks of tough mountain life. Outward Bound had tested his survival and backcountry skills, assessing his ability to lead kids through endurance camps. He was convincingly qualified, but the net result of his sojourn proved to be more profound. On his return, Tiger looked even more constrained and crowded to him, it seemed. The road had opened in his absence and the valley was beginning to fill with new rigs and personalities. I was elated to have him back, my heart grown even fonder.

A letter had been waiting for him, postmarked California, from his high school buddy Ron. Aside from regular newsy letters from my mom, there was seldom mail in Tiger's P.O. Box 553. I knew little about Ron except that he'd been a goofy kid, one of Wilber's few Jewish friends in school. Wilber had visited him in Santa Cruz in '69, while Ron was in college there and living in a crash pad full of beach hippies. It had been an eye-opener for both of them. The California scene was a caricature of itself: surfing, drugs, free love, hot babes, live music, and a laid-back life of legend. There were no rules, as long as you avoided the cops. The hippie mores there were looser than Colorado, Wisconsin, practically any place in the country. I knew they'd lived large, indulged and drifted from chick to chick. They'd had a blast. But Wilber had had his fill of the decadence and come home to Colorado. At a safe distance, he was excited for news of Ron's life, living vicariously through the post.

As I watched, he slowly turned the pages. He smiled and chuckled at first, but then his demeanor shifted. It turned out Ron's old lady, Suebi, was pregnant. A baby, responsibility, and marriage: The whole idea scared the shit out of Ron, and it seemed to be freaking Wilber out as well. Ron and Suebi lived in a commune in the Sierras. Sounded to me as if Ronnie was living the dream: mountain commune, love, baby. The natural course was cool, right? Shouldn't we celebrate Ron's good dharma?

A few days later, after we'd reestablished our simple routine, during a quiet moment on the porch, Wilber told me that it was over between us. My knees gave out and my heart seemed to burst. My breath stung and came out in gulps. It was too much, he told me. "We're just too close," he said, "and you're too young."

My young intuition told me that his heart said otherwise, that he was actually terrified by the intensity of his feelings toward me. He was crazy in love, and love was making him crazy.

"I need some space," he said. That made more sense, and I told him he could have it.

"Love one another but make not a bond of love: Let it rather be a moving sea between the shores of your souls." Kahlil Gibran's prayer came to my mind. But I didn't really feel peace. I was shattered.

The conversation ended there. Just as our spring bloom was producing the fruit of summer love, Wilber broke up with me. Our kitchen love nest became my lonely bunk. Within a week, he had explored the abandoned cabins in Tiger, picked one, fixed it up, and moved in.

I read the book *Be Here Now* over and over… and resolved to Be.

> *"You don't have to have that urge*
> *That desire,*
> *That unfulfilled THING,*
> *Just let it be,*
> *Just be be Be Be more more MORE"*

I thought of my sister Betsy, older and wiser and struggling as well. She and I had always pulled each other through the mucky times in life. We had been confidante, protector, and mirror to each other forever, and I realized that I needed her at that moment.

June 5, 1971
dearest betsy
how are things w/you? i love you. what are you doing? I get a letter from mama almost 3 times a week. it sounds like they've got a heavy trip planned for idaho this summer.

summer is slowly showing it's colorful face up here. everyone's smiling. i was convinced it was here to stay until it snowed yesterday while we were sauna-ing. all our best friends are being thrown out of mining cabins they've been living in all winter, so there are 20 or more beautiful people living in cars and tents waiting for hot weather. tiger, none the less, is still hangin' on. everyone is working hard at different locations around the county, while I stay at home, to cook, clean and keep the general feeling of togetherness between 5 men, 3 women, 12 dogs and 7 cats (including 5 kittens and 5 puppies). i've been getting into staying at home + cleaning, baking bread, washing in the stream w/a funky old washboard.

the stream has just opened up and flows right behind the sauna. so, out of the sauna, it's only a short run and a flying leap into ecstasy. really fine!! as the sun appears from behind an immense front of storm clouds, the snow melts down the sides of the mountains and the clear blue streams swell to form expansive ponds for swimming. though the water is just barely unfrozen, sometimes you get so dirty or so hot sitting under an intense sun, that it's perfect for swimming.

As new chick-a-dees migrate into our tight community of breckenridge, wilber and i have had a hard time keeping it together. as happens to many boys come springtime, wilber starts eyeing every new girl who waddles by. i sit back and wonder where we stand, as wilber sees his new love, sandra. i still love him and feel that this love of his is just a whim and that he'll realize his love for me soon enough. she is the sexy, seductive, city-type freak who lures men into her bed and never experiences a permanent relationship. if wilber wants to "do a thing" with her it's fine w/me just as long as i'm not shat upon in the process. one positive thought, i'm learning so much by this experience. (Sandra has a 2 year-old girl and no old man.)

if wilber and i are still together all summer we plan on doing a geodesic dome to live in, out in the woods and near a really fine stream. i really love him, bessa. we haven't made love since he met sandra, so my mind is blown.

still i want you and whoever you hang out with to come and visit us sometime soon. i really love you, bessa, and miss you terribly. instead of me visiting you in jackson, which i dread, how about you coming down here. you would absolutely love it, especially now w/ all the flowers and blooming aspens and color. i haven't seen you in over 6 months. that calls for a reunion wouldn't you say? please come down any time. ask in Breckenridge at the Gold Pan Restaurant how to get to tiger. come, please. I love you and miss you.

how is jackson hole these days? crowded? are all the same people still there? probably not. i'd love to see that country again, i just can't get into those people. i love you, please come, non xo

CHAPTER EIGHT

With the coming of summer, the valleys had come alive. Word had leaked, or been shouted, in New York, Denver, Austin, and Albuquerque, that Breckenridge was a haven. Hippies heading west turned uphill toward a free and wild place. As alpine flowers poked through dirty snow, wanderers in VW vans, crafty-camper-pick-ups, and barely running jeeps churned the muddy mining roads. Suddenly, the sanctity of Tiger, Muggin's Gulch, Wakefield Mine, and other miners' squats was transient and vulnerable. The roads opened and Summit County folks went through a major shake-up and resettlement. Unusable mining shacks were torn up to fortify the chosen ones. Ready materials—window frames, doors, beams, and siding—were in abundance and free for the taking.

Bert Ray, Roger, Andi, Jane, and Brother Paul abandoned Wakefield, trucking up Swan Valley and reclaiming the "Storyland" mining cabin on the North Fork. Kid Shileen built a tree house up the Middle Fork. El Paso parked his tipi in a wildflower meadow. Sandra, Vala, and Joyce were still at Jumbo. And at the top of a steep draw, a long hike from the road, Bob and Denise nested in a mine carved into the hill. Bien rejuvenated a cabin at Tiger, with a stylish nod to his Native American, Japanese, and French heritage. Tiger became the gateway to a community of fine folks. At its entrance someone posted a sign: "SLOW! God's Children at Play."

But all was not right. Living in the same small ghost town as Wilber tormented my broken heart. I was unable to move on, as Wilber apparently had, to quell the physical yearning touched off by a whole host of sensory cues. At the end of each day, I would listen for the trucks heading home, my body trembling at the rumble of his '54 Chevy. Torturing myself, I would crane my neck out the kitchen window to see him pull up at his new cabin. I'd hope not to see two heads silhouetted in the pickup's window, hope he wasn't starting a girl-of-the-night habit. But it was always just Wilber, with faithful and trusty White Cloud in the back. I'd wait for him through dinner as the Tiger folks showed up for food and friendship, but Wilber had his own kitchen and stayed away. It seemed he had really made the break. Sometimes, Joe or John would wander down to hang out with him, and on weekends they'd all disappear to higher ground. On the nights he didn't come home, I knew he was with Sandra at Jumbo. When that pattern became more frequent and I couldn't stomach the pain, I'd hitch a ride to town.

The bars and byways of Breckenridge became my home during the cool mountain nights. I wasn't looking for romance—I was still in love with Wilber—but I had deemed getting stoned and hanging out to be the best salves. And I had plenty of company. The town had swollen, the streets and bars filled with new faces and attitudes. Matthew and Martin's friends arrived from Pelham with rowdy and youthful abandon. Out of wagons and vans they piled: Chaser, Plum Fairy, Bourbon, Boguananda, Baron Munch-hausen, come to our town to set streets and spirits on fire. They brought that raw, tough New York edge along with a new style of drug: street drugs. We had been mellowed and mind-altered with weed, peyote, and mushrooms, but from the East came the blistering and ragged effects of speed, mescaline, and the ultimate party drug, Quaaludes. After a winter of long Tiger nights spent sinking into warm comforts, familiar highs, and the dragging lull of conversation, we were dancing wildly and desperately on Main Street in Breckenridge, seemingly unable to stop. Live music and jukebox tunes flooded from the bars. The nights were warmer, the air thin, and the starry skies enchanting. We whirled and boogied until dawn some nights, a free-for-all of men in suede and denim, women in street-sweeping dresses, all in stompin' boots. When we tired, beds were found in town, or rides bummed back to Tiger. We all had work to do come daytime. But our nights were free with the love of friends and the good vibes of the times.

After my plea, Betsy had come. She and Dede drove down from Wyoming, curious about what little sis had gotten herself into. Seeing how peculiar my life appeared to them made it all the more impressive to me. It was the first time I'd had to explain myself: my life, my friends, my duties and joys, my newfound pain. Betsy loved it. Dede was unsure and worried about leaving me amid the instability—my big sister, protective, sweet, and concerned without being judgmental. When they left after a week of summer frolic, Betsy promised to return.

When called on, a bunch of us would head up the ski hill to John Topolnicki's trailer on Peak 9 for day work. A famous local photographer, John prided himself on traipsing the backcountry for one-of-a-kind shots, selling postcards and posters to tourists. He'd hire us to roll and pack posters. Sitting at a long table on the sunny scree of his yard, we'd get stoned and listen to *Maggie May*, *Tears of Rage*, and *Midnight Rider*. Topolnicki paid little and flirted shamelessly, but with the great Tenmile view and the easy cash, we didn't mind a bit.

Joel and Kathy blew in from the southeast, a backwoods couple fleeing the low country heat of summer for the cool mountain clarity. They set up camp on the North Fork and hung out at Tiger when they could. They were older, maybe even thirty, the dreaded age of distrust, but they carried a quiet wisdom that we welcomed. We grilled them with questions about living in the south: Arkansas, Louisiana, and the Carolinas. Their well-honed marriage fascinated me. In the staid conformity of my parents' social circle, I hadn't witnessed true union, like this, defined by passion and respect. I loved watching it work.

One lazy afternoon Cheryl, Susan, and I were sitting on the stoop with Kathy and Joel, taking in the sun and tokes of hash. An easy rap flowed among us. It was warm and soporific, and we were feeling good. I got up to check on the bread rising by the stove, to turn and knead it. While inside I heard a car pull up. Its engine sputtered and stopped. Car doors opened and creaked to a close. A conversation began. The kitchen window was ajar, and a strange voice commanded attention. "Do you know the end is near? Have you accepted The Truth?"

I peeked out. Two dudes—boys, really—in drab, ill-fitting suits stood near a dusty sedan with the *Watchtower* in their hands. This was a first. Jehovah's Witnesses. In Tiger! I was stunned at their gumption. My immediate reaction was familiar. My father's words came to me like the words of God himself. His crazy theories bounced haphazardly around my brain like Ping-Pong balls, gaining speed and volume. "Nope. We don't believe *any* of that spiritual, religious, and theocratic bullshit! We have the power. We create our own lives. All religions, and those who buy into them, are stupid." But the voice I heard from the stoop was different. It was Kathy, with Joel as backup, who took on these invaders. She engaged them, her words rich and powerful.

"Yes, I believe," she began, her voice steady. "I believe in God, in Jesus as my savior. I believe in justice, in heaven and hell, and in salvation. And in the Old Testament."

The boys held up their New World Translation. "This is *the*

Bible," they stammered. They were young, easily disarmed by the rational tone of her discourse.

"You can have your beliefs and I can have mine," Kathy continued, still calm. "We can both live in God's light; however it is true to *us.*"

"But there is only one way!" Now they were getting pissy. They were not here to hear, they were on a mission, to witness and preach. "Armageddon is imminent, you will be destroyed. *We* will live in Christ's Kingdom forever…" They were spewing their script, and scriptures followed. I hid in the kitchen, kneading and listening.

Kathy spoke from the heart. She was sure and thoughtful, easily ten years older than these upstarts, but she was at the threshold of her patience.

"My father is a Baptist minister," she finally said, her voice breaking with emotion, her private world breached, "in Alabama. I grew up in a devout home. Don't preach to me." I was impressed, and not a little ashamed. It was the first time I'd seen true faith, and thoughtful, respectful spirituality. At that moment, I envied Kathy and Joel their beliefs, their feelings, their faith. They weren't stupid, hypocritical drones. Anger rose at my father and his Ping-Pong theories. I would have to work to silence them, I thought, to rewrite them in *my* image.

One morning I found myself with a case of ripe peaches from Paonia and a vat of pancake batter. My boys ate all they could, and then the folks from Storyland and the tipis began the daily flow, heading to their jobs. They slowed at the smell of fresh cakes and hot peaches. For several hours that morning, I served plate-sized peach flapjacks and spoonfuls of butter, doused with hot maple syrup, through my kitchen window. When the last car headed down valley, the waning of rock 'n' roll 8-tracks faded and the summer dust settled on our ghost town, I returned to my chores with a renewed sense of purpose and importance.

Somehow, even without the love of Wilber, this was my Summer of Love, brimming with the passions of hundreds of high and happy folks. I was free, making my own way and living fully, day-to-day. Mountain ascents were planned at the Pan on an evening. The next mid-morning, volunteers reassembled for Pan coffee before lacing up hiking boots, donning packs full of survival gear, and piling into various rigs. Summer high-altitude saunters in the Rockies could quickly turn to gale winds, pelting hail, and crashing lightning. We always kept an eye to the weather, which raced in from the west. Tripping to hot springs, western slope orchards, and concerts, up sandy dunes, and down river canyons rounded out that summer.

With the valley filling and the traffic growing, parties and gatherings grew around Tiger, too.

One day, Ellen landed in the second cabin. Drifting in a cloud of pastel Indian cottons, thin sandals treading mountain dirt, cheery blonde braids swinging free, she was a delicate and ethereal being, in contrast to Tiger's knuckle-raw grittiness. Her clear, pale blue eyes shone with love of Maharishi Mahesh Yogi and Transcendental Meditation. Ellen was a devotee, trippy, free and one-hundred-percent natural. She exuded peace.

Joe had taken a fancy to her and led her up to Tiger. I don't think he, or any of us, knew in the beginning that she graced a different plane. She was nonsexual, not seducible, but warm and irresistible. Wilber, Joe, and John adored her; to us all she was a gift. We were all in love with her. To the riff-raff of the new Breckenridge, Ellen's patience and faith were disarming. But she was humble and nonjudgmental; she quelled the irreverent feelings of even the crustiest hippies. As my new friend and guardian angel, she exuded the serenity I longed for in the tumult of my heart. She guided me through my season of dread. In her presence, anger and gloom lifted and I gained focus. That summer we spent our days eroding my pain, adjusting priorities and replenishing her generous strength. The high mountain hikes and hot fragrant saunas released my clogged spirit. Raw veggies and fresh fruits, sizzling saunas and icy creeks, meditations and yoga postures were Ellen's drugs and she was my pusher. For a few months, my party nights woke to cleansing days with Ellen, celebrating *Jai Guru Dev* ("Victory to the Greatness in you.").

In Ellen, we saw the path to inner joy and true grace. It was the goal of our generation, but few would ever attain it. I think we all dreamed of joining her on that other plane, a place she'd risen to through her devotion and discipline. Lazy and uncommitted, we tried to take some of her passion into our hearts. But with the distraction of jobs, filling the larders, and building our futures, we never quite reached the path of serenity and material abandonment.

As we prepped for our lives free of conformity, we heard that Buckminster Fuller was speaking at the Aspen International Design Conference. Ellen knew of the connection between Bucky and the Maharishi, their mutual respect and devotion. We'd heard of his "Spaceship Earth" theory in the *Whole Earth Catalog:* that we are all cohabiting on one very limited astral vehicle. "Man is going to be displaced altogether as a specialist by the computer. Man himself is being forced to reestablish, employ, and enjoy his innate 'comprehensivity.' Coping with the totality of Spaceship Earth and universe is ahead for all of us." We surely had to go, so we planned a grand excursion of many days. Ellen, Joe, Cheryl, John, Max, and I filled vans with food and drugs for the pilgrimage.

It was my first trip west, since I arrived in February. Perhaps I should have expected to see mountain valleys green and inviting with lakes and trails, but I was blown away. The route to Aspen, over Independence Pass, wound through a carpet of alpine flowers. Stopping on the pass summit at sunset, we tumbled out of the van, leaping and dancing with the sheer delight of it. Dropping to our bellies, we took in the soft newness of summer, the moss, phlox, and forget-me-nots. The air was thin and dizzying, the scent intoxicating.

When night fell on Aspen, we gathered at the feet of the great Bucky Fuller under a glowing geodesic dome along with hundreds of other visionaries, and we heard his plea for smart, eco-pure housing and living. We sat on the green earth, holding our collective breath as he spoke. The energy was electric. Outside the great, sustained tent, a rowdy crowd whirled in psychedelic haze as if at a rock concert. Whatever the gathering, in those days, the Rainbow People were always present, in a sense, tripping on psychedelics and distracting.

"Earth is a spaceship," he told us. "It is a certain size and capacity and can not exceed this capacity. If humanity does not opt for integrity we are through completely. It is absolutely touch and go. Each one of us could make the difference." He seemed to be speaking into our souls. Buckminster's message to the crowd of American youth nearly lifted the dome off its stakes, such was this seventy-six-year-old's enthusiasm for the future.

"Sustainability is a much broader theme than just environmental issues and has to be addressed by all nations as time goes on." We got to our feet, howling like wolves at the barnyard gate, cheering his message and promising to be his champions.

A genius and a master, he reignited our goal to homestead, and soon.

While I waited for Wilber to reignite his commitment to our homesteading mission, I decided to hitchhike north to visit my parents. From my mother's letters I knew that they had indeed moved back to the West and were building their log house on an Idaho mountaintop. It'd been more than six months since I'd seen them, and I felt ready to reengage now, full of my independence and fresh sense of self. The reunion, however, proved to be more of the same old crap. My dad greeted me by plunging all my clothes into BIZ, soaking out the grime and stench of my new life as if that were all he could see of it. I greeted my mom with the news that, even though we weren't currently speaking, I was going to marry a man called Wilber. How, she wanted to know, was I going to marry this man who obviously didn't want me? I was glad to spend time with my younger sister Sarah, to forge what felt like the beginning a new friendship, freed of our nuclear family's dynamic. She was cool.

They were living near the new house site, which commanded a fine view across the valley, over potato and pea farms to the grandeur of the Grand Tetons. The sun rose and lit the peaks in alpenglow, burning the fields with a dry heat all day, then set behind the Big Belt range, softening the evening as heat emanated through the night. Of course, it was a special place—my parents always lived in special places. Down the hill in a small grove of quaking aspens, several canvas tents had been propped on wooden floors. In the largest, a pioneer's kitchen complete with wood stove and coolers made for civilized dining on camp grub. In my parents' tent, lit by elegant kerosene lamps, their genteel antique furniture hinted of home. Navajo rugs softened the floors. Sarah's tent stood nearby, in a cluster of other small tents, as did a makeshift outhouse. Bears, skunks, and lazy wildcats frequented the camp. This was a strange scene for my parents: homesteading in the new West. There was something old, something new, and something wild about it. Sarah was none too happy at the prospect of wild animals in the night. I had to sympathize and I appreciated her courage.

All in all, despite my newfound maturity and liberation, my father's disapproval stung, my mother's pity hurt. They were both glad to see me, after so long with little contact, but completely confused by my choices. I shared information sparingly and didn't stay the two weeks I'd planned on before hitching my way home.

CHAPTER NINE

B ack in Tiger, my Summer of Love was facing an Autumn of Despair. Ellen had met the love of her life, a guru-hazed man who took her back to Vermont and reportedly rendered her even more blissful. I was—we all were—happy for her, and hearing her news I suddenly decided I had tortured myself enough. As the summer cooled, Wilber's resolve appeared immovable. I started talking about moving away, to Denver, and he was unresponsive. Humiliation bumped against my broken heart. I had to go.

Slowly, carefully, I packed for a complete separation—Cheryl would leave Martin and fill my space in Tiger, she decided. On a lonely Friday in September, after a night of heavy, tragic good-byes with my friends at the Pan, I bummed a ride to the suburbs and a flophouse of pleasant repute. Once again, I had no idea what was ahead for me. The change was typical of the ebb and flow of commune life. But would it mean a better future for me? Who could know?

In a well-worn, comfy bungalow on Denver's south side, my hosts, Dave and Monica, welcomed me with kindness. They were always willing and generous with those of us who crashed on the floors or couches of their porch or living room. When we'd come to the city on buying sprees to King Soopers and the head shops around Denver University, theirs was an open house. We could spend the night or two, or not at all; they flowed with it all. In turn, our men folk could help finish a languishing house project, while the ladies cooked up fresh veggies and ripe fruit. We'd wash it all down with tall tales and beer, laughter and music. We brought a rough and sweet mountain high to their mundane urban lives, and they embraced it and us.

On my first night, we sat on a warm porch and greeted new faces. The city-sidewalk flower children burst with suggestions and ideas for my new life. Talking to the others, I came face-to-face with the truth. What jobs awaited a high-school dropout? I hadn't considered jobs, hadn't ever really had one. Waitress in some rat-infested diner? Bagger at King Soopers? Washing mats at the car wash? These hippies were working odd jobs, or just milking our hosts. Not a good idea, not my style. A new reality began to sink in. I could never afford this decent neighborhood on my potential income, and I was unfamiliar with the rents and chores of the city variety. How much was rent? And what were the chores? Hauling water and grinding flour were unnecessary. This was a bad idea. And the weekend bore it out. Uninspired queries for jobs and permanent lodging gave me no hope.

Dreary Denver turned out to be a poor choice for a recovering spirit. There were no stars in the continually lit city sky. Suddenly and surprisingly, I missed my darkness. Cars raced by at all hours, sirens blared, and faceless voices chattered. I missed the solitude of my Tiger. Attempting to find sleep that first night, trying to will myself into this new life, I felt the city closing in on my choices. It was beginning to look like I'd had a bad run. In my self-imposed exile, I felt fear again, and I knew that I'd taken a wrong turn.

I'd made great friends and gained a wealth of knowledge at the University of Tiger, my school of choice. I had invested more energy, emotion, and care in those two seasons then anywhere, anytime in my whole life. And I'd been rewarded with forever friendships and a home. I felt like a schoolgirl running from the prom because her date danced with another. Hadn't I grown beyond that? Wasn't I done running?

By Monday, I'd resolved to go home. Hitching a ride back to Breckenridge, I landed in the Gold Pan on a gorgeous fall afternoon. Susan from Tiger was waitressing.

"Man, am I glad to see you." She was oddly enthused and friendly. "Wilber has been bumming out all weekend, drivin' us all crazy! Said if you didn't come home, he was going to Denver to get you!" I looked around the Pan; heads bobbed in assent.

"What?!" I stammered. My heart leapt. Could everybody see it? "What, why, how?"

"Yup, you better get back out there."

"I'm headin' up the valley now," El Paso said, the sound of Cupid in his voice. With a freaked-out sense of disbelief and an uncontrolled hope, I bounded into the van with my worldly belongings. My heart pounded and flipped in my chest. Susan better not have been fucking with me! She'd never liked me. Could this be a sick game? Her final blow? As we twisted and bounced up the soothing, golden Swan Valley, I contemplated this possibility. Imagining the reunion ahead, the prospects, the risks, my many fantasies come true, my knight in shining denim, I was cautiously ecstatic. The possible outcomes of this day blew my mind. Wilber and I really hadn't spoken for three months. When I had finally been convinced of his disinterest, he was missing me? Certainly his wanting me home was not one of myriad options I had considered.

Tiger was quiet and ghostly. I pulled my stuff out of the van and thanked El Paso, who returned my Cheshire grin and chugged off up the valley. The air was heavenly, scrubbed clean and ripe with a frosty eagerness. I spun in place to view and smell the mountains. With my adolescent sense of timing, it felt as though I'd really been away, since leaving Tiger "for good" just three days earlier. I had mourned it, dramatized, and wailed over it. Now I was back and the comfort of the familiar made me choke a little. With my hope of a brand-new beginning, the old place appeared keenly fresh. The shabbiness was perfect compared to the city grit and glitz, and I was happy for it. I noticed every blade and needle, every shingle and stovepipe, each a treasure I could not take for granted. Whatever happened, I was back.

Cheryl, Bourbon, and Andi were in the main cabin when I peeked through the door. Happy and surprised, they embraced me.

"Far-fucking-out," Bourbon crowed, "You came home! Wilber's gonna freak out!"

"Has he seen you?" Cheryl was ready for the gossip. "Does he know you're back? How was Denver?" We fell on each other with a weekend of news and gossip. Confident in my change of plan, I was glad to be back in the absolute comfort of my friends. We were together again.

Before long, with the lengthening of the valley shadows, we heard the rigs returning from the day's work. Tuned to the sound of each, I held my breath. Bertie's dry walling van stopped to pick up Andi. Kid Shileen's VW and Zipperer's Dodge Ram rumbled up the road, churning up dust, waving and tooting as they passed. Finally, I heard the unmistakable sound of the '54 Chevy entering Tiger, stopping and going silent in front of Wilber's far cabin. Joe and John pulled in with the Volvo; we could hear them talking and laughing as they headed to the creek for a swim. Bourbon, Cheryl, and I rapped on about nothing, fighting back the exhilaration of the moment we expected, trying to stay cool.

Suddenly, with a rush of sun's fading rays and a breath of anticipation, the door swung open. My back was to it; my view was of the suddenly pale faces of my pals. They looked up, their eyes bright and knowing. They continued, even sped up, their chatter. At once, two rough and warm hands touched my shoulders, a faint sigh burst from deep within me. Cool, I thought, stay COOL. I could feel Wilber's belt buckle and strong abs, pressing into my back, the familiar cotton T-shirt brushing my neck. His hands caressed my vulnerable shoulders, tightening into an "I'll never let you go again" grip. I could feel his resolve meld with mine. No words could have spoken with such intensity.

My friends stopped their awkward chatter, got up, and left, I guess. We were alone when Wilber reached around and kissed me, passionately, convincingly. I went limp, except for the sparks shooting out my toes and goose bumps rising on my skin. He took my hand and led me outside and down the road to his bed. This time, when he took me, it was for good. I knew it, he knew it. On that loft, in that isolated cabin, under a cool autumn breeze, we committed to each other as much as we could before minister, rabbi, guru, family, and friends. The struggles and pain of the summer melted like butter on the sill, and we rejoiced in having found each other again. As complete and silent darkness enveloped us, we vowed to never lose sight of this blessing.

The next morning, after seeing Wilber off with a packed lunch and a lingering kiss, I surveyed my new perspective. The view from the fourth cabin was different, with a clearer panorama of the old mine and the future. It was as if I was turning around and surveying my past, all that I had learned and lived here up the road in Cabin #1. It had been my classroom, with empathetic teachers and enthusiastic seekers. They had been my family. We had shared everything. Now, Wilber was my family and our survival would depend on our creating a separate, singular unit. It wouldn't be communal. For the first time in Tiger, there was a private cabin, set apart from the group living of yore and yon. At Cabin #4, friends might have to knock and be invited in. Of course, they always would be welcome, but the "ours" was a new beginning.

Heading back in through the tiny, rickety porch, I beheld a collection of chunky objects wrapped in bright Navajo tapestries: an armchair, a wooden crate, a trunk. A potbelly stove, small and sufficient, was tucked into the corner and led to the kitchen, where Wilber's handiwork shone. Weathered-wood shelves were lined with jars of teas and grains. A particularly handsome wood slab held a rusty old porcelain sink, and a tiny cook stove centered the room. It was stoked and the teakettle was steaming. White Cloud curled in his warm place. Wilber's cabin, into which I had never set foot, only dreamed of, was super cozy. I was home. Crawling back into the loft, my packs slipping up behind me, I unloaded my stuff and tucked it under the eaves, neat piles of my clothing and security.

Then I noticed a further loft space, under a skylight and well plumped with fabrics and pillows. Gently I crept into Wilber's secret, a place he hadn't shared, and discovered a shrine. My Jewish old man had crafted a sacred place for worshipping the Guru Maharajah, the 13-year-old guru we'd all been talking about that summer. I'd had no idea. While I was meditating with Ellen, he'd been sitting lotus-style before a photo of the little master, burning candles and incense and intoning his own consciousness. I was impressed, and humbled. With each unveiled element of his pad, I was so much more in love. That day I discovered new levels of Wilber, and I admired each. I made a promise to myself to always be worthy of the love that he gave willingly. Through our separation, Wilber and I had grown up. I had found serenity, lost the urgency of commitment, and grown to value myself as a partner and friend. Wilber, I thought, had learned the importance and comfort of a strong and smart woman, and proved he had the integrity that his friend Ronnie lacked. I got to work nesting. And we got down to planning our future, not the horizons and dreams of a commune, but the future of two.

Over the next few days, word spread of our reunion. Our friends were blown away and called it a miracle. They had not suspected Wilber's turn of heart, any more than I had, but were relieved that their favorite love affair was again high on love. They had counted on it once, had been cheated by its loss, and felt a certain security in our reconciliation. It gave them hope, it seemed. Many of the hippie chicks and dudes in town were spacey, loose, and funky. Commitment was not hip, free love reigned, and drugs were the elixir of good lovin'. Wilber and I were outside of that, now, tight in our little union. I felt the change: in his arm when he'd usher me across the street, or in his earth-shaking smile that parted a crowd in the Pan.

That fall, Betsy shook her bad boyfriend in Wyoming and came back to our commune, this time to live. In fact, I had insisted she come. She'd been enchanted with Tiger during her summer visit, the endless party and the character of its occupants. Unlike Jackson Hole, the Swan Valley folks were less about proving their athletic prowess and grooviness, more about surviving and creating an alternative. A stunning, gentle blonde, Betsy exuded a trust and tenderness that drew the groovy to her. Throughout our childhood, I had counted on her for initiating friendships. Betsy and I would pick them, she'd ingratiate them with her delightful humor and charm, and then I'd swoop in. We had a good laugh about that pattern when she moved into Tiger.... I had found the friends this time. Now she could reap the benefit of my friendships.

She settled into the main cabin, happy in my old loft. Her room-mates, MaryAnn and John—Maxine was gone to the city, pregnant with John's child—were happy to have her and her help in the kitchen. We worked some shifts at the Gold Pan, hiked in the as-pens, sweated in the sauna, and played. Betsy found fast friends in my Pelham pals and enjoyed her days and nights of freedom. Joe, Stuart, and Susan were still hunkered down in the second cabin. John, Joe, and Stuart were busy with their successful new enter-prise, Swan Valley Painters. In a twist of irony, Sandra from Jumbo had fixed up the cabin just east of us and began stocking her own wood and supplies for the winter with little Vala, without benefit of a man. Liberated, we may have been, but it was still nice to have a man to heat the bunk on those long winter nights. I was glad she hadn't been able to steal mine.

The hint of a coming winter blew in as a blatant warning: morning ice on the pond, snow in the hills, and arctic breezes through the drafty cabins. Wood was being split and stacked, extra insulation stuffed in cracks, and early sunsets meant bringing in more kerosene for the lamps. Banked stoves glowed red with welcome heat. In the deep of an October night, Wilber and I were awakened by the crackling sounds and glow of an uncontained fire. We could see the flicker of flames through the windows. It was coming from Sandra's cabin. In the same moment, she and Vala were bounding through our door.

"It's in the goddamn wall," she screamed. "I pulled away the wood, but, Jesus, I dunno. It's fucking out of control. All our shit's gonna burn!!" She was hysterical. Wilber was in motion. Sandra took Vala into the refuge of our cabin. I ran into the icy night in my socks, following Wilber. He would need backup. Inside Sandra's cabin, the nightmare unfolded. The 100-year-old wood was on fire, the wool/vermiculite/newspaper insulation was smoldering, and the kitchen was in flames. Wilber looked for the source, and we pulled out as much wood and stuffing as possible as we threw water into the center of the fire until it stopped smoking. (Luckily there were full five-gallon buckets inside.) We looked over the blackened room. "Vala's gone back to sleep," Sandra announced, reappearing suddenly. "Is it cool if we crash with you tonight?" Of course. We were all too tired to sort this out now. We would help her clean things up in the morning.

We had all settled back into a deep sleep when Sandra's cabin exploded. We jumped up, all of us yelling and running outside to find the cabin engulfed, all gone. Quickly, we set about saving our own, not 20 feet away. The rest of the night was a blur. Joe, John, and Betsy—everybody was there with buckets, blankets, and shovels. When we climbed back into bed, for the third time, early in the morning, we smelled and tasted of smoke, fiberglass, and sweat. Our first attempt at saving Sandra's cabin had only dampened the fire. The old boards and insulation must have smoldered, heat and combustion intensifying until sparks started to fly and the walls exploded in flames. Needless to say, Sandra and Vala would have been blown to burning bits had they gone back in. The tragedy was not uncommon in these cabins built with questionable and very old materials. We learned caution that night and were blown back on our omnipotent heels. Sandra and Vala were relocating and scavenging for a very long time.

This is Tiger. It is home for a dozen people, several dogs and one amazing kid called Waller. These folks would like their road plowed like everyone else, but they may be snowbound this winter. (See editorial.)

Tiger Town residents lock horns with Commissioners over snow removal

CHAPTER TEN

Tiger folks were planning for the road closure and the isolation of deepest, longest winter. Wilber and I began thinking beyond, preparing for the ever-pressing goal of self-sufficiency. The ground froze. We continued buying food with money made on construction, but we felt the hypocrisy of our existence. This wasn't self-sufficiency; it seemed more like opportunism at the cost of our beloved mountains, which were steadily being carved up for ski hills and condos. We were disgusted and saddened, but the money was easy and we were happy. Or were we? We lived in a society, loosely framed, of transient boomers. Our friends and co-habitators were in constant flux. We had talked about permanency, but our dream was always set in a warmer climate, with shorter and milder winters. We were searchers, and the pursuit of the dream was far from over. The perfect life, we felt, would involve a grand farm in the south, where we could work and water the land to its lush and abundant production. But the future had to promise the peace and nurturing of the high mountain summer. Wilber and I were addicted to that.

From somewhere in his past, maybe his summers at the family cabin in the Rocky Mountain foothills, Wilber had acquired a passion for mountain meadows, and for horses. His ideas for further self-sufficiency training settled on a horseshoeing school he'd read about near Denver. In the horse country of the foothills, Vern Ollinger at Hillcraft School was in the business of passing on the ancient craft, technique, and horse sense. He worked from a coal-fired forge, and anvil-hammered custom shoes were his pride and joy. No fancy footery, this was the real thing. Wilber was intrigued. He envisioned this as a potential pastoral livelihood—no more building condos and tunnels for him—and applied for January enrollment.

Several of our dogs had mysteriously gone missing that fall. In November, a local hunter shot White Cloud to death. Deep despair at the violent death of his best friend sent Wilber into a whirlwind of anger, bordering on vengefulness. White Cloud had been a faithful and loving dog. Found in the White Cloud Mountains of Idaho, he'd been Wilber's constant and dependable playmate for three years, just the beginning of many great years ahead. White Cloud would climb any mountain, ford any river, and attack any porcupine. Wilber was sure that, in death, he was raising hell, chasing picas and quill-less porcupines in doggie heaven.

I held Wilber as we cried for White Cloud and his time stolen from us. He felt the loss so powerfully, I wondered at its origin. Then he mentioned his Opa, his mother's father. He'd lived in the family home from the time little "Frankie" was born. They'd been close, slept in the same room, and Opa had made his breakfast every morning. It was clear that theirs was a strong bond, and his face brightened with the joy of remembrance. When his Opa died at age eighty-eight, Frankie was twenty and away at university. He'd been inconsolable at the news. Five years later, my sensitive man was still suffering that loss, devastated to have missed his good-bye. I asked him to tell me more about Opa, and the door suddenly shut. I was told, quite directly, never to bring him up again. Opa's spirit lived protected in his heart, not to be touched or shared. With White Cloud's death, that pain had resurfaced, begging to be resolved. Was it possible?

"Tis better to have loved and lost than never to have loved at all," wrote Alfred, Lord Tennyson. Made sense to me, but then, I had never lost. Not having been given unconditional love, my heart had never filled. My grandparents had barely been in my life and died in my early youth. I hadn't suffered loss. In fact, no one really close to me had ever died. My mother's parents lived nearby and holidays were shared, but Granddaddy died when I was ten, Bumese six months later. I remembered his embrace and soft chuckle, comingled with the image of St. Nick. Of my grandmother, Bumese, my limited memory was of a lonely and sarcastic woman. My father's parents were mostly absent, living in the Far East. I saw them twice. Aunts, uncles, and cousins were plentiful, but none could be counted on.

I watched Wilber go through his more recent loss of unconditional love as if I were listening to a foreign language. Maybe the fuller the heart, the slower it heals, I thought. Wilber was a proud, loving, thoughtful, and good-humored man, a man whose character I considered irreproachable. I wondered if I, like him, had unconditional love to give. I wanted it, that depth of acceptance and care. Wilber gave it, my friends gave it, and I would learn how to give it back.

The loss of our dog, it turned out, wasn't an isolated incident. The dogs of the Swan Valley were disappearing. The resort developers in fledgling Breckenridge were threatened by the hippies and worried that our sloppy presence would upset property values. But

killing our dogs was beyond despicable. We knew they were trying to get rid of the "undesirables" and many of our good friends
had now moved out of mining cabins and into their vans and tipis, keeping one foot ahead of developers. Many had moved away
completely. We were safe with squatting rights from the owners of
Royal Tiger Mine, but the animosity had served its purpose. Just
as the moneyed populace had hoped, the hippies were fleeing the
bad vibes. The community was changing once more, but this time
things were getting nasty. We were sadly but more resolutely determined to be on that wagon train heading downhill, to warmer
climes and further opportunities.

In December, before the snow got too deep, Wilber was called
to Cherry Creek in Denver, for a command presence at his father's
sixtieth birthday. Since our future was heading toward family and
forever, I asked if I could go along. Wilber said yes, but I could tell
he didn't want me to; facing his parents as a hippie, not a doctor
or lawyer, was bad enough. Showing up with a young chick on his
arm, the repercussions would be brutal. I had no idea why he was
so worried, but I was about to find out. I knew his parents were
immigrants, having fled Nazi Germany and Austria in the early
days of World War II. Though I knew little about Judaism, almost
nothing in fact, I was a polite and sensitive young woman. I'd had
Jewish friends in school. I'd visited Auschwitz with my parents. I
knew the horrors. I'd been around. I promised to call him Frank,
since he'd been named after the president who'd rescued his parents
from the gas chambers.

I spent days picking out the right look and cleaning up. My
whitest waffle-weave long johns tucked into tall army boots and my
handmade Indian print snow-sweeping dress made my best birthday costume. I wove my brown tresses into a thick waist-length
braid, imagining how impressed they'd be at the sight of me. My
wool-lined jean jacket had been fancied up with a red velvet collar,
finished with my favorite embroidery stitch. I never wore make-up,
so they couldn't think me a hussy. Although I had no deodorant,
perfume, or hair spray, I was nice-looking, simple, and well bred. I

was sure they'd like me. I sure wanted them to.

"Don't SEET on zee COUCH!" Frankie's mother's thick German voice boomed from the kitchen. "Eet cozt me eine zousand dollarz." His father shot me a challenging glance, then disappeared toward the food, where Frankie had gone to challenge his mother. *Oh, this* was a good start…

"Go ahead, sit on the *fucking* couch," ordered Margaret, in a whisper. She was Frankie's sister, down from Boulder, and already seated in a velvet armchair. We'd met many times and I liked her a lot. I think she liked me too, even though, on meeting her the previous spring, I'd asked how old she was. She didn't scoff at my rudeness and told me that she was thirty. She laughed at my shocked response: "But you look so young!" Anyone over thirty was untrustworthy, *period,* but she didn't fit that cliché. A female version of Frankie, she flashed her intense brown eyes at me, equal parts daring and welcoming. Dressed in a long woven skirt and dark cowl-necked sweater, she looked like a more mature version of me, identifiable at a glance as a woman living on her own terms. She reminded me of my much-older cousins who would dress mysteriously in black and dance the Frug and Watusi on our linoleum kitchen floor during holiday gatherings.

Margaret was an artist, cool, funky, and very, very funny. Her friends had built an artist's commune in southern Colorado called Drop City. It was a hillside of geodesic domes, homage to Buckminster Fuller. Committed to their art and the shared experience, the Droppers built their domes out of salvaged materials, pooled money, clothes, and food, and lived a minimalist life immersed in their craft. Margaret visited them rarely, not being the co-living type. When the Droppers came to Boulder, she told me with a laugh, "They sometimes stayed with me. What was mine was theirs and what was theirs was mine, but they had nothing." Like Frankie, she had chosen a life that disappointed their parents, and humor was how they survived.

I looked at the couch in question, taking in its shimmering aura of pale gold and feeling somewhat like Linus, though not blissfully unaware of my filth. Though familiar with this response from my own family, I was surprised by the assault on a guest. It bespoke their fear of my permanence. If only they knew....

"Come on, Nonnie, sit down," encouraged Margaret, rolling her eyes. Sparky, her beloved mutt, sat at her feet. She distractedly stroked his head. I took to a wooden cane chair instead, sitting gingerly.

"Und keep zhat filtzy dog off zee furniture!" More missives wafted into the room along with a whiff of brisket. Here were Hansi and Fred, the parents of my darling lover.

The evening never loosened up. A delicious but demanding dinner, on what happened to be Shabbat, was full of ceremony and chants I knew nothing about. Couldn't Wilber, I mean Frankie, have warned me? Was he setting us up, waiting for fireworks? No matter—we made it through. We even spent the night. Since the '54 Chevy had broken down on our way there, we were kind of stuck. Frankie was more than a little humiliated.

In the morning, Fred and Frank went off to Colfax Avenue and bought a new 1972 Chevy three-quarter-ton pick-up. Shiny green, with a big wide bench seat and a much bigger bed, it was a strong and grown-up vehicle despite its lack of a four-wheel drive. Given our idea of farrier school, our move toward independence and Wilber's loss of White Cloud, responsibility and accountability were in order. A note co-signed by Fred enabled us to make the purchase. Consumerism, yes, but an investment: in us, in our freedom, in our dream.

One evening not long after that intense Neumann family visit, after dinner in our tiny snowy home, our talk turned toward commitment.

"Do you think we should have a baby?" Wilber said, completely out of the blue. I was still seventeen, uneducated, technically an adolescent, being asked to consider motherhood. My man, my love and my future, was gently requesting my opinion. There was no pressure in his question, delivered in the sweet tone of affection.

"Yeah..." I responded instantly. "I think we should." I knew at once that this was the next best step for us. A baby, a new life, a bright hope. If he wanted it, I was sure I wanted it, and it would be a wonderful thing. We'd think about it some more, though what with my inconsistent diaphragm use, who knew what would happen and how soon. As Christmas approached, I thought of the possibility as a gift—a baby to brighten the next holiday season!

In early January '72, we moved to a tiny back house in west Denver. Every day, Wilber drove out to Golden. He loved farrier school. Vern turned out to be a curmudgeon, tough and humorless, but Wilber respected his style and his amazing skill. And he excelled, of course. I'd talked my way into a fancy French restaurant, downtown on newly renovated Larimer Square. I sold myself as a cook, lying through my teeth once again, and they put me on the line as sous chef. I thrived as well. Taking the bus into town, to work the lunch shift, I saw myself in the working class, and loved it. I was having fun, working alongside a staff of young folks who gave a serious attention to quality. I learned a lot, and was proud.

Most fun for me was setting up our little home. For $130 a month, our darling rented bungalow was perfect, if temporary. Our humble furnishings, plus a few oddities from Hansi and Fred, made the place homey; a welcome retreat contrasted our busy days. There we focused on each other. We read to each other from *Be Here Now* and *The Whole Earth Catalog* and began to craft our self-sufficient life. I was knitting, baking, making a home. Wilber was learning to weld, shoe horses, and repair engines. We hoped to be able to barter our skills in the country. Our backwoods education was in high gear, even though we were living in the big city. On my eighteenth birthday, I unwrapped *The Joy of Cooking* to find a short but poignant inscription: *"To Nonnie, Happy 18th m'dear (hint, hint), love Willy."* The life-long tool was appreciated and instantly useful. We had Margaret and her friends over for dinner, and friends came down from Breckenridge. With an electric fridge and stove, meals practically made themselves, and I loved the convenience. Hansi and Fred never crossed town to see us, but we went there when invited, and I thought I sensed an easing of the father/

son tension and a general warming toward me.

I was timid about making the right choices for furnishing and feeding our lives, but I needn't have been. Wilber taught me the importance of being direct, self-assured, and clear. He approved, encouraged, and cared. He was sensitive to criticism, since his father had been a tyrant. He liked being appreciated, and he treated me in kind. He valued my input and supported my decisions. His dry wit and savvy humor were charming, but he was intent and serious about his approach to protocol. His moral judgment never wavered. Now that I was going to be his woman and mother of his child, turning on and dropping out were off. We tuned in to our new reality. We clung to each other with a desperate passion, and filled our intimate moments with heady promises.

The sense of urban isolation inspired frequent trips to the mountains. We'd drive the truck on Friday evening up and over Loveland Pass, always tricky and especially so at night. *American Pie* and *Take Me Home, Country Road* played on the radio and we clamored to be heading home, *"to the place we belonged."* Betsy was living in our cabin, and friends were scattered about the valley. For news and friendship, we skied familiar trails and found scenes little changed. We were glad for the tea and toke, and understood this would only ever be a visiting place for us forevermore. In late February, when we found out I was pregnant, we went to the mountains for a proper announcement of our eternal commitment. Of course, there was a mid-winter warming and a pre-wedding party at the Gold Pan. All the remaining hippies came out of hiding to celebrate for and with us. We danced and ate, and laughed until it hurt. The Pan was in fine form and it was a joyous reunion. Unlike many members of our generation for whom pregnancy was not necessarily a prelude to marriage, it was a natural next step in our devotion to each other. More people were having babies than having spouses. The American family was being redefined for some, but not for us.

Telling our parents was a bit of a different story. Wilber took the opportunity to go alone to Cherry Creek for the bomb dropping. It went as he expected. What they said I'll never know, thank goodness, but he returned that night only to report that they were not very nice about it. Visits came to a halt as they took their time to get over the shock. Hansi was an adoption counselor for Jewish refugee babies and families, and Fred was director of the Jewish Family and Children's Service of Denver. They had both worked hard, as immigrants and refugees, for their Ph.D.s in psychology. Obviously, the fact that their first grandchild would be borne by an uneducated Goya was a weighty stone on their lifetime of disappointments and pain.

I expected drama, yet relief on my end, when I made the call to Idaho. My dad had taken to calling himself the "Main Man" to his still-single daughters. Very loosely referring to himself as the Number One male in our lives spoke only to his perceived importance, not to any burden of caregiving. I knew he'd be relieved to pass that torch to another, in my case especially. I'd been a liability, and now I'd be off his back permanently. No turning back from the family way!

I figured my parents would ultimately be glad. So I called collect. My father's policy was never to accept collect calls, unless they were emergencies. He answered on the first ring.

"I do NOT accept collect calls, unless it's an emergency," he informed the operator, and me. True to form. And he hung up.

Suddenly, I lost it, crying and choking in bursts. Being pregnant did that to me. I asked the operator to try the number again, collect.

"Only emergency calls!" he blasted the operator.

"But, Daddy," I sniffled, "I'm pregnant (sob), and I'm getting married (sob-sob)."

"Well, Mista, if DIS ain't an emergency, I dunno WHAT is! Yo betta takes dis call!"

Thank you, sensitive operator.

"Oh, all right," he sighed.

He passed the phone to my mother right away. She and I discussed wedding plans, at their ranch, with a nondenominational judge. My sisters would come home for sure, Wilber's family, of course. But when? As soon as possible. Wilber would graduate from Farrier School *("from what?")* soon, and we'd be traveling to look for a new home *("where?")*. Needless to say, the train had left the station.

Now, my consequences bespoke my options. I was pregnant, soon to be married in my parents' home. I had sworn I'd never go back, but going home with my new Main Man, for the rite of passage, was all forward motion. I would show my parents that my quest for a life of meaning had yielded a fine man and a hopeful future. I knew my father would welcome the rite of giving my hand permanently to another. He loved me, within the confines of his narcissism. I wondered whether my mother still cried herself to sleep. After the years of challenges in our relationship, I hoped they would be relieved and act proud.

Chapter Eleven

The gloom of a Teton Valley winter hung on into March. When we arrived with the bridal party, Betsy and John, I couldn't help but flash back to my first impressions of the place. It was September 1969, and as our small Frontier Airlines twin engine bumped and banked out of the clouds, I felt we were dropping into another world. High school in Wyoming! We glided over the open range, and grasses and river rolled endlessly north and south. Dry buttes stood sentry to the east, the green flanks of the magnificent Teton Mountains to the west. The gray mat of clouds hung low and muted the colors of the season. As we deplaned, the scent of molding hay and pines wafted in on a light breeze. I didn't recognize it then, but those would be the recurring scent memories of my life. The Rocky Mountain West had stolen my heart forever.

Despite our idyllic first impressions, Jackson Hole was full of the tackiness tourism, then and now. My parents' new town of Driggs was even more dismal. In the brown and white cold of spring, the one-horse town was depressing until you'd been there long enough to call it quaint. That took going to town with the folks and letting them show you around, meeting everyone. Coburn Drug, Sessions Grocers, Teton Mountaineering were the hub of the community and not hostile to hippies. The Mormons had accepted my parents into the valley. They were not welcomed, but neither were they shunned. That was the way it was.

"Boy, that judge is in for a new experience," my mother had said in one of our few planning chats. Judge Willis Moffat, local officiator/barber, would join us in holy matrimony. My mother would make a turkey dinner; Dede, who cooked at Blackie's in Jackson, would bake a whole-wheat carrot cake; and the flowers could only be the simplest available. That was exactly what we wanted. Wilber and I had shopped for wedding clothes in Denver. My hand-embroidered Mexican "gown" from a Colfax Avenue head shop and his new cowboy shirt, boots, and dress corduroys were fresh and simple.

No amount of describing could have set the scene that greeted my fiancé when we arrived at the barn the first night. Kenny (my dad, father-of-the-bride, and soon-to-be-grandpa) was there—we'd alerted him from town—standing in the bright semi-circle of barn light in his signature wool toque and bulky down coat. His posturing bespoke his fear of this new man. His greeting was awkward and brief. His machine was revved up. The Ski-Doo snowmobile was puffing with power. Its Ski-Boose, a trailer sled, attached and waiting. The driveway to my parents' new hilltop log lodge was unplowed in winter. Loading, shuttling, and returning people and supplies from barn to house by snowmobile was an effort rewarded with an unobstructed and sweeping view of the county and the Grand Teton peaks. It was bitter cold and getting dark. We had to start moving people and luggage up to the house.

Betsy hopped on the Ski-Doo with our dad while I piled in the Ski-Boose hanging on to bags and gear. At the house, my mother waited with Dede and Sarah. The aroma of roast something drew us in from the porch. (I had forsaken my vegetarian diet at a bridal shower at the Neumanns a month earlier. Arriving in my newly pregnant but not yet showing state, I smelled bacon—not kosher, but yummy—and couldn't hold back. I got down with a pile of pork and never looked back.) After hustling our stuff onto the porch, Kenny slid back on the Ski-Doo and roared off to retrieve my groom and best man.

Betsy and I entered a house new to us, but full of mementos and memories. Furniture and fabrics from colonial Connecticut mingled perfectly with art and accessories of the Wild West. When we embraced, my mom seemed a bit uncomfortable, yet relieved. I felt that familiar blend of love and judgment. An impromptu gathering of her children was joyful, but the shotgun wedding of her pregnant teenager was fraught and dubious. Within an hour of meeting him, she and Kenny had taken the measure of Wilber, and their pleasure and relief gave way to a casual evening, with story-telling of shared passions: mountain living, fishing, hunting, and surviving. Warm laughter and classical music filled the cathedral ceiling and set me at ease. I was proud of Wilber and my parents for embracing each other and our future. We awaited the arrival and introduction of Hansi, Fred, and Margaret. We still had the wedding ceremony to face. The easy mood would be tested.

Our wedding day dawned overcast. Wilber and I awoke in separate bedrooms, meeting in the hall for a private snuggle before the requisite western breakfast. A somber sky dropped large light snowflakes on the porch. The call went out for skiers. Who wanted to try Grand Targhee Ski Area, at the foot of the Tetons and famous for feather-light powder? Wilber looked at me, knowing I'd not stand in his way, but sensitive to the occasion. I nodded assent, of course. Soon he, John, Betsy, and Dede were packing the snowmobile, with Kenny happily in the lead. As we watched them disappear down the hill, my mother turned to me. "Well, Nonnie, you've finally done something you said you would. Good job." The sideways compliment (a reference to my unfulfilled childhood ambitions—Mt. Everest climber, Olympic skier, rock 'n' roll singer, and so on) surprised and confused me. I was marrying the man of my dreams, a goal stated long ago, but no one would believe that we'd planned the pregnancy. My success and pride looked like a mistake. Sarah and I settled in for a catch-up day, and helped Mommy prep the wedding feast.

At noon, a call came from the ski hill requesting a few more hours of skiing. The wedding was scheduled for 2:00; could we push it back to 5:00 in consideration of amazing powder? Of course. "Just make sure the groom makes it back in one piece," was my reply. The Neumanns were on their way with my dad. We could entertain them for the afternoon. Most of the wedding party was skiing. What could we do? Needing some fresh air, I walked down to the barn to welcome my new in-laws. Beleaguered by the town, motel, travel, and remoteness, my city-savvy new family needed encouragement to face the unexpected snowmobile ride. Not only were they not going to a good Jewish synagogue wedding, with familiar mores and vows, they were being ordered onto a sleigh by a jolly bearded man. Christmas, Christians, and blasphemy must have merged with their disappointment, and they figuratively threw up their mittened hands. I felt bad for them, though I was feeling as jolly as my dad.

The shuttle process began. Hansi sat gingerly behind Kenny on the Ski-Doo, Fred settled solidly in the Ski-Boose. With the roar of a two-stroke engine and a skid of snow, they were off. Margaret and I followed, hiking on packed snow, chatting and laughing at the scene. But at the big curve of the hill, we heard the engine whine in effort, then saw the shifting weight and the Ski-Boose slowly flip, sending poor Fred into the deep snow. There he lay sputtering and flailing while Hansi moaned about Marjorie Morningstar and her last hope of lost tradition. By the time Margaret and I could control our hysterics and join the scene, Kenny had helped Fred to his feet, and Fred had decided to walk with us. Humiliation was an inauspicious beginning. But it was really just a clash of lifestyles.

We walked slowly and made it to the house just as Hansi was settling in for tea with my mother. They were all unsurprised by the wedding delay; what else could go wrong? Judge Moffat was cool, so we'd make the best of it.

"We're just so pleased with Wilber and glad to have him in our family," my mother said, trying to soothe Hansi and recover the mood. Her pleasantries fell on Hansi's already disbelieving ears.

"Vhat?" was her confused reply.

"Oh, we so enjoy Wilber and are thrilled for their future." My mother continued her struggle for social grace.

"VHAT?" Hansi stepped back. She had begun to comprehend. "My son's name ees Vilma?" My unsuspecting mother looked pleadingly in my direction. Had we forgotten to tell her Wilber's real name and the importance of using it? Oh my! What a start. Making the best of this we weren't, so I sat down to explain. Margaret and I tried to minimize it as a silly, temporary thing, but Hansi and Fred were not pleased. How could their son forsake the name of their liberator? They didn't and wouldn't get it. Why should they? I wished Wilber/Frank would get back soon. We needed his broad shoulders for this.

Pleasantries and humor helped us weather the afternoon. By four o'clock, the skiers had returned safely, showered, and dressed. The judge had arrived. Flowers were bunched and beribboned. Places were taken. Wilber and I had not planned for a ring, but my dad had. As we met at the end of the hallway/aisle, he turned to me with a twinkle and a smile.

"This is my mother's wedding band," he said, opening his hand to reveal a tiny platinum ring. "It was given to her by my dad more than fifty years ago. I want you to have it." And he placed it in my hand. So with my bouquet in my left hand, my grandmother's ring clutched in my right (my "something old"), my wedding dress ("something new"), my sister's shoes ("something borrowed"), and my eyes standing in for the "something blue," I took my dad's arm and marched into my perfectly untraditional wedding.

Photos show the judge grinning as we kissed before the picture window, the gorgeous backdrop still shrouded in clouds. No matter. The celebration and wedding dinner followed, culminating in a sense of relaxed joy, perhaps resignation for some. Night closed in quickly after the six-thirty sunset, so Wilber and I walked Hansi, Fred, and Margaret back down to their car. Returning to the house, we found the wedding bed prepared by my parents in their room, a fire in the stone fireplace, and champagne in a bucket on the hearth. A very romantic and thoughtful surprise.

We awoke to the tableau of my sisters and parents chattering over pancakes and coffee. As we entered the room, they looked up and faked a blush, as though we'd been virginal newlyweds instead of pregnant cohabiters. We all laughed hard at the irony. Soon, we'd begin our "honeymoon," which for us meant not a vacation but a search for a new home and community, our first adventure as a married couple. We headed out that day with a thirst for all the possibilities in our grasp.

Early April meant true spring in central Idaho, in the lower elevations and gentle river glens. Climbing the panhandle, we found hopeful options in Lewiston and Kooskia, gardens already growing and saner-than-Colorado pricing. We toured with and without realtors. Fine areas, verdant properties, and old homesteads were plentiful. Wilber found abundant horses for his shoeing work, and I sensed the crafty handwork of busy women. In an instant, we thought we'd found the nesting place. But meeting locals and catching the vibes, we felt the folks were too provincial, and found we might not be welcome. Community was important to us, and we sought like-minded and hard-working hippies, freethinking spirits. On further inspection, the valleys proved deep and dark. In the majestic cedars' brush with the fog and the forest's quiet mossy undergrowth, we forecast the social claustrophobia and cold damp of winter. So we continued on.

Eastern Washington was too dry, western too wet. Cruising the coast, we camped on the beaches of Oregon and Northern California and huddled against the chill ocean breeze. Sand in my sandwich and beachcombing for shells took me back to Cape Cod and spring visits when we had the beaches, blustery and winter-swept, to ourselves. Stopping in all viable towns, we found endless homesteading possibilities. But mostly, being in the family way, we were blown away by our yearning for the comfort of home and our family at Tiger. So we headed home via Eureka, stopping at the commune Wilber's friend Ron had been encouraging us to join.

It was in the Sierra foothills and had been touted as a true nirvana, full of Santa Cruz hippies, free and harmonious. When we finally found it, we weren't disappointed. We were dazzled by the scene: The green pastures ran with goats, the hillside sprouted an enormous garden, the Yuba River gurgled over granite, and the hippies freed themselves of clothing. It was a bit of a reunion for Wilber. These were folks he'd known from his 1969 beach bum daze. Ronnie, now settled as husband to Suebi and father to Sunshine, appeared the leader and puffy-chest proud. California hippies were different to me, not like the Texans and New Yorkers I'd come to love in Colorado. They were laid-back dreamers, and a bit overly cool. Blonde, beautiful, tanned, radiant, they seemed like the chosen ones, an idealized tableau of a hippie commune in 1972. Rather than being tempted to stay, Wilber and I found ourselves homesick for our Tiger family. Amid the protests of the Bridgeport Garden folks, we headed over Donner Pass, through Nevada and Utah, and straight into the friendly arms of our hearty mountain freaks. We had made a stab at independence, but we weren't quite ready.

Back in Breckenridge, P.O. Box 553 was brimming with wedding presents and the Gold Pan erupted in applause. A fine homecoming. The mountains near Tiger were full of our best friends that summer. Bertie Ray, Bro Paul, Jane, Roger, and Andi were still in Storyland. El Paso, Sandra, and Vala had hooked up and settled into his tipi at the North Fork. Tipi Chuck was also in, well, a tipi, across the creek from Tiger, close to the sauna and mine ruins. Maxine had given birth to Shanti, and they occupied Jumbo, now with Tami. The Brown's Gulch gang, Annie and Bernie, Steph and Tinker, had survived the invasion, we were glad to see. Betsy still lived in our Tiger cabin, most recently with a Pelhamite called Plum Fairy. Cheryl had met Roger, a quiet guy from Indiana with his head screwed on tight whom we all loved, and they'd headed to Alaska with the salmon run. Kid Shileen had taken a summer job on a fishing boat in the Gulf of Alaska.

But Tiger, we found, was overrun, with more cabins inhabited and a slew of unfamiliar trucks, freaks, and dogs. It wasn't our home anymore. In the midst of all the craziness, Joe and John decided it wasn't theirs, either. With the success of Swan Valley Painters and a new Chevy Carry-all van, they were in need of a place with electricity and security in which to run a successful painting business. So they drove over Hoosier Pass to Alma and found a new community, a town of dedicated workers. In fact, some of the locals in Alma were actually locals, born and raised right there. Some worked in Fairplay, some in Breckenridge. Joe and John bought an old Dodge dealership and garage on Main Street and moved in. The apartment upstairs was deluxe—big kitchen, bathroom, and two bedrooms. Below, in the working garage, a giant gas heater hung off the wall and blew warm to cool air around the voluminous space. Working on trucks, vans, and cars suddenly became a joy. Everyone loved the Alma Garage and went over the hill often just to experience it (and its showers and cooking).

We were glad for their success.

Chapter Twelve

Still, we needed a place to settle for the summer. Wilber and I had the tent and a fine camping routine. We parked the truck near Storyland and followed a game trail to the west. It was probably late June. Aspens were shyly tipped with the iridescent glow of green leaves still growing, and the grass was damp, long, and fragrant. The air almost stung with the sharpness of departing winter, long dormant life responding to warm sun with new growth. The sun felt good, through thin air, and its long arc toward the western ridge brought memories of the last summer of love. We found a clearing in the aspens, near a small creek, overlooking another field of flowers and the long Swan Valley. Paintbrush, larkspur, columbine, daisies, and phlox crowded and scented the place, leaving just enough room for the tent and a hammock. We were home and went to unpack the truck.

For the next weeks, I was a bird with an egg, building a nest. Wilber went back to work, building tourist condos at Copper Mountain and leaving me carless by day. I stayed up-valley and built a mellow environment for our growing fetus. Of course, if I wanted a ride or some company, there was always someone at Storyland wanting for a visit, a baking partner, or some music making. But I was busy. The ground around the tent was raw, virgin, had never been nested. I walked around and around to mat it down. I piled fieldstones in the creek to dam it for a basin. The water was brilliant and cold. I would wash and gather water there. I had an old enamel tin pan, big enough for washing dishes, vegetables, and, later, a baby. When my day's work was done, I'd sit with my back to a tree and the world at my feet and read about babies.

Wilber crafted a summer kitchen, out of barn wood as always: cabinet set between two aspens, a weathered board for the table, hooks for the hammock, a cooler near the creek, our Coleman stove on a log. I dressed it all up with nuptial dishes, pots and pans, linens, and potholders. I found a vase amidst the wedding presents for wildflowers for the table. The more permanent tent setup included a foam bed with wedding sheets, matching towels, and crates stacked with clothes. Toaster, blender, bronze sculpture, and other useless but thoughtful gifts stayed in the pickup's bed until they could be donated elsewhere. We had all we needed. We loved our little site. It was romantic, simple, and perfect. I thought this would surely be the best home, and time, of my life. Later, I'd find out I'd been right.

Quiet evenings with Wilber were composed of campfire dinners, blazing sunsets, and projects by kerosene lamp. We talked of the baby nightly, contemplating where we'd go when the summer waned. Some nights we'd go to Storyland for music with Mark Haynes. Or we'd head down to El Paso's tipi, on nights when Mike and his Gold Pan Boogie Band would rev up a generator and play in the meadow. Music could be as loud as needed; all the neighbors were at the party. There were no rules. On one of those epic nights, while they drank beer, toked pot, and ate Sandra's tasty Texas tamales, some partook of acid-laced wine. Dancing wildly around the tipi fire pit, they twirled and shimmied. The night grew frenetic with psychedelic energy and music. Suddenly, Paso, totally loaded, did a flip over the fire pit, landing in the fire and burning his arm badly. The music played on, the dancing continued, while Sandra nursed him with potions of goldenseal and vitamin E. That's just how it was.

The Lord of the Universe, the now fourteen-year-old guru, had reentered our lives. With his vision of a perfect union and initiation to the Knowledge, he had inspired the formation of the Divine Light Missions worldwide. In July, he hosted a gathering of disciples in the desert near Montrose, Colorado. We were all going, and excited about it. We drove down in the panel van, "Swan Valley Painters" emblazoned on the outside and eager hippies with food, blankets, and hopes inside. We arrived to a scene of mellow chaos. Gated and fenced, the festival was a no drug zone, and we all had to get rid of our contraband before entering. Some people were smoking up their stash, but most were appropriately reverent and respectful of the reasoning: We were all going to get high on the love and the light of our guru. Almost immediately we heard the chant that would resonate all weekend:

"The Lord of the Universe has come to us this day,
He's come to show us the love,
And he's come to show us the light
And he's come to show us the way … back to our fathers."

We filed in and found a campsite off by the fence to the north. There were nine of us: Joe, John, Betsy, Plum, Martin, MaryAnn, Bien, Wilber, and me. It was hot and dry to those of us who had come from the land of creeks and wildflowers, but the sensation of being deprived of landscape and color only moved us closer to the holy one. The weekend took place in slow motion, full of many languid sittings and meditations, culminating in a daylong lineup to kiss the feet of Guru Maharaj Ji. Betsy and Martin were skeptical, doubting this young boy and yearning for drugs and fun, not abstinence and devotion. Martin found the Rainbow People, of course, just outside the fence, their camp a riot of color and music and drugs, and he was gone. While the rest of us lined up for absolution, Betsy wandered into a tent gallery of photos and relics. As she studied the art, a young round man entered and stood with her observing the photos. Later, she realized she had been standing with the Lord of the Universe.

"I just looked at him and tried to feel something, but didn't … He was just a guy, a kid." She was clear and, in my attempt to transcend, I knew she was right. Back up the Swan we all went back to work and play, and the holy one faded from memory. It was fun while it lasted.

We'd go to town sometimes, to hang out at the Gold Pan, shop for food, and see friends. Occasionally, we'd spend a Friday or Saturday night at the Pan or the All American, dancing and partying. For me, it was reminiscent but totally different from the previous summer, when my loneliness tempered my every moment of joy. In contrast, I was now on the arm and under the watchful eye of my husband, a place I'd dreamt of when I'd boogied alone through my perceived freedom. Safe, glowing, and loved, I danced in my sweet Willy's arms.

One night at the Pan, Quaaludes made the scene. I wouldn't do any, and no one offered, though it looked like the stupidest fun. Everyone was falling down, silly and heady with experimentation. Someone picked me up and swung me (I couldn't remember who, but Wilber said he'd beat the shit out of 'em). That night in the tent, I cramped and bled and Wilber rushed me to the clinic in Dillon. At seven months pregnant, it was a bad sign, and we were scared. They laid me down and conferred in hushed tones. I worried, but Wilber was resolute. *What's meant to be will be.* Luckily, they were able to stop the pre-labor and we retired to our meadow. It was a sobering moment for us all. We realized it was time for us to leave the field, to find our next home—and a nursery.

We'd thought long and hard about the commune and the hot, fertile land of the Sierra foothills. We'd heard from Ron that the corn, tomatoes, and melons were ripe to bursting. We were still buying our food from King Soopers, so the lure of California bounty appealed to our hunger for nature and simplicity. Our new Sioux tipi, ordered by my parents as a wedding present, was ready. In the nearby forest, Wilber and Joe chopped down the requisite lodge pole pines, peeling and drying them into perfect tipi poles. We'd live in our tipi, amidst the garden harvest, along the Yuba River. Once again we packed up to move away. This time our thoughts turned to family and values.

Chapter Thirteen

The land of plenty. From the high, dry, and cool valleys of Colorado across the high, dry, and hot deserts of Utah and Nevada, we drove through the changing waves of extreme environments. Suffocating days and chilled nights, endless sun to vacant horizons, we rolled over hill and plain wishing for a breath of cool air through the open windows. The oven blast continued. We were tired and hot and dragging our collectively pregnant bodies to our new home. The still-new Chevy truck was loaded with our worldly possessions. Domestic gifts from our wedding, relics of previous lives, and travel gear crowded the bed. The fresh tipi poles and big stretch of white canvas that would form our next home were strapped to the topper.

We were a cliché of the '70s, hippies in search of the free life and good times descending on California. We were the 20th century version of the pioneer, moving faster and with more stuff, but with the anticipation and wonder of our ancestors. We were happy, young, and poor, and we were inspired by change. We didn't know how we would be received, how we would feel about the place or people, how we'd adjust to the California life. We'd had a short call with Ron, on the ranch's single phone, and he'd said we should come—there was plenty of room, and extra hands were always welcome. Molly was caretaker to a 640-acre section of dry foothills; the land belonged to a rich friend in Santa Cruz. She'd invited her friends, including her boyfriend, Dave, and Ron and Suebi, to live self-sufficiently on the life-giving South Yuba River. Like so much of the West, a watered desert became an Eden in no time. Still, we had our questions and doubts, but mostly we were excited to be bringing forth life in the land of plenty.

Up, up, and over Donner Pass, down I-80 into California and into the wealth of life budding, growing, and ripening as we passed… The basins, farms, rivers, and small forgotten towns cascaded before us. Fresh, fragrant air rushed in our windows and filled the cab with a new feel. It smelled of scrub pine and possibilities, and hope replaced the tiredness in our veins. The town names made us laugh in excitement. Emigrant Gap, Gold Run, Yuba, Placerville, Washoe, and Rough and Ready summoned a time when tipis and mining shacks coexisted in these hills. This was the California version of our Colorado mountain-mining life.

We had directions and the memory of our visit in April. Rolling across the hilltops in the foothills of the Sierras, we were blown away to find that the purely green, tender, and bracing splendor of spring now lay brittle, golden, and flat. The relentless sun had scorched the grassy hills, the berry brambles, and the rattlesnake dens. We bounced along, as the narrow, broken asphalt of Bitney Springs Road carved hillsides and ranches. Eventually, Pleasant Valley Road delivered us to Bridgeport. There the road ended at a barricade protecting the self-proclaimed "longest single-span wood-covered bridge in the nation." The graceful structure of weathered pine and Douglas fir timbers dated back to 1862 and had been deemed unsafe for cars. Thus the abandoned community on the South Yuba River had been reduced to a few ramshackle buildings and a public parking area for river swimmers.

There at the river, an oasis welcomed our squinting eyes. Through the trees and across a small draw, we saw a garden climbing the hill, a green swath on a brown wasteland. Ahead a tall red horse barn rose to a hayloft peak, its wings bustling with chickens and goats. Beyond the stonewall, the main farmhouse had sprung to life with signs of use. The river and creeks were feeding the shores of this sanctuary, which needed only the simplest of refreshments in order to thrive and grow. Water, once flooding the mountain gulches in Colorado, was precious here, and we saw why. Nearby, tucked in by a great oak, another small, old farmhouse looked alive, with a VW van and laundry decorating the yard. We went to greet Ron and Suebi. We were anxious to catch up and settle in.

We'd arrived in the midst of a heat wave. It was August and due to get hotter through October. The resident group was small, tight, and totally cool—the strain of shared life had already sent some revelers packing, but the remaining group was steady. Ron, the pot farmer, was a funny, quirky bulldog. Suebi was his old lady, wiry, feisty, and a total earth mother. Sunshine, their nine-month-old boy, was cherubic and spoiled. Molly, the gardener and caretaker, wore short golden ringlets, a full-body tan, and a strong will. Dave, her old man and our token draft-dodger, was tall, dark, and intense. Richard, lanky guitar player with sandy beard and tresses, came and went on important missions. There were others, of course, escaping the Bay Area and landing in Bridgeport for a few days or weeks. It was the summer of '72 and all freaks of the hippie persuasion wandered the hills in search of a meal, a bed, and a toke. Bridgeport had all that and more.

To find the perfect tipi site and learn the lay of the land, Wilber and I hiked the neighborhood. Behind Ron and Suebi's cottage, past the barn, up on the knoll, in the middle of the field, we explored for days until we came upon a spot beyond the garden. Nestled between the creek and a tall bramble was a private grassy clearing and the ideal nest. We unloaded our stuff and began to build our home. Everyone gathered to raise the tipi frame, rainbow-bright ribbons waving from each lodge pole tip. The skin, perfectly white, hung gracefully. Inside, the light was magical. Wilber's brilliant Navajo blankets draped the platform bed, matted the grass floor, and lined the clothes bins. The liner went up, but needed no insulation now. The sides were rolled to capture the breeze off the creek and the door flap left open. Wilber built another rustic kitchen, with a sink, upper shelves, and pot rack. I fashioned curtains from wedding sheets to hide the lower shelves, slop bucket, and dishes. There was always a canning jar filled with garden flowers on the kitchen counter.

Gracing a half-acre hill, the organic, biodynamic garden was a wonder to us. Terraced and companion planted, it was a grand verdant staircase. Potatoes planted with beans and sunflowers, tomatoes with nasturtiums and herbs, melons with borage and cucumbers repelled bad bugs and attracted helpful ones. Stronger leafy plants shaded delicate growers from the hot California sun. Wilber and I would soon learn that not only were the plants good growing companions, they tasted great together, too. Dave had fashioned a gravity-fed watering system from the creek behind our tipi, brilliant and back saving. Wilber was pleased to have his hands in the dirt and learned pruning and propagation quickly and eagerly. Weeding, watering, watching, and planting were everyone's work, begun anew each day. And the significance of putting a melon in the garden fridge early was soon proved. We all enjoyed it at days' end.

I milked the nannies of our twenty-three-goat herd at dawn and dusk daily. Well into my third trimester, I'd waddle across the farm to the barn, before anyone had risen from his or her stoned nirvana, to a waiting herd of bleating nannies. My maternal instinct forced me out of bed early to relieve their engorged teats and to feed the growing herd. It was my job. I would slop the buckets of fresh milk to the main house and its kitchen, where the cheese, yogurt, and ice cream would be made, eventually.

While the scorching days were filled with farm work, we dipped early and often into the cool, wide river. A short walk from the barn, the river emptied from the glen beyond and settled onto the granite rocks, a natural architecture comprised of ancient fallout. Silver, aqua, and turquoise stone and water soothed and strengthened our wilted bodies. In dewy morning and late summer's evening, we bathed and basked on the cool rocks, lolled and drifted in the chill water, always cosseted by the gentle canyon and swathed in a hot breeze from the glen. This was our salvation. Pregnant and hot, tired and restless, I found solace in my daily soak and short walk along the riverbanks.

The garden invited strangers. With a colorful Pick-Your-Own, hand-painted sign at the driveway, "Bridgeport Organic Gardens" was open to the public, attracting tourists and locals alike. It was too hot and strenuous for the confines of clothing, so we often worked naked, but a sarong or pair of shorts always hung nearby for a quick cover should customers arrive. We were perpetually on guard for a family or uniformed soldiers from Beale Air Force Base. Visitors of all persuasions could wander up the drive to pick tomatoes or buy watermelon at the stand—a rough octagonal porch— or visit the communal dinner table at the heart of the garden. In these instances we were all salespeople. The invasion of our privacy was a small price to pay for cold hard cash.

We were almost totally self-sufficient, buying only frozen orange juice to flavor our smoothies. Veggies of all sorts were traded for flour, honey, and staples. Mint, watercress, and blackberries crowded the creek behind the tipi. We would roll down to Maryville and the heat of the plateau to pick the nuts, figs, apricots, peaches, and pears we dried, canned, and devoured. A few days of picking in the orchards could be traded for bushels, enough ripe and juicy fruit to sate our summer yearning, the remainder canned and frozen for winter's delight.

Wilber shod a few horses and bartered for hay and feed for the goats. We joined a Lamaze class at a community center up the road and, though we fit in as a pregnant couple, we stood out in this traditional community. We took the lessons and techniques as seriously as anyone, but when the teacher told us to toughen our nipples by discreetly exposing them to the sun for a few minutes every day, we had to laugh. At Bridgeport, tan lines did not exist.

With the soft babbling of the creek and our tipi secluded from the others, we bonded as a family while awaiting the birth of our child. In our private haven, we read baby books, discussed names and plans, practiced Lamaze, and studied home birth.

Suebi and Ron's son Sunshine had been born in the central California hills, in a tipi. Although her labor was a torturous 40 hours, she believed, "I am a woman and will toil with the birth of my child." Her fearful story was featured in the "Birth Book," which she proudly loaned to me for my earth mother preparation. A collection of more fearful birth stories from women around Santa Cruz, the book included graphic photos of the implausible: giant-headed babies emerging from tiny birth canals. As if from the pages of *National Geographic,* the voluminous, radiant women appeared as my future. Interspersed with *A Short History of Childbirth, Female Sexuality, Prenatal Care, What to Watch For, On Imprinting and the Formation of Love,* the personal stories were moving, grateful, and spiritual. They were real, too real, but all connected by a cord of love and the gift of life. I had to focus all of my innocent inexperience on hopeful outcomes.

There had been a tension between Suebi and me, or maybe between Suebi and everybody, since the start. In the free spirit of the commune, we all had ideas of our own, and we were free to express them and be unconditionally heard. That was the theory, but Suebi was judgmental of my instincts and opinionated at every turn. She was aggressive with her advice. I found her intimidating and felt myself responding with a tinge of anger when she assessed my plans, our plans, to raise our baby. I did need Suebi's help, as she was the only mother around. But I took control of how she gave it. She would lend us Sunshine's crib, since he slept in the family bed anyway.

As the youngest woman in the commune, busy testing my own mind, I often turned to Wilber with my doubts. He encouraged me to be myself first, his partner next, and ultimately a member of the farm. There were a myriad of events before the baby came, along with the emotional prep work such a transformation entails. But there could be no baby things, it turned out, no crib, no diapers, and no clothes in the tipi until the birth was complete and everyone safe. Wilber was superstitious. And unbeknownst to me, a long-standing Jewish superstition dictated that drawing any attention to a baby before it is born brings bad luck, or the "evil eye" to the family. Apparently, the risks outweighed the inconvenience of delaying our preparations. We could get all that stuff later.

The community midwife was a friend of a shoeing client: Mary, whose Scottish accent had the comforting lilt of my childhood nanny. With several wee bairns of her own, and many successful deliveries in this Sierra community to her credit, she seemed a good fit. We liked and trusted her as an older, wiser guide. I was eight months along when we first visited Mary's farm/clinic. She listened to our heartbeats—perfect—and the size and shape of our little fetus seemed to jibe with the due date. Gently, with calming concern, she told us the baby was transverse, lying across my middle, hip-to-hip. Wilber was anxious. What did that mean?

If I went into labor with the baby in this position, we'd have to go to the hospital—horrors!—and a Caesarian section would be necessary. She asked if we wanted her to turn it. She could try to settle the head down toward the birth canal. If we waited, the baby would only be bigger and harder to turn. She seemed completely confident that the time was right, and Wilber and I concurred. Lying on her table, I felt so vulnerable, but Wilber's confidence helped put me at ease.

Mary closed her eyes and palpated my womb. Then she began— gently, slowly pushing bottom and head, turning the baby ever so slowly. It was the weirdest sensation, like my whole insides were rotating and flipping. The pressure was immense, not painful but invasive. When she was done, she opened her eyes and smiled a beam of satisfaction. We breathed. She instructed us that the baby might bounce back to its chosen comfort place, but to hope for the best: that it would be happy in the head-down position. We left her a basket of veggies from Bridgeport, but as we headed back to our farm, we were full of worry.

Later, we thought it strange to have had that procedure done on our first meeting with Mary. Our time to birth was so short. Was it perfectly natural, or had we gone against the order of things, like rhythms and rotations? From that moment of manipulation on, I was super conscious of the baby's movements and the new kicking pattern: right into my stomach! We stayed generally aware and I was careful about my movements, though in truth we had no control over whether our baby would stay comfortable in its new placement.

CHAPTER FOURTEEN

Sept. 1972

Hello folks—

Your phone call last night came at an odd moment. Lots of company, crying babies, myriads of thoughts zooming through m'brain. Nonnie is almost 8 months pregnant now, very big, incredibly active, and in good spirits. We had the baby turned by a very fine mid-wife, a woman from Scotland whom we hope shall deliver the baby next month.

Today is really a fall day, the weather is cooling down, plants grow a lot slower and nights creep in at 7:00 PM. It's really beautiful to be in an area of oak & madrone trees, lots of lizards & snakes, blackberries, horses, gardens & goats. Nonnie really feels relieved to be away from the cold, and I feel relieved to be out of Breckenridge.

I've been milking cows & doing some horseshoeing and have decided not to actively participate in the union carpenter work. You have to be in the hall every morning by 7:30 and the work they send you to is ungratifying concrete slabs that hire carpenters to pour cement.

At any rate, the tipi is really acquiring the lived-in look, and is very homey now. I'm still curious as to the effects of winter on a baby here in the tipi & still undecided about a move into a more solid roof. I don't want to, but it's rather difficult to decide about life-styles with a baby very nearly here. It always works out as planned, but recently I have been curious as to what will lay in store.

Those kinds of thoughts really confuse a person because of their inherent insolvability: my only consolation being that other fathers to whom I have talked remember clearly those kinds of feelings when they were in my situation. Certainly those remembrances don't clarify anything, but to realize that nothing is uncommon helps me smiling accept all the newness.

Nonnie & I feel comfortable and as she progresses she seems to get stronger, more smiling and much more profound with her insights. I listen to her more and more, as she seems to be getting wiser all the time. It is so gratifying to have that kind of rapport with someone, especially if that someone is very close to you. We both hope you can come out after the birth if all goes well. I can't seriously think of your arrival until I see, touch, hear & feel baby. I'll keep you posted on all kinds of goodies should they arise. Nonnie sends her love too.

Stay well & happy new year.

Frank

Life on the farm was good and productive. We called it Eden

and it was. The gardens were in full harvest. As my pregnancy ripened, our commune family called me "two cantaloupes and a watermelon." All in fun. Life in the tipi was good and simple. The occasional mouse in the grain didn't bother me. Bugs were insignificant, and mosquitoes an expected nuisance.

Rattlesnakes, however, were my one true nemesis. I hated them. I feared them. I could not touch the page of a *National Geographic* if it featured a photograph of a snake. I had avoided living in snake country all my life, but now they plagued me everywhere I turned. I'd awake to find them curled up on a warm sunspot on my rug. I'd hear them when I rinsed dishes in the creek. I'd see them on the barn trail in early morning. Others, who did not fear the snakes, rarely saw them, and wondered at my frequent sightings.

One afternoon, late in my pregnancy, I was walking along the farm road, trying to see my own feet over the rotundity of my belly. The road was dappled with low autumn sun and I meandered. Suddenly, within my view, a rattlesnake stretched across the lane. I jumped, I hopped and I ran, wobbling and swaying, all the way to Suebi's cabin. Inside I slammed the door and, panting, collapsed.

"What the fuck are you doing?!" Suebi was indelicate in her surprise.

"Oh my God, there's a huge rattlesnake chasing me!!!" I screamed. "Didn't you see it?" Just two weeks ago, Suebi had shot a rattler as it slithered toward Sunshine, sleeping on a blanket at the base of an old oak. Surely she'd want to get right after the snake chasing me.

"Rattlesnakes don't chase," she corrected me, as usual. "It probably didn't even notice you." Why me, I wondered. Those disgusting creatures were out to get me, and I was NOT being paranoid!

Strangers and friends flocked to the now golden hills of the Sierras and the cool azure waters of the Yuba, always in pursuit of a mellow retreat. The public came regularly to buy fresh produce. In hindsight, it must have been one of those customers who saw our enormous crop of pot and alerted the police. The stunning and healthy *Cannabis* specimens, camouflaged among the tomato and potato plants, were unremarkable to casual observers, but someone must have recognized them.

Ron had tended them all summer. They were his plants. But when the squad cars pulled up that September afternoon, Wilber and I were heading for our truck and Ronnie was conveniently absent.

"You live here?" one of the four state troopers bellowed at us. "Where are you going?" Innocent and more than a little naïve, we answered honestly.

"Yup, we live here, over in that tipi," Wilber replied. As he pointed toward the tipi, across the garden, he realized his mistake. His shoulders visibly slumped, as his gaze settled on our Chevy truck and its Colorado plates, an easy getaway. Another retort came to both our minds: "No, we're just shopping at the farm stand." But it was too late.

"Get in the car!" they ordered as they handcuffed Wilber. Handcuffed. Wilber??

"What?" We were both genuinely surprised.

"You're under arrest for cultivation of marijuana," one of the troopers said as he turned to me, my face doubtlessly contorting with fear. I looked around. A surrealistic haze clouded my peaceable view. In my peripheral vision something moved, and I clearly saw Ron crossing the field, hurrying away from us. His pot, his escape. My husband was in handcuffs and his old buddy was scurrying away, his true character on his sleeve.

Just then, Molly and Dave came out of the garden shed, clothed.

"You two, get over here," an officer ordered. "Who the hell are you?" Molly had no choice, as caretaker, but to own it. Soon she and I were in the back seat, hot and scared. Wilber and Dave, in the other car, were already reeling with worry over Dave's fate. Our draft-dodger was in grave danger.

My mind still reels with the memory of being in that cop car, pig mobile, fuzz bucket. As we turned onto the main road I saw Ronnie running, low and fast, toward his cabin. Molly and I were separated from our men. I could see the back of Wilber's head as we followed the first car speeding away up the hill, out of our Eden and into town. We'd rarely been to town and I was instantly disoriented. But when they drove into the concrete underground of the ominous city hall, I knew we were in trouble. Pulling us out of the back seat, the dirty pigs pushed us into the elevator. Cu-clunk! I thought of a bad action film. The door closed. Up and up we went, scared and mad. Pulled before the desk, we gave our names and addresses, our ages and stats. Molly was cool and controlled; I was scared to death, scrambling to follow her lead. It was the first time I'd seen her fully dressed in a long time. She looked respectable, like a hard-working farmer: her nails filled with dirt, her fingers tinted green from tomato plants, and her golden ringlets heavy and matted with sweat. Before we saw or talked to Wilber and Dave, they led us into a "holding tank." A hollow and earnest rat-tat-tat-tat-cu-CHUNK! sealed our fate. We were *Women in Chains*, felons, and throw-away-the-key inmates. I, in my fragile state, began to sob. Confident, strong Molly comforted me. We needed to stay cool.

"My baby will be a ward of the state," I whined. "This is it." I pined for my utopia by the stream. I grabbed the bars on the eight-inch-square window in our steel door. I rattled the door, priming for my movie close-up. I peered between the bars. Down the hall, Wilber was peering back from his cell. *Bonnie and Clyde!* Blowing kisses and winking, he was trying to send me some hope and resolve. I was trying to smile back and return some signals his way when the door burst open. With but a very few words, we were led out to sign papers and told to leave. Leave? But our men? Their door hadn't opened. I didn't want to leave without them. Molly nudged me; we had to sign for our release. Soon, we were with Ron in the van and headed home.

The days to follow were filled with calls and laws. We knew Dave had to be released as soon as possible, before his status was known. As soon as the fuzz pulled his records from state, they'd see his draft status. Before we knew it, he'd be serving in Vietnam or a federal brig. Trying to live a safe and simple life had just gotten complicated, and weird. Why had Ron been hiding while his best friends took the rap for his pot? How could he have handed Dave to the pigs like cattle to slaughter? Not to mention sending his best childhood friend and his friend's wife and unborn baby into jail? I held my tongue, but my trust in him was forever damaged.

"Dave should have gone to Canada when he had the chance," moaned Molly.

At some point the boys were released and came home. I was struggling to stay calm, for the baby's sake. We heard something about a new law and the legality of personal possession. I think a fine and a wrist-slap were involved, but in my slowly expanding naïveté, I was just so thrilled to have Wilber back that I didn't care. The pot plants were gone from the garden, torn from their happy place by the angry hands of the law. Ron was forced to pull his wild plantings from the woods before they matured. He hung them dramatically—in effigy—in the barn. Ron and Suebi were getting freaky: his guilt and exposed weakness, and her increasing over-enmeshment with Sunshine. Wilber and I started spending more time nesting in the tipi.

CHAPTER FIFTEEN

One night after an awkward but tender lovemaking, my labor began. I got up to pee, as usual, but as soon as I stooped in the cool grass, I felt the power of muscles initiating. Strange but intense, no question about it. I woke Wilber with the warning, "It's starting." He was cool. Trusting me, trusting nature.

"Good," he said, as he lay back down.

I lay beside him, and soon mellowed with the soft rhythm of his breath. I fought for sleep, knowing I'd need my rest in the day (or days) ahead. Fighting didn't work. Instead I rested, relaxing through the stream of mild contractions, becoming one with the ebb and flow. I cocooned with my awakening motherhood, treasured the moments of calm. My mind came alive with vivid images of an infant, precious and vulnerable, cradled between us, worthy of all the purest love we could give. A baby swinging in the tiny hammock my parents brought us from Guatemala, me singing and soothing with old family ballads. Our newborn swaddled to his daddy, pacing the trails of the farm. I imagined the new and welcome purpose a baby would bring into my life: the care and feeding of a tiny person who would depend on my every action and demand my every attention, day and night. A normal eighteen-year-old might have suffocated at the prospect, but I felt only joy, knowing I would share it with the man I adored, trusted, and admired. In counterpoint to my still-forming motherly instincts, Wilber's age and experience brought an undeniable weight to the enterprise. I was soothed by and counted on his confidence.

Suddenly, my joyful dreaming shuddered awake as my uterus tightened with a painful intensity. Chilled and shaking, I huddled in my own fetal curl. Trying not to wake Wilber, I breathed shallow and quiet. My Lamaze relaxing techniques reminded me to start at my toes, easing each muscle until I felt I could melt my cervix. I focused so intently that I actually began to enjoy my mellow, private preparation. I was tripping on the light fantastic. Still two weeks to my due date, but I was ready. As the first shards of sunlight popped up over the garden, I remembered the goats. I nudged Wilber.

"It's time," I whispered.

"Time for the midwife? Time for the oils and massages?" He woke with a start, but then sensed my calm. "What *time* is it?"

"Yes, all that, but right now it's time for somebody to milk the goats," I smiled as I prepared to blow off my chore for the first time in two months. I was ready for that, too. Though I'd loved the responsibility, the billies were getting ornery and the nannies were in heat. Even the thought of the stench was enough to make me retch. I'd have a well-deserved break.

Wilber was dressed and hopping out the tipi door in moments. Before long he returned, having woken the commune to the beginning of our birth day. Between mild contractions, I reflected on the many birth stories I'd heard in the past nine months. From my mother, who was a natural birth pioneer in the '50s, to Suebi and her hellish saga, one thing I knew for sure was that there would be extremes: excruciating pain and blissful lulls, endless contractions and primal screams. Forceful contractions, involuntary puking and shitting, sweating, swearing, thirst, and exhaustion had been the common reminiscences of new mothers. I did find it comforting that older women seemed to remember little—my mother now only recalled how darling each of her four infants were.

I knew that within a few hours after Wilber's return, the tipi would fill with our friends. Mary would also be there, along with the trappings of her midwifery. I looked around to be sure there would be enough space. I rose to sort the accumulation of our lives, to move the trunk and arrange a table for Mary, and my water broke right over my favorite Navajo rug. My first major involuntary action was perfect, for with it I gave up control and began to really listen to my body. As if on cue, Wilber ducked into the tipi and laughed with me. In the few minutes of privacy, before the crowd gathered, we tuned in to the moment. We were both ready. It was nine o'clock on October seventh.

From here the day slid into a kaleidoscope of faces, chants, oils, massages, guitar playing (was Richard back?), and contractions. Always the contractions, coming in waves that would strike with force, then subside to a sea of tranquility. My body would respond in a grateful collapse, relaxing to await the following assault. Suebi and Molly made sure of a constant flow of teas, fresh water, and food for the attendants, some of whom I didn't recognize. Could they be tourists who stopped in to Pick-Your-Own? Did Suebi have to bring steamed broccoli? The smell made me gag. A mild irritation at the chatting and laughing did not interrupt my focus. Through it all, the attention of Wilber and Mary never wavered. Elasticizing my perineum with warm olive oil, massaging my lower back with Skin Trip, smoothing my hair away from my face, they were with me and only me.

Unaware of time, I was surprised to find it dark enough that we needed the light of the kerosene lamps, and then realized that twenty-four hours had passed. Bright warm day had blurred to amber dusk, then to black moonless night. Stars flickered bright between the tipi's smoke flaps, constant as ever, witness to the cosmic shift occurring here. Soon it would be another new day. I moved around the tipi, alternating positions and views. A fire glowed in the pit, illuminating faces and expressions.

"I've changed my mind," I whispered to Wilber, his ear ever eager. "I think I'm gonna do this thing *another* day." But it was too late. The contractions started coming closer together, almost continuous, and stronger. *Transition.* I breathed, and panted, and relaxed, and tensed, and cried, and drooled. After several hours of intense, relentless transition, I heard Wilber's concern, and the midwife murmured that my cervix was almost 10-centimeters dilated.

"Do you feel like pushing?" she asked me, between my panting and pleading.

"Yes, YES, I do!" I said. "I think I do..." I mumbled, hoping I'd given the right answer. It was my first time, and I felt my instincts working against my worn-out brain.

"Right-oh." She seemed relieved. "Okay, Nonnie, dear, and with the next contraction, give us a great big push. Let's get this baby out!"

Everyone gathered, like a team in a huddle, like we were going to do this together. I was too polite to say anything, but thankfully Wilber told them all to step back. He knew I needed to breathe and protected my little space. I felt the next contraction mounting, the tingling of a cramp, the flood of anxiety, the forceful convulsion, the sharp climax. They held my shoulders up and I pressed down, pushing against my anus, my bladder, and my perineum while Mary urged away the tissue to make room for the head. For the next three hours, I persevered like this with each contraction. Hundreds of times I pushed with all my might, feeling my legs being torn apart and my crotch shredded and bleeding. The only apparent change was my dwindling energy. The baby's heartbeat, my utmost concern, was still strong.

Finally, for the first time, I saw the worry as Mary looked to Wilber. After three hours, the cervix was unchanged. After all this, the pushing may have been premature.

"The cervix might be frozen at almost ten centimeters," she worried, "or the baby's head could be stuck with the cord in the birth canal. Maybe she should go to the hospital."

"Could that have happened when you turned the baby?" Wilber followed her lead.

Those ideas, those sounds came to me as if through water. I didn't understand. I looked to Wilber and saw his agony. People started leaving, looking helpless. Someone mentioned a stretcher, gathered blankets, and rushed outside. The warm glow of the tipi turned instantly mute and cold, with an air of foreboding. The crowd's festive energy and giddy anticipation evaporated into the dark and I was scared. A change was coming, doom hung in the air.

"Am I in danger? Is the baby okay?" I must have been wondering out loud, as Wilber stopped making arrangements and came to my side.

"We're going to the hospital." He spoke slowly to be sure I got it. "Mary thinks it's time."

"Everybody's going?" My concern for the energy continued.

"No, Poms, just you, me, and Suebi." He used my childhood nickname, and I was comforted. Of course, I wanted Mary to come with, but I knew her gift, her craft was illegal in California. We must be careful to protect her.

Soon, four or six strong but frantic friends were hauling me across the field and garden on a makeshift stretcher. The transfer from tipi to truck was quiet but rough, and our pickup was soon hurtling and bouncing toward Grass Valley. The quaintness of the country road, with its holes and heaves, became a form of torture, and the noise was deafening. Ron drove too fast, and Suebi and Wilber held me on piles of blankets in the pickup's bed. Bumping along on the thirty-minute ride, I realized that I hadn't felt the "urge" that comes with natural birth. The only urge was my mental anguish, and my impatience to be done. What could have been different, had I waited for the "urge"? We would never know. Above I saw the stars that had guided my final hours of tipi labor; I squinted to make contact with them between the trees. They were a certain comfort, steady and twinkling. Turning my gaze to Wilber's brave and beautiful face, I saw sorrow and regret as we rushed toward the unknown.

When we pulled up at the Emergency Room entrance, I felt like a cow going to slaughter. Nurses pulled me—to them just another hippie with a botched home birth—up the ramp and onto a cold metal gurney. In the delivery room, bright lights and cold rubber gloves probed and prodded me. Gone were the glow of candles and the touch of caring hands. When the nurses cleaned my perineum with icy Phisoderm scrubs and roughly shaved my pubis, reality hit: Our hope of a tipi birth was over. We had surrendered to the establishment.

"Labor has stopped progressing, probably that bumpy road," Dr. Waechter sneered as he went for the Pitocin. "Give her Demerol. Then an epidural to put her out of her misery." Wilber was being stripped and scrubbed—dirty hippie—and I felt like a naughty child who'd been caught and punished. Unfamiliar with the hospital options, I was in their hands now. My only concern was for my baby; I'd let the doctor have his way.

Wilber arrived finally, angry and frustrated. While this process had deadened my physical pain, his had been heightened, and we were both feeling the loss of a coveted outcome. Within a few hours, many pushes, and a snip-snip, a head crowned and a baby slipped forth. The epidural had worn off just in time for me to feel the birth, thank goodness. Relief, rejoicing. A boy! Beautiful and healthy. At 3:16 on the morning of October eighth, we were able to relax. The staff hovered: snipping, clamping, stitching, cleaning, weighing, testing, probing, and confirming our baby's perfection. Six pounds, eight ounces, and twenty-one inches. Wilber hovered, waiting impatiently for his baby. I felt the numb of exhaustion and drugs as I was transferred to and collapsed into the hospital bed.

Wilber brought our new baby boy and laid him on my chest. Pale wisps of white fuzz covered his tiny round head. His blueberry eyes fluttered open and lolled. Little baby acne scattered across his strong nose and petal perfect lips. Wilber rolled back the swaddling and we examined his skinny legs, long toes, starfish fingers, and wrinkled tiny hands, kissing each in turn. His little mouth searched blindly, rooting in air, and then latched on strongly; he nursed right away, a certain relief. Instantly, I was glad for my Lamaze coaches' advice and my tanned, tough nipples.

Throughout the morning, I slept in fits, waking to find Wilber gone and my infant boy sleeping off the birth trauma in a bassinet at my side. As we dozed, soft-stepping, starched-white nurses came and went, catering to our every need. It was strangely comforting. My spotless, uncluttered room with private bath was a luxury, foreign to my wilding eyes. As I snuggled into my crisp sheets, adjusted my hydraulic headboard, and reached for the TV remote, my self-serving joy felt guilty and shameful, but I let it pass. I deserved a break, didn't I? When my baby cried, a nurse scooped him up, checked his tiny diaper, and brought him to my waiting arms. When a candy striper arrived with the day's menu, I greedily ordered: meatloaf, peas, gravy, mashed potatoes, and spumoni for lunch. And fresh milk? Cow's milk? Yes, yes, bring it, please.

Wilber had gone to fetch my mom at the Reno airport. We called her Noonie, the new grandmother, a nickname of her given name Anne. Her parents called her Little Annie Roonie after a popular 1920s movie, and when her baby mouth formed Roonie into Noonie, it stuck. In my family, names were assigned at the hospital, but nicknames morphed with personalities. They were the monikers by which we identified. My yet unnamed, or nicknamed, baby slept. I was just settling in when I heard loud voices in the hall.

"That's my family in there." Wilber bristled at the staff. "And I'll see them whenever I damn well please!" Mumblings of a nurse or orderly signaled a response I didn't hear. "What do you mean I'll have to put on a shirt? This *is* a shirt, a fine goddamned shirt!" My smart and sensitive husband, my new baby's father, burst into my room in a sleeveless undershirt (a "wife-beater"), jeans, and boots. He looked like he'd just hopped off a rodeo bronc, sweat and dust lacquered to all that bare skin, and his wild-eyed, anti-authority expression made me tense.

My mother snuck in behind him. Quiet but watchful, she glanced around his bare bicep. When she saw my face, she rushed in for a joyful reunion. Wilber lifted the baby out of the bassinet and handed him to my mom, who looked luminous and young. I was so glad to see her.

"We're outta here," Wilber pronounced. "Get your stuff." Visions of juicy meatloaf with gravy-sodden potatoes danced in my head along with the bathroom, clean sheets, air-conditioning, and showers. My mind was awash and distracted with temptations of modern convenience.

"Right now?" my mother and I responded in unison.

"But wait," the nurse jumped right in. "You can't go until the doctor checks her and the baby and releases them. He'll have instructions for you. The baby's only a few hours old. He won't want to let you go." I sensed my mother's agreement over my shoulder. She respected Wilber, but she also knew the grueling first days of motherhood. In her mind, a stay of five days, not five hours, was expected.

"I can take my family outta here whenever I please," Wilber retorted. He was calming down, but he wanted his way.

"And we'll need a name before he can go home," the nurse continued, suddenly reconnecting with her authority. "I have to fill out the birth certificate."

"Well, his name's Wyatt," he said with an eye to me. "Wyatt Neumann." It was a good name, we'd talked about it plenty and it seemed to fit this six-and-a-half pound bundle.

"And a middle name?" she suggested.

At that, Wilber, who'd already started pulling my things out of the closet, turned on his heel, slapped his butt, and, with a nod of challenge and reason, said "Levi! Like the jeans…" He waited for a response. The nurse was writing and mumbling as she hustled out of the room. My mother and I turned to each other and I grinned to let her know it was all right. In that moment I believed it was a *great* name, Wyatt Levi Neumann, a strong and noble name. (I didn't know it then, but this was Wilber's nod to his heritage and tribal roots. Having abandoned Judaism and all his parents' conventions, he had named his son for the priestly tribe of his people, the Levis, even as he chose not to have Wyatt circumcised.)

We waited impatiently, some of us for Dr. Waechter, some of us for lunch. Finally, he arrived, bossy and doctor-like, and dressed us down with instructions that would fill a book. Of course, the nurse had it all on mimeographed sheets. "Walk often and everywhere, resume normal activities right away, cook, clean, and don't stay in bed. Don't take baths, use a squirt bottle when urinating, watch for bleeding, and keep the stitches clean. For the baby, he has not been circumcised, so you must be diligent about keeping the foreskin clean, and watch and clean the umbilical cord connection."

As the doctor was spewing the instructions we knew were in our books back at the tipi, Wilber paced in the small room. My mother hung on every word like her life depended on it and I imagined my very untraditional housewife role. "Resume normal activities." Like milking a dozen-or-so goats? "Don't take baths." You mean in the dishwashing basin? "Walk often." This would be the half-mile to the bathroom? "Cook." Over the Coleman stove? "Clean." With water from the creek, heated on the Coleman stove? Was I the only one who wanted to stay here and be waited on? Just for a day? Still, I knew the challenges ahead would be met with the joy of being home with friends, peace, and a healthier environment for us. So, time was a'wastin' … We were soon loaded in the truck and headed back down to our new life on the old Yuba River.

CHAPTER SIXTEEN

"Wyatt Boo-Boo, with the Boo-boo-boo-berry eyes…"
My mother stayed in the main house and was welcomed by all the hippies. Everyone loves a mother, especially a mother with a naturally non-confrontational style. Several times a day, I trudged the distance to Ron and Suebi's to use the bathroom, then back to the tipi to cook. Noonie was sweet and helpful with Wyatt, but she took the doctor at his word and allowed me to keep at the cooking and cleaning. As I labored over chores and distances, she sat in the tipi and knit a little sweater.

Wyatt was a darling, a good and happy boy. In the end, however he arrived, he came to us in perfect form, and Wilber and I welcomed his innocence. He was easy, thank goodness, and he slept and ate well. When he woke in the middle of the night, crying, I'd rise to change him in the cold tipi. Propped on the trunk, with a candle or a flashlight reflecting off his little bottom, he wailed at the injustice. Quickly redressed and rewrapped, he nursed and slept between us in solid comfort.

Second to visit was Wyatt's other grandma, Oma. She came with a delicate yellow blanket she had knit, and instructed "send to me for laundering." But she came without Wyatt's Opa, whom I believe was offended by the non-circumcision, though no one ever said. Oma was awed by our lifestyle and by the fact that my mother drove her to and from her motel in our three-quarter-ton pickup, like it was a Country Squire. I imagined she was revisiting her recent bad memories of the wedding transport, along with her wishes for her little Miss Morningstar. But she was kind, in a pinched and shocked kind of way, and crazy about Wyatt. When Kenny came with Sarah, he brought a football, on which he'd scratched "WYATT" with a marker, and a box of Cracker Jacks. I was offended by the stupid gesture (Doesn't Wyatt really need a Snuggly or a savings bond?), but I tried to stay cool. As usual, his behavior led me to anger and confusion. Life had been uncompli-cated without him, and the novelty of his visit wore thin quickly.

Poor Sarah was the most uncomfortable. I tried to make it very mellow, but I saw her dismay. As a high school junior, she must have been disgusted by my choice to be a mom and live with noth-ing. I should have been college-bound, like her, looking forward to dorm living and dating. I wanted her to see that being a mom was good and satisfying so she could go home with a calm heart. I knew that once they'd gone, I wouldn't think of them. I didn't know whether they'd think of me. In the meantime, I hoped Wyatt warmed them to the possibility of our good future.

Before long, family retreated and friends dwindled; some even moved away as autumn descended on the river bottom. When a hard frost threatened to settle with the dawn, the harvest of frag-ile crops began in earnest. Canning and freezing filled the main house kitchen, our overstock of goats was sold, and the leaves that were green turned to brown. People moved on. After the drug bust, summer's glow and growth faded, and the change began. Tipi life was fragile for an infant. Cold and wet pervaded and the life that had been so joyous became close to miserable. Wilber and I considered our options.

All that we'd learned in the past three months, an essential "Be Here Now" of California wildness, had been based on a journey of hard work and on the particular bounty of the golden state. We'd been apprentices in the art of caring for gardens, farm animals, babies, and others. We'd lived the textbooks—the *Whole Earth Catalog, Living on the Earth, Rodale's Gardening,* and *The Foxfire Book*—and experienced the options. Gravity-fed watering, goat breeding, cheese making, dome-building, shake-splitting, tipi-living, home-birthing, and tuning-in to the land had kept us busy, hearts and minds. We'd lived a workshop of sustainable independence, built on the generosity of mother earth, the landowner in Santa Cruz, the other hippies, and our dogged determination to be free. Free of grocery stores, free of regular employment, free to simply make our way, we had become addicted to the freedom and the satisfaction of hard work. Living hand-to-mouth had taken on a new meaning. If we didn't grow it, barter it, or bake it, we didn't have it to eat, to nourish, and keep us strong.

But freedom was now becoming the problem. With the gardens harvested and the sky's seasonal dripping begun, the grooviest place in the world had suddenly become a major bummer. To boot, we were again reminded of what it meant to squat on someone else's property, to depend on an owner's whims, and to have no rights. The anonymous owner, Molly's friend, wanted to sell his land, and everyone had to go by year's end. Molly and Dave quickly moved on, back to real jobs on the coast: she as a landscaper, he as a cabinetmaker. It would be easy for them; with no family or trappings, they could slip in and out of society, as he needed. The vibrant commune at Bridgeport Gardens was reduced, abruptly, to us in the tipi, Ron, Suebi, and Sunshine in their cabin, and Richard occasionally in the main house. The demise of summer in the foot-hills was dark and dismal, and it stank. The stench of rotting plants and rutting goats hung in the valley. We tried to be cheery, but this was bogus, and the glimmer of our highs faded with the withering garden. It was sad and we worried over the changes. As the tipi sagged with the weight of rain, Wilber, with no work to do, was feeling the heaviness of his new responsibility. I stayed focused on Wyatt, my darling growing infant. The more our daily needs became tedious with drizzle and dampness, the more the bright and simple moments with him filled my heart.

In early November, Wilber heard of a carpenter job, a remodel, in Lake Tahoe. In desperation, he took it and we loaded up in the pickup. We could live in the house under construction, and the idea of living back in the mountains for a few weeks sounded simple and kind of cool. The thought of a little construction money, which we knew would be good, sweetened the pot.

But our confidence outshined the realities of our new opportunity. Arriving in Tahoe in broad daylight, we drove the strip as we searched for the address we'd been given, the contractor's home. Blindly entering sin city, our eyes were pried open to the reality of our new town. Casinos, bordellos, strip clubs, and bars rolled by, and once again I was struck by my own naïveté. The sights disgusted me, and I wondered whether deep down I really was a prude. At the boss's house, we got directions and instructions, along with a look of concern from the boss's wife, peering over his shoulder. Up the snowy gravel roads, the snow banks grew tall. The trail narrowed to a half-finished chalet, and we were surprised to find the house open, wide open, with only partial siding and roofing. There was a kitchen of sorts, some furniture, and a bathroom in our makeshift home: the daylight basement. The scene was far more depressing than Bridgeport, so I sharpened my focus on Wyatt and tried to imagine it acceptable. After all, we had music, lots of goose down and wool, and food from the farm. Besides, the money was good—boomtown money. "This is temporary" became my mantra.

The weather promised comfort, 40° and sunshine for the first couple of days. Like a chinook, the warm breeze filled in and snow melted off the roof, settling in puddles in the basement. Wyatt and I snuggled in sleeping bags and walked hills bathed in autumn splendor. But the weather soon turned—it was November, after all—and cold blew in through the open walls. Wilber hammered and sawed in tense harmony to my moods. There was little for Wyatt and me to do but stay under cover and shudder. He cried, I cried. I knew Wilber was doing his best for us, but I freaked out. The money was overrated; this was no place for an infant! I begged to go home to the tipi.

Yielding to the strain, Wilber packed us up again. After a painful two weeks, he took us back to Bridgeport. In our absence, Richard had stayed in the tipi. Not a big deal, I thought, but the sight of our now unkempt and sodden home challenged my sense of generosity. I was overwhelmed, and more crying ensued. We lived with tiny Wyatt in the rain. We shuffled to Suebi's for showers, using her oven for baking. One afternoon, I stepped out of my shower to find Suebi nursing Wyatt. Sunshine was over a year old, and still nursing, so she had milk. But not for *my* baby! I was furious, and I stood up to her for the first time.

"What the hell are you doing?" I barked.

"He was crying," she murmured.

Seeing my infant at her breast blew my mind and made me sick. Free housing for Richard, free milk from Suebi? Maybe my spirit was just not free enough if these were the rules of commune life. I grabbed Wyatt from her and rushed back to my home, to clean and reestablish my own personal form of freedom: non-communality. Wyatt and I hunkered down while Wilber continued to look for work. From Santa Cruz we heard that Richard was in the hospital with hepatitis. We worried for him.

Thanksgiving came with great plans, the harvest of many moons. We could give thanks for a season well worked. Suebi and I toiled with vegetables, herbs, and cheeses, creating a memorable meal for those gathered. Cleaning up before dinner, I went to the bathroom and noticed that my pee was red, really red. I called Wilber, who looked into the toilet, then into my eyes (which were yellow). He said, "Nothing to worry about. Maybe you ate some beets?" But he was just trying to calm me down and knew instantly that I had hepatitis, like Richard. As soon as the harvest was celebrated and dinner consumed, we headed for the hospital. Though he was still pissed at the medical machine after the birth debacle, I could see Wilber was scared by my symptoms. He uttered not a word. He knew the danger and rushed me to the ER, Wyatt cradled in my weakening arms. Again the rough and steep road carried us away from home and toward the scary unknown, faster this time.

Hepatitis A was the diagnosis, and the staff stepped well away from us all. Again, we felt like dirty hippies, and I guess we were, though we weren't heroin addicts, sex addicts, or undesirables. The doctor ordered ten days of hospitalization in isolation, and they whisked Wyatt and me into a sterile room. White sheets, private bath, meals-to-order, but this time I was not eager for it. Instead, I felt lonely and confined. No visitors, no escape. My condition was critical and the staff worried for Wyatt and me. The instructions for my stay were strict and dire: not a drop of body fluid between mother and child. Thankfully, mother's milk was exempt. Incessant washing and careful bathroom habits were required. If my saliva, blood, or urine touched him anywhere, anytime, he could get the disease. He could die. No kissing, no tears. His five-week-old life was completely in my hands. I flinched at the severity and intensity of everyone around me, but not at my orders. I could handle this. And it wasn't my fault that we were quarantined. But why me and not Wilber? Thankfully, the doctor made that clear. The hepatitis came from Richard's improperly washed dishes, from a fork, or a cup. The bacteria attacked my newly postpartum, weakened, and depleted body. I hadn't been able to fight it. But I would now.

While we were in the hospital, Wilber and Ron were working hard at making money with the firewood business. Then in the fracturing of our commune, Suebi walked out on Ronnie and the baby. Suddenly a single father and lost, Ron was staggering. Suebi's departure didn't surprise me. She had been intolerant of so much, now her son's father added to her list. What really surprised and sickened me was her abandonment of Sunshine. I knew Ron was weak, that his and Sunshine's survival at Bridgeport was dubious. When Wilber brought me the news, I saw how its effect would spiral outward, envisioning a further disintegration of our commune. I worried for Wilber and our home. In the meantime, our hospital routine had become a comfort; we were looked after, cooked and cared for, and all my attention was lavished on Wyatt. A forced confinement in the tiny sterile room was a relief amidst the strains of the dying commune.

> *Early November 1972*
> *Dear folks:*
> *It's been nice talking to you and hearing your good spirited voices. Nonnie and I think often of returning to Colorado but for now we really cannot. First, we have dental appointments in December, second, the weather is too beautiful, and thirdly, the confusion here in California has us so intrigued that we are both rather spellbound.*
> *Ron & Suebi broke up last night after 5 ½ years. Right now he is friendless, alone and with Sunshine. There are 10 goats, his household and parts of his life to rearrange. Everyone else is gone and after the thriving community that was here this summer, Bridgeport seems haunted. Ron & Suebi & Sunshine came here initially, helped to start things rolling and it seems a number of people drifted in, took advantage of the situation and then left when the thrill was gone.*
> *Right now we feel that we would like to be with him because he is our friend. My memory is not so jaded that I cannot recall the private hell that is tugging at his brain. It is very depressing indeed but also serves to strengthen Nonnie's and my appreciation for what we have in each other.*
> *Of course, I'm used to such conditions as we found in Tahoe and would have stayed on, but Wyatt cried all the time because of the icy cold that was all pervasive. Nonnie hated it too just because there seemed no reprieve from the wind. The house was cold*

all over and there are only so many hours one can spend inside a down bag nursing a very unhappy little boy. I thought at first I would send them down and stay on. But now I really want to be with my family. Nonnie needs a great deal of help. Her motherly responsibilities are so great that it would be hard to take on the gargantuan chores of tipi life besides. I really could use the money but priorities do not always lend themselves to financial rewards. Nonnie really does not want to go back up there at all. The incredible decadence of the gambling & whoring depresses her and she doesn't want Wyatt in that environment at all.

So we may stay here and cut firewood. Ron figures we can get $85.cord – he did last year anyway. So if we cut 8 cords a week we could make a little money. I really want to see him get after it lest he stop and stagnate in his depression. So after that little hustle we may go back east to Colorado. Also Dad I forgot to thank you for the savings bond for Wyatt. When it matures, I plan to deposit it in his very own account so he can have the same kind of options afforded me when I became of age. It was really thoughtful of you.

Take care,

Love, Nonnie, Wyatt & Frank

During a dry spell, Wilber and Ron broke down our tipi, packed up the stuff, and dismantled our kitchen. I was glad not to be there to witness it. It was sad, with a bit of a tail-between-our-legs feel. As soon as I was released, we'd be heading home to Colorado. This California happening had turned sour, and we were just not committed enough to the state to stay. But it was the first time we'd really run from something. We had two months of sultry nirvana, then the bummers got us down: the pot bust, the birth debacle, the Tahoe surrealism, the hepatitis, and now the end of the commune. It was just not meant to be. Ron and li'l Sunny were going back to Santa Cruz, following Molly, Dave, Richard, and familiarity back to the coast. Wilber had been there and knew it wasn't for us. We'd be going home, though we were not exactly sure what that meant.

Chugging over Donner Pass in a blinding blizzard, I got a sense of what the party of 1846 might have endured, the loss and desperation, though our passing took half a day, not two and a half months. We crossed the desert once more, the brutal heat of summer now turned to winter's bitter cold. The entire states of Nevada and Utah were blanketed with snow, and the road wound through a shifting ground blizzard. In contrast to our last pass across this wasteland, we coaxed warmth out of the pickup's vents and tried to keep Wyatt warm. We were thin-blooded and thin-skinned from our California living. We carried on, again anxious to find what waited, singing along to our adopted theme song, Lynn Anderson's rendition of "Rose Garden."

> *"So, smile for awhile, and let's be jolly,*
> *Love shouldn't be so melancholy...*
> *Come along and share the good times while we can.*
> *I beg your pardon, I never promised you a Rose Garden ..."*

CHAPTER SEVENTEEN

We weren't headed for Tiger or the Swan Valley this time. We'd heard stories of cabins being closed and hippies run out of the hills. Our destination was Alma, just seventeen miles south of Breckenridge, in Park County. At 10,578 feet, Alma was the highest incorporated town in the United States. There our beloved Tenmile Range ran into the Mosquito Range and five 14,000-foot peaks melted into this high desert plateau. Dry hills were littered with the remains of the Pikes Peak Gold Rush of 1859. The gold, along with silver vein of Sweet Home Mine, built the legends of the pioneers that still haunted the valley. Originally named Buckskin Joe, after the guy who found the gold lode, the town was devastated in 1861 by a smallpox epidemic. Early inhabitants literally washed the gold out of the rocks of the South Platte River. Tailings piled high along the river drainage. The wind blew down from the peaks unhindered. Incorporated as Alma in 1873, it was a mining hub with a population as high as 5,000. A century later, with a resident count of 140 and slowly growing, Alma would be our home.

This was where Joe and John had bought their garage, when they'd run south over the pass to build a life away from the ski town development of Breckenridge and environs. A checkerboard of abandoned miner's cabins, Alma was now brimming with color and life. It was the happening new community, where people actually rented and owned places. Most of the freaks from the Swan Valley had followed Joe and John over the hill, where Alma was welcoming to influx of any kind. Their homes were secure. Many drove over Hoosier Pass daily to work the old jobs in Breckenridge—still developing and raping, but the money was good. We'd check it all out and find a new nest.

The last time we'd returned to Colorado, it was to the bloom of summer; this time, we returned to the dead and cold of winter—but into the warm and welcoming arms of our friends.

Joe and John invited us to live in the office space of their commercial enterprise, downstairs in the Alma garage. We took it. In spite of the picture window looking out on Route 9 and a blanket tacked over the opening to the giant workspace, it was a private getaway. With electricity, gas heat, and a bathroom, we were living in comfort. Up an open iron stairway perched the apartment where Joe, John, Stuart, and Susan lived with Martin and Mary-Ann. Alma's Only Bar was the new Gold Pan, and Janet and Patty were doing their thing there. Silver Heels Pizza made a mean thin crust topped with an olive-oily spicy sauce. The general store sold basics and gas, but Breckenridge, 17 miles north, was our town, not Fairplay, just 6 miles south. Our allegiance was still over the pass, no matter the conditions or time of day.

The Neumanns requested a visit, to officially welcome little Wyatt and belatedly celebrate Fred's birthday. We arrived in Denver on a cold December night, to a cool audience. Auntie Margaret was funny and dear but awkward with her tiny new nephew. *So what does a two-month-old do, anyway?* Oma and Opa were sweet with the baby but not so warm to us. Had it been a year since we met? So much had happened, and changed. In Fred's face, I saw a year of turmoil and anger, disappointment and insult. Couldn't they forgive Wilber when confronted with this innocent infant? Or maybe that was the problem: They saw the failed son and his child-bride, with the innocent non-Jewish grandson, no money, and no plan. I felt like we were the uninvited interlopers. As usual, they huddled in the kitchen kvetching in German about our lives, our choices, me. Again, Wilber reminded them that his childhood German allowed simultaneous translation of their sentiments, from their lips to my ears. The visit was short, and we were glad to leave. Back on Interstate 70, heading to our home and the warmth of our community, I shook off the pressure of their expectations, though I'm not sure their hard-working, strong, committed son ever did.

In Alma, the days stretched on through December as we renewed friendships and old patterns. It was so good to be with old pals and known personalities. Though a bitter wind blew relentlessly up Route 9 and battered our picture window, we were warm and comforted. Joe had been in Costa Rica, exploring and adventuring during the off-season for painting. John had been home with family in Wisconsin and was back for Christmas. Stuart had been painting interiors and Susan had continued her sewing and repair business. Our relationship remained strained; her dislike and dismissal of me were a constant irritation. Neither of us had the energy nor compassion to change it. My showing up with a darling infant must have further soured her feelings. She and I had shared her sewing machine in Tiger, but it was now apparent that I needed to get my own. Wilber and I had heard of a warehouse in Leadville full of treadle bases and Singer machines. You were welcome to pick your base and head, and the crotchety old owner would put them together, shine and oil 'em up, and make them yours for a mere 85 bucks. We drove over and I spent the day scouring the cavernous building while Wilber and Wyatt charmed the old man with their warmth and wit. I scored a beauty, another tool we would use toward the cause of our freedom. Back home I began making Wyatt's overalls and altering my own clothes. I sewed a nylon and down sleeping bag from a Frostline Co. kit to replace my silly cotton one. I stitched up a storm.

Martin and MaryAnn were a refreshing new couple. He was ever funny and crazy, she was sweet and mellow. She and I became good buddies; her quiet confidence made her a trusted cohort. We spent the days cooking, sewing, and playing with Wyatt. She was like a sister of the same age and interest, another strong and able woman. The long, dark, bitter winters at 10,000 feet culled out the wannabes and left a rough and tumble community of mountain ladies.

During Wyatt's first winter, a wider group of ladies decided to gather their energies at a Tea Party once a month. To hang out and let it out with our closest girlfriends, we'd trudge into one of the secluded cabins, ten to twenty ladies in our finest dresses, hats, and mukluks, and one baby. There we would huddle with mugs of tea (whiskey) and crumpets (joints), crammed into a cabin turned sweat lodge. Someone played music. We sang and swayed. Wyatt cooed delightedly, passed around the women's circle, and snuggled by aunties. We'd gossip, share intimacies, and forge new alliances. It felt good and important to know the women who lived far and wide, or across the street. The energy of a season's toiling oozed out of us and we laughed until it hurt and the day turned to night. The Ladies' Tea Parties became a tradition of legend that winter, a welcome escape.

Our men were spending their days hanging sheet rock and finishing trim in the condos, working around the Swan Valley Painters. Most evenings they spent hanging on the bar at the Pan, drinking beer and bitching about work, blowing off the steam of their days while seeking news of the wider world outside. We had no access to TV and little radio, and we didn't trust the newspapers. Still, the men made it their business to know what Nixon had done, what was new in Southeast Asia, and the progress of our ideals. While we gossiped about new squatters, who was sleeping with whom, and our own sex lives, our men were solving the world's problems.

Nixon had been reelected and sworn in, then implicated in a spying scandal they were calling Watergate. His top aides had quit and run. There was talk of a peace treaty with North Vietnam, and we had a feeling that we may have been heard, though too little, too late. On January 27, the United States and North Vietnam signed the Paris Peace Accords. Withdrawal of our troops was imminent. Over 50,000 young Americans had been killed in Vietnam, along with untold numbers of Vietnamese, and the damage and shame could never be undone. Timothy Leary, labeled by Nixon as "the most dangerous man in America," sat in solitary confinement at Folsom Prison. He continued to write and spread his beliefs. Abbie Hoffman, co-founder of the Yippies, was arrested for intent to sell cocaine. And Gloria Steinem was gathering steam and support with NOW, the National Organization for Women, and the House and Senate had passed the Equal Rights Amendment. In the case of Roe v. Wade, the Supreme Court voted to legalize abortion, paving the way for safe and subsidized choices for our generation. Though not an antidote for free and irresponsible sex, the decision would save many lives by taking illegal abortions out of the back alleys all over America. Governor George Wallace, white supremacist, had been shot and paralyzed. It seemed as though a revolution might actually be taking hold. Our men came home from work exhausted, but bright with hope.

February 1973

Hello:
For the moment I'm working and don't see much of Nonnie and Wyatt. I was home early tonight so Wyatt and I were down in the shop. He's airing out his little seat, and being a good kid. I've been really happy with him and for the most part he's been really happy too. He really loves mama and his beaming mama

really loves him too. Hardly ever a diaper rash and when it hits him, it only lasts a few hours. Anyway, the happier he is, the happier we are. So it helps to smile a lot.

Weather has been super mild for the area and things have worked out smoothly. First folks I worked for beat me for $60, but since then we have been able to do most things that we wanted. As soon as this job in Vail is finished some of us are going to ski from Alma over to Aspen. It's been awhile since I've done any mountaineering and I'm anxious to go. It's so easy to fall into complacent ruts and sometimes I must stop and look around and remember why I came to the mountains. Nonnie will probably truck over with Wyatt and we will stay for a day or 2 to downhill ski (Wyatt hasn't been yet) and taste the good food over there. It should be real exciting.

Don't know if we'll be able to make it down in March but hope to see you all in the near future.

Much love, Frank

When we'd camped long enough in the garage office, I took it on myself to find a new home. With MaryAnn, I braved the constant biting wind, hiked and searched the crooked lanes of Alma. With Wyatt in the Snuggly, we surveyed abandoned cabins on abandoned streets, seeking good roofs and straight walls, intact windows, and evidence of plumbing. We'd peer in the windows and rattle the doorknobs, afraid at first of the ghosts that might lurk, but growing bold as we checked out dozens of potential livable spaces. Some were adorable, quaint Victorians with porches and root cellars; some were just four walls and a roof. We noted the addresses that had potential and went to the county courthouse in Fairplay to complete our sleuthing. With the owners' names and phone numbers in hand, we called and called but had no success even though we offered to fix up their places, patching roofs, painting, and gardening come spring, free of charge. The owners had heard that the town was growing with hippies, and apparently they didn't want to rent to *them*, to *us*. Their cabins weren't worth anything and they liked it just that way.

In our wanderings around the town, MaryAnn and I were eventually drawn to the old Alma Hotel. Also abandoned and in need of care, the building suddenly looked promising, and, given our recent hopes and disappointments, we turned to it as a possible home. The garage was crowded; maybe MaryAnn and Martin needed a new place, too. By then she and I were pros at finding owners and not shy about calling. Within a few days we had called, coerced, and cajoled the hotel's owner, and Wilber and I had committed to leasing the Alma Hotel. We were thrilled—a space and a business of our own. It was an urban commune; complete with large gathering rooms, a commercial—albeit dated—kitchen, and lots of bath and bedrooms. There was even a sweet little room for Wyatt. In the month of January, MaryAnn and I cleaned and rented the rooms and set up the kitchen for feeding the tenants. Martin and Mary-Ann took one room. Roger, Bien, and Cass-the-photographer took others. We'd let four rooms by the month and the rest by the week or night. Sixty dollars a month for the room and thirty for food gave us plenty for expenses and free rein on the meals. MaryAnn and I planned and shopped for dinners for our diners.

Our customers were mostly hungry men, famished after swinging a hammer all day. As the goddesses of the kitchen, we'd pore over cookbooks: *Vegetarian Epicure, Tassajara Bread Book,* and my ever-present kitchen companion, *Joy of Cooking.* We planned elaborate family-style meals. Our big extravagance was the bi-monthly trip to Denver or Boulder for supplies. With the $150 from the tenants to spend, we were on a lark. Wilber would take us in the Chevy or we'd hitch a ride in the Swan Valley Painters panel van. Down and out of the mountains, we'd discover the air light with warmth and heavy with city scents. We'd peel off our wool and our long johns and dance through Green Mountain Granary, filling bags and jars with goodies. We kept to our carefully prepared list, but we'd always reward ourselves with a treat or two for the effort: a fresh bottle of Skin Trip, a loofah, or a bag of dried pineapples.

Back in the rarified air of Alma, we'd have a banquet the first night. Perishables were used in sequence. Cabbage, potatoes, and dry beans could wait. We'd steam asparagus, broccoli, spinach, maybe make a quiche or a fresh tomato tart. Later in the week, our pressure cooker would whistle daily with the beans, rice, and grains that were our staples. Though I was the one in charge and did most of the cooking, MaryAnn and I loved to experiment. Our failures became legends, sometimes inedible, but served with a flourish— like my first soufflé, at over 10,000 feet, a sodden mass of egg and cheese with bits of limp spinach. Delicious! We loved the work. Wyatt was happy in his highchair, mashing scraps with his eager gums. Still nursing every four hours, he loved all foods and the pleasure of the feeding-time ritual. Our workspace was a warm, bright, and joyful kitchen, with a bank of windows to the east, unobstructed views across the South Platte. A service bar opened into the lobby, with a view to the card tables, fireplace, and picture windows onto Route 9. Colorful with fabrics, posters, and the flow of hippies, our lobby became the new clubhouse south of Hoosier Pass, and it was the reason for our #1 rule: No pot smoking on the first floor. We were happy to have the company, but we couldn't afford the suspicions of the local law. We were running a business, after all.

Noonie came to visit in March bringing an air of Her Ladyship to the Alma Hotel. Sharing motherhood and all its endeavors, we finally found time and commonality. She loved Wilber and the two of them connected in their mutual admiration of Wyatt. She and Wyatt could sit all day entertaining each other, with food, balls, and kitchen gadgets. An old-fashioned mom, Noonie was happy as long as everyone smiled, held cultural discourse, and ate well. Simple pleasures were her ambition, and she was welcomed and appreciated. Though I'm sure she was relieved to see indoor plumbing and electricity in our lives, she brought no judgment to our "family" structure. I could see her concern when Wyatt was passed among the grubby working hands of our friends for a collective caring. But he held sway as the only baby in town, and a babbling, smiling five-month-old begged squishing. Noonie was his attendant for three days, and I was sad to see her off at Stapleton Airport.

Construction work was plentiful, the money too good, and the hotel was grand. But life was not simple. Our friends' ever-changing soap operas embroiled us, their dramas complex and seductive, but their unmarried, uncommitted, and discontented lives were exhausting. Party drugs were changing: LSD had led to peyote, pot to downers, speed to more speed. This was the moment when Richard Nixon famously declared: "America's Public Enemy No. 1 is drug abuse." Hard drugs—heroin, cocaine, and reds—hadn't found their way into our little neck of the woods, not that I knew of. We were off the beaten path, a box canyon away from the migration route from east to west. And, despite the occasional emotional turmoil of our friends, we had found respite in our little nucleus. We were cocooning, and we liked it that way. There was a certain comfort in our Breckenridge/Alma family, a comfort we had missed in the slick grooviness of California. Everywhere we went along the Tenmile Range, we would run smack into someone we knew and cared about. There was a safety in our numbers.

March 1973

Dear folks:

Sorry we missed you last time down, but we were so busy that by 7:30 when all our trips were finished we were tired, Wyatt was cranky and Cherry Creek seemed too far away. I decided to go back to work anyway, which is probably best at this point. We have rented the Alma Hotel and the huge deposit required to get the keys have left us pretty near penniless.

But the building is beautiful and full up with all our friends (whom you cannot tolerate). We like it here and hope to be able to swing free rent out of the venture. Nonnie is managing the place and doing most all the cooking and seems very happy. Wyatt has lots of people around which is just the way we want it, and he is in his own room now.

He is getting so big that it almost stuns me to watch him grow. Tonight he ate pea soup and cottage cheese and really loved it. We fed him yogurt and eggs too. It isn't warm and soft like the titty, but at 6 months he's got to start pulling away from infant desires. Which means a little less sucking and a little more searching for other forms of entertainment.

I have done some downhill and cross country skiing, have been working on some fine hand-made doors for John, Joe and Stuart's garage, will soon be taking a welding course over in Breck, working on my car which runs very poorly and holding down this job. Both of us are very busy and we are doing a lot of eating out and movies. I guess the more you make, the more you spend and soon we are going to have to get down to the fine art of saving. But car payments, new tires, etc., etc., are killing the budget. Only 13 payments left – and that's some relief because if I can't get the damn thing to run I'm gonna sell it and get a 1966 Dodge pickup – when trucks were not burdened with inefficient and wasteful air pollution control devices that don't work.

We may travel down to Arkansas to look at land. It's supposed to be very fruitful soil and relatively cheap to Colorado standards. We are getting anxious again to seek something out. Hope you are in good spirits and taking life easy. May is Mother's day and your birthday so I hope to see you then.

Write soon, F

Wilber and I realized that a place of our own, where we could build a barn, a forge, a greenhouse, a root cellar, big gardens, could be a home of our making that no one could take away. We knew starting over would be tough, but we were focused on the future, and the idea of a true homestead was a powerful goad. Once again we began to talk privately and in the group about a move to warmer climes, as we had from the beginning. By the end of our lease, we were ready to strike out on our own and find that utopia where we could afford a piece of land and begin to build a life.

Wilber's beloved grandfather Opa had left him a bit of ground in his will, up the pass from Alma. We'd gone to look at it and had found a bare, hard plot, higher and dryer than Alma. We couldn't imagine subsisting there, so we sold it for a down payment on land elsewhere and thanked Opa Seligman for his contribution toward our freedom.

Wilber had made good use of the Alma garage by building a camper shell onto the pickup. Wood-sided, with Plexiglas windows and a hand-split cedar shake roof, it would be our home for a while. A plywood platform in the truck bed hid the trappings of life on the road, stuffed into boxes and crates below, while on top a foam pad beneath my childhood poppy-patterned quilt made a cozy nest for the three of us. It was a darned good home. Like military strategists waging a battle against our own homelessness, we emanated vibes of success. We were primed and outfitted for the siege.

Again, we would tip our caps at Colorado, say farewell to all our friends, and set off to find our true home. It was the eighth time we'd packed up and said good-bye in the eighteen months since we'd left Tiger. Still, I thought we were pretty stable. Wherever we went we were a family, trusting and in love. Like the natives before us, we would pack our horses, strap baby Wyatt to the travois, follow the great buffalo herds and the grass shoots north, and savor the rites of summer. From my childhood's extensive travels, I knew that an itinerant exploration could be a thrilling vacation.

As we mapped out our quest, north seemed a better bet for the summer. The Wyoming, Montana, and Canadian Rockies were a raw version of the Colorado mountains we loved. British Columbia held the cachet of being wild, sparsely settled, and far-flung, yet English-speaking and temperate. Arkansas could wait until fall, when it had cooled a bit.

Before leaving Alma, we climbed to the top of the nearest 14,000-foot peak, Mt. Lincoln. We'd been up a similar peak the summer before, when I was pregnant. I recalled the hike as tough and stunning, definitely worth doing again. In early summer, the wildflowers grew close to the rocks in bright green velvet pincushions. The hills were dappled with the hot pink of phlox, the cool blue of forget-me-nots, and the stark white of cushion-plants, and I could identify both the flowers and their medicinal qualities. When they warmed in the sun, the intense fragrances of the struggling blooms wafted on the alpine breeze. We were heady with the scent and the thin mountain air. I carried lunch, Wilber had Wyatt in the Snuggly, and Joe and John led the way. As we crossed snowfields, scree fields, and wildflower fields, the views were stupendous. The sights kept us going, but we were exhausted. We were healthy and young, and we'd lived above the tree line, but we were not mountain climbers. It was a tough climb. Every rise was a false summit; you only had to peek over its top to see the next "summit" beyond. But the biggest surprise awaited us at the top. When we finally reached the summit, we looked south and saw jeeps and people on the top of Mt. Bross, the peak to the south. They had driven up! Driven all the way. I had to laugh. Though we were proud of our efforts and strong muscles, they were enjoying the same view, maybe, but not from the same viewpoint. As Wilber and I held Wyatt close, we surveyed the peaks and valleys of our past, and I looked beyond our confident little tribe to our unfamiliar future.

I murmured words that were oft used by my savvy husband: "It helps to smile a lot."

CHAPTER EIGHTEEN

To begin our journey north, Wyatt and I would take a bus from Denver to Idaho and spend a few weeks with my parents at their new ranch house. Wilber would meet us there in two weeks, after he spent some time with his parents, filling the camper with food from Green Mountain Granary, digging camping gear from his parents' crawlspace, and calming them down before leaving the area. This trip was to be pivotal. We didn't know when we'd be back. We arrived in Denver for Shabbat, and Wyatt and I said quick good-byes before the Greyhound pulled out on I-25, northbound.

I hated leaving Wilber. Our little family was so strong and tight, and now that Wyatt was sleeping in his own room, and eating at the table, Wilber and I craved connection and private time. New motherhood and the business of running a hotel had left me tired and distracted. A road trip with my husband promised a chance for us to renew our marital bond, and I missed him already.

As the Greyhound rolled through Wyoming and up the Ho-backs, we passed Granite Hot Springs, the rustic pools filled with memories of wild high school parties (just three years ago!). The Tetons surged into view, images from my colorful past rising up along with them. Jackson's antler-arched square reminded me of hours idled away while tripping on acid and smoking with my meager clutch of compadres. When we climbed off the bus, with all my motherly paraphernalia in tow, Kenny and Sarah were there to meet us, the Dodge Ram rumbling behind them. Noonie was home making dinner and we were just an hour from the ranch. We piled in, all a-jolly, and I was suddenly glad for my family. They were good-looking, healthy country folk. Their love for us was palpable in their genuine welcome and their shared anticipation of what lay ahead for us in the coming weeks. Unlike our times at the Neumanns, where any visit was a chore, this felt simple and good. Would Wilber feel about my family the way I felt about his? For his sake, I hoped not. After a few weeks, time would tell.

Yet, as I settled in, the bloom would fall off the rose for me too. Soon I began to feel the telltale effect of my proximity to my father. It was the feeling of being sucked into a cult, the sound of his voice piercing my subconscious and letting loose a flood of sensitivities. I was back in the Kingdom of Kenny. Even before we were over the Teton Pass and entering Idaho, I could feel his church surrounding me. I hadn't forgotten his powerful influence, but I was surprised by the ease with which a look, a tilt of his head, or a subtle sigh could drag me back from years of independence. I steeled myself against his control. Again, I missed Wilber, yearning for his love, confirmation, and protection.

When we were kids, the cry "Daddy's breathing" was sufficient to send a spasm of terror through the house. He had told us that when he was really, really upset, he would take ten deep breaths before acting or speaking out. We could hear him from afar, in through his nose, out through his mouth, and we'd scurry and hide in fear. Our best bet was to run for the backyard or our rural Connecticut winding road, lined with old stonewalls, fields and woods beyond. That was during his silent phase, just out of the mental hospital, when he spoke only the absolute truth, *his* truth. Breathing still precautioned his behavior.

At the ranch, supper was ready: my mom's famous macaroni salad and a thick, juicy steak. At this western ranch, meal meant meat. All manifestation of animal, wild or domestic, appeared as centerpiece. My mother crafted a creative display of veggies and starch around the meat-of-the-day for balance, but meat every morning, noon, and night? Wilber and I lived as light carnivores, a good burger or fried chicken being the occasional treat.

After a good tight hug, I looked over her shoulder at the new, old home they'd built on this hill. During the rush of the wedding, we'd passed through so briefly and chaotically. Now as I anticipated my next two weeks, I could imagine hours of reflection in the arms of my past. African spears, Tibetan weavings, Western art, and Samoan seashells complimented Queen Anne furniture and my mother's delicate cross-stitch creations. Here, I would recall and relive the enduring good, and smart bits of our past, as well as the haunting trouble.

As expected, my parents had planned as much as the valley could offer. Noonie was happy to stay home with Wyatt while we hiked, fished, floated, and generally explored the Teton splendor. It was their second summer in the county and they'd not only plunged into the wilderness, but had bought up a couple of other secluded ranches for Kenny's entertainment. He loved the hunt, the negotiation, and the purchase of a good piece of land for a good price. Undiscovered and undeveloped, the Idaho side of the Tetons, in their opinion the best side, was just as funky as God and the Mormons prescribed. Unpaved, unimproved, and not on any airline route, Teton Valley was an unspoiled, unlimited playland to my parents—and an inherited, demanding farmland to the locals. The sleepy towns of Driggs and Victor offered bare necessities, and Co-burn Drug served a fine Fresh Lime Freeze, the reward for a hot day's activity.

Kenny, Dede, and I hiked Teton Canyon, rode ill-mannered horses up Mahogany Creek, and floated the Teton River in search of trout and a cool dip while Sarah worked and Noonie entertained Wyatt, or vice-versa. While we hiked, my dad would occasionally spew his delusional theories on life. Dede and I refrained from comment, changed the subject, avoiding the rant beyond. But he was in a talkative phase. Far from the "I speak only when I have something important to say" mode, which had been awkward and unpredictable, this new version of Kenny was mostly a relief. He was almost normal, as long as we could monitor his ramblings.

He could be charming and informative on the subjects of history and wildlife. He loved to turn people on to his world, to captivate them with a grand tale. He would spin yarns teeming with cowboys and grizzlies, dark nights and campfires. Nothing gave him more pleasure than sharing a story (true or not) with the un-initiated, especially Easterners, along with a helping of my mother's wild huckleberry pie, buffalo salami, or his Dutch-oven chicken. Kenny was an entertainer from way back, from the nights of lamp-shade on the head and dancing 'til dawn. We couldn't help but be drawn in by his jokes—"So, this guy walks into a bar, see..." His perfect delivery had us laughing even as we rolled our eyes, before the punch line even came. He and my mother had shared wit and humor for more than twenty years. Sometimes I thought of it as their salvation.

Best of all was spending more time with my sisters. Though Betsy wasn't around, Dede and Sarah and I had the space, for the first time maybe, to share the intimacies and confidences of our lives and loves. We had matured, yes, but mostly we had grown away from being a unit of four little girls in matching party dresses or school uniforms. We were close in age, four of us born within five years, and our father fostered competition between us. As we moved through the ranks, we had followed lock step behind each other, through schools, lessons, and sports. Even our friends were the siblings of our sisters' friends. In our last year together, on our trip-around-the-world, we'd grown our hair waist-length and shared clothes and dazed expressions. By the end of that romp we might have looked, and acted, like quadruplets! It wasn't that there had been great expectations for us; in fact none at all, but neither was there celebration of our uniqueness. Now, we had each sprouted a unique life, no two alike. It'd been five years since we left Connecticut, years of turmoil, years of change. We had all come out damaged, each in a different way, but incredibly strong for it.

Sarah was working in the pea fields, her last summer job before her senior year of high school. Her boyfriend was a football hunk, a Driggs local, Mormon and sweet. After sophomore year at a free-thinking boarding school in New York, she had become the only non-Mormon at Teton Valley High. Having resourcefully gotten herself excused from religion class, she was happy to sit in her car, smoke cigs, and share pot with the kids when they were released from God, but she was alone. She was not one of *them*, the gum-snapping, high-hair-teasing, polyester-wearing local girls. Did she want to be? I felt badly about having left her as a fourteen-year-old, alone with our parents. I had not ever taken the time to protect or even know her. But maybe she was stronger than I.

After her one-year stint in New York, Dede had followed the family west, shedding her boyfriend and her preppy past to find something unique. She was working in Wilson, just over the pass, as head chef at a popular haunt called Blackie's, and was now living with one of the local climbing/skiing junkies. In the winter, she taught tourists' kids to ski at Jackson Hole. In summer, she played in the rivers and mountains of the Tetons, chugging around in her yellow VW bug. My golden oldest sister's life seemed rife with success, romance, and adventure.

Betsy was still living with Plum Fairy in San Francisco, the national heart and soul of hippiedom. What we heard from her was surreal and exciting. Living in the Beat Culture of North Beach, she and Plum were digging it. Allen Ginsberg, Herb Caen, Lawrence Ferlinghetti, and Mimi Fariña were there. Several of the Pelhamites were there, and they'd become quite a community. I imagined her in that scene—Betsy, the easy and delicate flower child, the sway of her long, blond hair and the dazzle of her graceful frocks. Would she survive the city? I hoped the Pelham boys would keep a close eye on her. I knew my parents had transferred their feelings of concern and shame from me onto Betsy. They worried about her choices, in Plum and in the city. They hoped for a life of better options for her. So why, when she'd asked our dad to send her to art school, had he not agreed to support her? She'd been devastated. And thrown from her passion.

My sisters were curious about my lifestyle and the woman, wife, and mother I'd become at just nineteen. My descriptions of Tiger, Alma, Bridgeport, and the lifestyles and friends there kept them rapt. Stories of the gardens, Suebi and Ron, Sunshine, and the jail, Joe, John, and the Alma Hotel gave them a taste of the tension and adventure in my chosen path. They could see that I'd grown and learned in the school-of-life. My place in the family as trouble-maker, attention-grabber, and dreamer had led me to a life of tran-sitory permanence. Proven as the rebel, I had taken my life by the shoulders and shaken it into something really special and full. I'm sure they were impressed that I'd lived in such remoteness: hauling water, chopping wood, bathing in a dishpan, and shitting in an outhouse. And I'm sure they didn't know what to make of it. I felt as though they were all wishing us well while simultaneously wait-ing for the other shoe to drop.

By the time Wilber arrived in Idaho to retrieve me, our truck/home loaded and welcoming, I had developed a temporary blind-ness to my family's foibles. I was so proud and eager when my dash-ing husband rounded the bend, in a cloud of dust, and pulled up to the back door. Wyatt and I were poolside; he was kicking from the edge, and he squealed at the sight of his daddy crawling out of the truck. Wilber had had a tough twelve-hour drive, alone and tired. We rushed to meet him. He scooped Wyatt up and danced him around, "Wydie, Wydie... How's my boy?" We hugged with the urgent reunion of our first separation, and his eyes settled on me, warm and still so seductive.

CHAPTER NINETEEN

"Don't park there!" Kenny called, pushing through the screen door from the kitchen. "No, no, you'll have to move." What a welcome! My persnickety father was foaming through his disgustingly cracker-crumb-speckled beard. What did he care, and why was he so gruff? It wasn't a good start, and I was surprised. Here was his first son-in-law, the first male in his all-female harem. Was Kenny peeing on the perimeter of his turf? Wilber was too tired and dazed to respond.

"We'll put the truck over beyond the garden," I jumped in, rescuing my husband from his first encounter with in-law abuse. (I'd had plenty.) This was no big deal; and besides it was hot and the pool was calling.

The next week rolled out with more valley exploration and what turned out to be a pretty peaceful visit. Kenny challenged Wilber with hiking, fishing, and intellectual jousting, and I thought he might have met his match. Both men were physically strong and agile, but Wilber was book smart as well as clever and witty. He'd been top of his class at University of Wisconsin, and I knew that higher education intimidated my successful, but untraditionally educated, father. They were in equally unfamiliar territory, however, when it came to healthy paternal relationships—they'd both had unloving, unsafe fathers, and the result was a mutual distrust.

But we were on vacation, determined to be civil, and Wyatt kept the ball rolling. In a house full of egos and needs, his were the loudest and most endearing. Dede and Sarah were smitten, and when they weren't working or playing with boyfriends, they could be found hiking with Wyatt in the Snuggly, hanging out by the pool, petting the horses, or reading the books of our childhood. With the menfolk often off running errands or handling chores (their version of bonding), my mom and I had some time to cook, bake, and talk. She was as easily entertained as Wyatt, and as long as I kept out the scary parts, she was enchanted with my tales. I didn't tell her about my almost-miscarriage, or the rampant drug use among our friends. Two weeks passed quickly and pleasantly.

Between picnics and rodeos, we got a call from Joe, who'd been looking for us and had found my parents' number by calling the Neumanns. He had sad and shocking news from home. We knew that the previous summer, the U.S. Forest Service had kicked the hippies—some friends, some strangers—out of Tiger. The most recent development was that Summit County (essentially, the developers) had succeeded in pressuring the Forest Service to burn Tiger down to the ground in order to keep the undesirables out once and for all.

We were heartbroken. What a waste. We had such beautiful memories of Tiger, and now the spirit of the place was ruined. I imagined the flames licking across the worn floors and weathered walls of our peaceful sanctuary, where we'd begun our dream and hatched so many ideas. I saw the visqueen melt, my kitchen workspaces aflame, and then the scorched ground around the wasted site of our love affairs, feasts, and meditations. I cried into Wilber's shoulder while he got angry. My parents had little sympathy; what did they know of the times? So we mourned alone and resolved that we would own our future, that no one could burn down our memories again.

The news further motivated our northern exploration, to the wilds of Montana and Canada. We bundled Wyatt into his car seat, basically a hollow aluminum tube that hooked over the bench seat, with a padded cardboard seat in yellow vinyl and a little steering wheel complete with horn. Toot-toot, and we were off. The national parks were our first destination. We spied bears from the truck, camped in the topper, and cooked on the Coleman, mostly in prescribed campgrounds, occasional campfires and ranger chats. It was a luxurious holiday. We all loved it, and even as bears roamed the camp at night, we slept cozily in our cabin-on-wheels. Wyatt was not yet crawling so commanded little space.

When we crossed into Canada, we encountered Banff and Jasper National Parks, marveled at the grandeur of Lake Louise and Mt. Robson. We rode the spine of public treasures, each one offering deeper ranges and steeper peaks, with thick lips of ancient glaciers. With Wyatt snoozing in a new frame pack, we hiked through the Valley of the Ten Peaks. A roar in the distance spun us around to the sight of a glacier sloughing and to the avalanche that ensued. I'd never seen anything like it. The power, felt from miles away, left us shaken. I hoped that no hiker had been caught in its path.

Venturing ever northward, we found the lakes bluer, the sky bigger, the trees shorter, and the people friendlier. We were blown away. Granted, we reminded ourselves, it was the height of summer in the north, no better time. But we were unexpectedly, spontaneously falling in love with Canada.

From Jasper we headed west into British Columbia and meandered along the Rocky Mountain Trench of the Fraser River. There we entered the boreal forest, the rolling lake-studded terrain of the Cariboo, and the wildest country either of us had ever seen. Not a tourist trap in sight, and barely a gas station or outpost. Thickly forested, sparsely settled, rough and rugged, this was truly the land of pioneers. The woods were so dark and dense that a person could easily get lost without the view of mountain or sun to help find a way out.

In the occasional spots where the wood was cleared, the farms grew rich, the livestock fat. Turning south on the Fraser River, we entered a valley of early settlements, dotted with way stations, hand-operated ferries, and service towns. Growth had been slow, and development a product of true necessity, giving us a feeling of the purpose of the place. We were impressed by the girth and life along its banks, the ancestral home of the river people, Lheidli T'enneh. White men had settled in Western Canada, an exploration that began in 1784 with the great surveyor and mapmaker David Thompson—long before Lewis and Clark left St. Louis in 1804. Yet still these northern reaches were home to only a hardy few. We preferred hardy to the ease of California. We respected the spirit and satisfaction of a hard-won life. Through Prince George, Quesnel, Soda Creek, and Williams Lake, we continued south. The scene got richer and livelier.

In Williams Lake, just for something to do on a Saturday, we shuffled into a real estate office. A nice lady in a colorful pantsuit and cowboy boots welcomed us to the home of the "World Famous Williams Lake Stampede." Nothing that interested a coupla hippies, but she kept on.

"You might stay on a bit, eh? Camp out by the river?" Sheila began to set the hook, dragging her "o"s in the Canadian way. "There's a good campsite, with real washrooms. Tomorrow, we can take a look at a spread or two that I just know you'll like. How about you come back here at ten, eh?" Well, why not.

She used her best bait in sending us to the river. Verdant and cool, it was a sight straight out of our dreams. Its gentle rumbling waters sculpted the Interior Plateau of the Fraser River, ranches and farms filling in the flats. A more productive terrain than the one we'd come from, a harsh but fertile ground. The whole area was appealing, including a small town with all the necessary services and light industry. Or so we thought until the next morning, when the air filled with the sight and stench of a plywood mill.

"Did you say those spreads were out of town?" Wilber asked Sheila, who was waiting near the office in a denim pantsuit. He nodded toward the billowing orange smoke.

"Yep, south a bit. Oh, that old mill, keeps the town alive," she said, her sales brain getting ahead of our doubt. "The northwest was built on timber, eh?" A new consideration for us, a cherished history of hardy families and livelihoods that had survived on killing forests, polluting air, and risking lives.

"So, you're not from B.C., eh?" she asked, assuming the position of so many we'd met—and would meet—in Canada. Her implied question, about whether we were among those Americans dodging the war in Vietnam, would forever go unasked and assumed. Wilber was definitely *that* age, but Dr. Schick had certified him 4-F, for his asthma. We certainly had friends who'd served (Stewart in Tiger), dodged (Dave in Bridgeport), conscientiously objected (John in Alma), and just flat lied or hid. We were anti-war of any kind, and the Vietnam War was a proven disaster that neither our "boys" nor the Vietnamese should have been dying for. For my part, I was young enough that my classmates had been unaffected. The draft lottery had ended in 1972, when I turned eighteen.

Soon we were loaded into Sheila's sedan, cruising south on the Cariboo Highway. Passing the old stage station, 150 Mile House, the central and only highway rolled north to south. Eventually it hooked east away from the old supply route, the Fraser River, and ran alongside the newer transport, the Canadian Northern Railway. The farms and ranches we saw along the road were simple and functional, very unlike the fancy chalets of Jackson or Breckenridge. Piled with rusty equipment and kids' toys, the yards also held huge gardens high with August's corn, beans, and broccoli. Some had orchards—ripe cherries, small apples, green pears. I elbowed Wilber and we both grinned.

About thirty miles south of town, the highway rose out of the geographic limits of the valley, up and away from the river. Knife Creek Road took off to the east. Sheila slowed as she turned onto the gravel-logging road, and we took in the view. As we pulled off the highway, the road widened and the scene narrowed. We were going into the northern woods.

"Nothing from here to the Canadian Rockies," she boasted, and I thought of those bears. "No roads, no towns, nobody!" We felt the emptiness of it as we drove on and on. One driveway shot to the left, but hard as I looked, I couldn't make out a structure, mailbox, or sign until we reached the creek.

"Whoops, looks like I missed it, eh?" Sheila laughed. We turned around and slowly retraced our route. There, just off the road, over a small rise, was a rustic, demure ranch gate. We drove through it and the road dropped us down to where the dirt driveway came to an end. Sheila turned off the car and we piled out to a humble, stunning scene. The grass was high and dusty, edged with trees thick and dark, but I'll never forget my first impression of Knife Creek: the sound of its unseen, vibrant creek and the sight of its hill, dotted with bright kinnikinnik bushes and quaking aspens. It was a precious setting, peaceful and pastoral, and Wilber and I were mesmerized. Wyatt struggled in my arms. He was ready for some floor time.

"There are thirteen acres, and the creek is the east border. The property goes north over that fence," Sheila went on, pointing past the corral, "and back across the road. About six acres over there. The barn is up the hill."

We spun around to behold what we both knew would be our new home—a small log cabin standing sentry over the yard, with a good strong front porch, framed and partially enclosed for summer and winter storms. An outhouse sat off to the south side, a shed to the north, and the corral beyond was full of manure, a fine garden plot. We ran to the creek, Wilber taking Wyatt on his shoulders. A beaver dam blocked the narrow crossing, and a fine fishing pond had formed behind it. Above it all was that colorful hillside—not part of the thirteen acres, but ours to meditate on forever.

We peeked into the root cellar, tucked into the hill behind the cabin. Its shelves and bins showed signs of use. I imagined it filled with our own homegrown potatoes, carrots, turnips, rutabagas, and onions, put in for the long winter. And beyond that the tiny log barn on its large flat field with a tidy paddock attached.

"Great place for a few calves or pigs." Sheila was reeling us in. She proceeded to answer all of our questions about the growing season, average rainfall, snow depth, and winter temperatures. Thirty-below-zero, no problem: We'd seen that in Alma. Snow wouldn't be deep, but it stayed for a long time, into March. Not a problem for us either, as in Tiger it snowed in July. No phone: For emergencies the nearest neighbor was "a fir piece" on down the road. No electricity and certainly no running water. By the time we'd scoured the property, including the piece across the road (a swamp of little interest), we'd been caught hook, line, and sinker.

We hadn't even stepped into the cabin yet, however. The porch felt solid underfoot, and the heavy split-log door was held in place by a padlock and a great iron bar. But the place was a mess, apparently hadn't been lived in for some time. It stank, whether because of the mold and dust or the mouse turds scattered across the stained and buckled linoleum floors, we couldn't tell. One corner drooped heavily under the weight of logs and a lack of foundation. We climbed the stairs, cautiously, to the two sleeping rooms. Large windows at each end flooded the otherwise dreary spaces with light and the welcome of mornings to come.

Reality gave our dream a little bit of a smack in the face, but we were still sold on the location, the size, and the remoteness. By the time we got back to town, we had made a verbal offer to the owners, a couple in Seattle. Not yet committed, we had the night to think on it. After closely inspecting the town, we packed up a special picnic and went back down Knife Creek Road for the evening. We pulled off on a quiet turnout and hiked every inch of the land. In the high-latitude late summer, the sun didn't set until after eight, so we had plenty of time to explore.

By morning we were back in Sheila's office to sign papers and pay up. The asking price was seventeen thousand, and our offer of fifteen five had been accepted. Sheila would take care of things and be in touch with us when we got back to Colorado. Opa's legacy was our down payment, and our owner-financed mortgage would be $136 a month for four years. That we could handle. With a packet from the Chamber of Commerce in-hand, after one final stop at the property for photos, we headed back to Colorado to plan out our future. We would have to emigrate, which could take some time, but we wanted to do this right—no sneaking around. On our summer vacation, we'd made the decision to become Canadians, to make a permanent move and build a life in the Cariboo. We couldn't wait to get started.

CHAPTER TWENTY

In late September, land-rich and cash-poor, we reentered the Colorado Rockies. We headed, of course, to the only place worthy of our big news: the Gold Pan on a Friday night. It was almost freaky the way everyone was always there. The news of our land grab came as no shock to our closest friends, but the finality of it was definitely the sign of a shake-up.

In the meantime, Wilber needed work and the emigration process would take time. We would be around for a while.

Rumor had it there was a building boom on over at the Vail Ski Resort, in Eagle County. Farther than Copper Mountain, too far for a daily commute. We decided to move closer, but the problem side of resort booming was that we couldn't afford to live near Wilber's work unless we squatted—and we were done with that. So we got in the truck and drove the 30-mile radius in search of a place where we could afford to rent. Leadville, famously known for the Silver King and Molly Brown, seemed a manageable distance, though it had seen its better days about eighty years before. It was a small forgotten city, of had-been businesses and woulda-been miners. At the top of a short pass, it was windy and cloudy most of the time. We were soon hooked up and moved in with a friend of a friend who owned a dilapidated Victorian in the middle of town. Jim was an engineer at the Climax Molybdenum Mine and a decent sort, but I was never sure how he took to having a baby, or a family, in his house. We had paid for his back bedroom, upstairs, and I took it upon myself to do all of the household's cooking in order to ease the toll of our disruption. There was just no keeping a healthy baby quiet.

Shortly after we unpacked, Wilber and I began planning a trip to his parents' mountain chalet for Wyatt's upcoming birthday. My parents and my sister Sarah were flying down, and the Neumanns were putting on a party, a valiant effort for the first birthday of their first grandson. The party would be a welcome distraction. My family had never visited Wilber's. We hadn't seen any of them since our summer vacation and hadn't yet told them of our Canadian future. Tension would be unavoidable, even with Margaret there to lighten the mood.

The Neumann's chalet, at the foot of Rocky Mountain National Park, was simple and stunning, filled with Hansi's handcrafted, alpine German furniture. These were the treasures she and her parents had carried from the Rhine as they'd fled the Nazis. On the walls, the character of Fred's Viennese family sparkled with sophisticated art and diplomas. The cultured heritage of the Neumanns and Seligmanns was apparent in the treasures they had salvaged from Hitler's SS. More so than their tract home in Denver, this cozy country house bespoke their histories and passions: Hansi's old barrel skis, Fred's polished violin. A true sense of Europe was alive in the two-story chalet. Their hearts, I felt, lived there, amidst the delicate heirlooms of their shattered past. We would have to keep a close eye on our marauding boy.

The party was a great success. It was good to catch up and to walk the foothill trail, and we ate well, as always. German and Austrian specialties were savored along with stories of long-gone mothers and grandmothers. As we'd hoped, Wyatt received the lion's share of attention. Boy toys filled the room—John Deere tractor, horses, and a barn from my family, blocks, books, and puzzles from Hansi and Fred, and a squishy teddy bear from Margaret. When the cake came out and was set on the tray of Wyatt's highchair, he attacked it. His face, arms, and OshKosh overalls were covered with chocolate frosting, and we were proud. We laughed while Hansi raced around protecting linens and furniture from flying cake. Finally, Wilber began to describe our British Columbian farm, and faces fell. The distance and the isolation caught them all by surprise. Fortunately we had no time to linger over judgments or chagrins—we had a three-hour drive ahead of us and Wyatt had to get to bed.

Back in Leadville, Wyatt and I spent our days roaming town looking for playmates. The City Park and library were comforting outings, freshly urban and exciting for us both. In the carpeted children's stacks, attempting his first steps, Wyatt hurtled from shelf to shelf as I replaced books as fast as he could scatter them. It was a jolly game. When weather permitted, I'd pile him in the stroller and set off to investigate the historic mines. We'd roll up black canyons, over tailings and into ruins, throwing pebbles into copper-colored puddles. On weekends, with Wilber, we'd hike the Mosquito or Sawatch Range and play on the shores of Twin Lakes. We took advantage of the new territory but had to admit we were lonely, being so far from home and without a home of our own. The added pressure of owning a perfectly good home and having left our hearts there in pursuit of money put us both on edge, and we struggled with the direction we were going. Thankfully, the Vail job didn't last and we moved back to Breckenridge without much delay. We'd been in Leadville for two months. I was sure Jim would miss the added income, but not the family messiness. The real story in the fall of 1973 turned out to be our nation's messiness.

On October 10, amid charges of corruption and scandal, Vice President Spiro Agnew had pled no contest to income tax evasion and scrutiny by the FBI and resigned from office. Gerald Ford had been sworn in as Vice President under Nixon, who'd been on shaky ground since the Watergate thing had begun in 1972. In November, Nixon told the world, "I am not a crook," the general response being, "He doth protest too much." There was nothing new to the general distrust, disgust, and disinterest we felt in our government, but our hopes of becoming Canadians alleviated our gloom. We knew most of our troops had been pulled out of Vietnam, finally, and sent home bearing the negative legacy of the war they had lost. It was a national tragedy, but not their fault, and they would suffer that jungle fever forever.

The horror film *The Exorcist* was released after Christmas, and Wilber and I went on a date to see it. I'm not sure what I was thinking, as I've never been so scared in my life. Images from that film brought back the night terrors I'd worked so hard to leave behind, and the evil of that Hollywood devil haunted me for six months. Wilber thought I was being silly, but he didn't know about my primal fears. They were suppressed, deep and untended.

The Eagles, Seals & Crofts, Marshall Tucker, Jim Croce, Joni Mitchell, Neil Young, and James Taylor soothed the craziness of the era. Men and women were writing our hearts into the ballads and sermons of our time. Words of protest, never resignation, connected us. *Can't You See?, Heart of Gold, We May Never Pass This Way Again, Desperado,* and *Time in a Bottle* reminded us to treasure the time and significance of our lives. We were passing out of the euphoria of the Swan and Tiger and heading to the necessities of structure.

Back in the Tenmile Range, Wilber found work on the mountain, throwing together cheap condos. As always, the pay was good, but our goals were grander. We would have to work hard in order to squirrel away enough to head back to Knife Creek. Not only did we need money to support us up there until work could be found, but emigrant status required you to have socked away a certain sum of cash to prove that you wouldn't be a national or provincial burden. We needed a cheap place to live. Someone suggested a cozy cabin in Monte Cristo Gulch, near the top of Hoosier Pass. We knew a clutch of great folks living near the mine there. On the south side of the gulch, a couple of huge cabins that had once served as homes for miners had been made into roomy communes. Our home would be on the north rim of the gulch, a 200-square-foot chicken coop at 11,000 feet. We'd save dough there, for sure. We took it.

Getting serious about emigration meant exhausting trips to Denver and uncomfortable nights at the Neumanns, with their repetitive and painful attempts to refute our independence and denigrate our choices. "Why Canada? What's wrong with southern Colorado? You love the San Juan Mountains. We're not getting any younger. How can you take our only grandson away from us?" None of the guilt tripping was new to Wilber. Ever since he'd gone off to college, they'd demanded that he call them every Sunday to check in so they could remind him of his failures. Hansi and Fred had "fled Hitler's henchmen" to come to America in 1935 and 1938, respectively. (In contrast, my ancestors arrived on the Mayflower in 1620. I was a fourteenth-generation American, and took my nation for granted.) They loved the country that had saved their lives and those of the few relatives who'd been able to escape. Though they were barely sixty, mortality was for them an intensely felt and very present burden.

We were a generation of revolt, and what we were fighting—American aggression, consumerism, greed—was in essence the cost of the policy that had liberated my in-laws. We were insulting their choices. They had named their only son after the man responsible for their survival, Franklin Delano Roosevelt. He'd gone and rejected the good name they'd given him—for *Wilber?* And now we were leaving. Their dramatics stung, though I couldn't help feeling bad for them. "They've always been this way," Wilber whispered as we lay on the pullout in the den. They wouldn't be stopping us from moving forward.

We needed a lawyer, forms, a sponsor (Sheila), and the cash. Of course, Fred was unwilling to help in any way. So we worked it out. Interviews were conducted in the Federal Building in Denver, which reminded us of our California drug bust. (We hoped it wouldn't remind the authorities.) We went for our official photos on a gray winter day, Wilber in his wedding best, me in an Indian print blouse I'd made. He said we'd probably get rejected because I looked like a hippie chick, but when we got the photos back we had to laugh. His resembled a criminal mug shot, while mine was of pure innocence. Either way, our plan was rolling forward.

All the while, back in the gulch, we were cooped up in a chicken coop at 11,000 feet. Wyatt slept in a drawer, and every morning as I'd start our tiny coal stove, the cabin would fill with sooty smoke. I'd have to stand outside in my Lanz nightgown and down booties until the cabin cleared. Most mornings it was -30° and pitch black. Water was nearby, and after ten minutes of ice chopping, I'd form a hole big enough to dip a cup in. There were benefits to our miserable life up in the gulch, and we tried to keep these at top of mind. It was free, it was temporary, and on moon-filled nights, it was fantastic. At timberline in the heart of winter, when the sky was brittle and clear, the moonbeams would light up the snow. It was so magical and cool, you really could "read a newspaper by the light of the moon," as the old expression went. The moon's phases had always been important in our transient, rural life, and now on full-moon nights, we would stroll up the gulch.

Still, it was lonely in our dim and shabby home. Daylight lasted only a few hours, and in that time the sun never shone directly on the cabin. In the afternoon, while Wyatt napped, I'd listen to the short-wave radio Fred had given us, one of the seven they owned. Spinning the dial, I'd tune into faceless voices telling tall tales on far-flung broadcasts. A cup of rosehip tea and a dose of Firesign Theater warmed the gloomy, semi-permanent twilight of my day. I was hooked on the characters' voices and tales of intrigue and would sit in the oak, leather, and horsehair rocking chair that Wilber and I had found in a mine up the Swan, nursing my hot tea and escaping for an hour or so.

Wyatt was taking his first steps, around our shrunken floor space and in the packed snow trail leading to our home. On errand trips to town, Wyatt would totter around the Gold Pan café while I read mail and sometimes called my parents or sisters. He loved the warmth and commotion of the Laundromat, pushing the cart along or falling into piles of toasty clothes. Wilber's workdays were long, beginning and ending in the dark that bookended spring's short daylight. If I wanted or needed to go to town it meant an all-day commitment. Luckily, we also had friends with houses in town, always welcoming.

In the two years I'd been in Summit and Park Counties, there had been a widespread coupling of the hippies. Many had come here together as friends and bonded over shared pasts. Many were newly seduced by free love, then fallen for the object of their affection, and committed, for now anyway. Some had rented houses, or apartments, in town and began acquiring possessions. Some were pregnant, and we were happy for the joy they would know. Babies were born and I was able to attend their births from a new perspective. Families were forming, and struggling. It was a new scene of domestic regard.

It was a rough and confusing time for our little family. Wyatt and I were alternately unhappy or sick, or both, an increasingly crabby crew. If Wilber's long hours were a convenient excuse for him to avoid coming home, I couldn't blame him. (Though I did.) When he finally did come home, he was often met with a frustration I'd built up over the days, and weeks. I was feeling trapped, and pissed about it. Things got so bad that at one point I took Wyatt on the bus to Denver to stay with Hansi and Fred, feigning the flu. I had to get away from the cabin and the darkness. After a good soak in their tub, we were cleared to sit on the golden couch. And in my moment of need, Wilber's parents turned out to be endearing and kind. Hansi was a marriage and adoption counselor, and she sensed that something was off without my telling her. "You and Frankie have a solid marriage," she told me. "You care so deeply and are honest with each other." I began to cry, and she urged me to go home and take care of my husband.

On the return trip, I resolved to work harder to focus on our Canadian dream. When we got to Knife Creek, we would clear the air of our divisive bullshit and make a real home, finally. We wanted the same thing. We'd been talking about it for years. Were we getting scared of the leap to independence and unwittingly trying to sabotage our future? I thought so. He thought so, and we returned to our hovel to hatch out our final plan and make up the best way we knew how, while Wyatt dozed blissfully in his drawer. We later realized we'd been celebrating our first wedding anniversary.

Somehow, while we were busy behaving stupidly, winter had melted off the trees and buds and birds were returning. We were sure spring had come to faraway Knife Creek as well. The garden must be in need of turning, the house calling for air and a good cleaning. It was time to go—our "Landed Immigrant" papers in hand, our cash accumulated, and our stuff packed and waiting in Hansi and Fred's Denver crawlspace.

Staying in Breckenridge was changing us. We had been heading out, our progress slowed by the seduction of big money, and one we feared would suck us back in indefinitely. We couldn't wait any longer; we would leave with the next paycheck. There would be no time for a grand going-away bash at the Pan; we'd already had several. We would encourage everyone to visit Canada. We set to work on our recovery. We knew exactly where we were going. Our spirits were craving flight, and we set our date. We would leave at the end of April.

CHAPTER TWENTY-ONE

We snuck away one early spring evening, stealing into the night with our soot-soaked possessions. Heading north on Interstate 25, we bopped along to the last we'd be hearing of the American Top 40 for a while. John Denver, Jim Croce, Buffalo Springfield, and America sang our national ballads and we sang along right to the 49th parallel. Crossing the border in Roosville, Montana was a trip. The officer at that outpost must have thought we'd wandered in from the set of *The Beverly Hillbillies*. I'm sure he would have welcomed an excuse to send us back, but our papers were signed and sealed. We were as good as Canadians, for five years anyway. Still, he wanted to take a look, so we let him. He and his pals rifled through the edges of our cargo while keeping a good eye on our reactions. We were cool. We had nothing to hide.

Knife Creek was as we'd left it, but another winter dustier. There were still patches of snow on the ground, a stagnant pink algae reminding us of the mountains. But that was where the similarities ceased. This place was flat and treed from horizon to horizon: no landmarks in sight, no peaks, no hills.

This was our new life, and we danced around the dirty, slanting floors. Wyatt hooted and laughed, following our lead. We dug around the barn. We crept up on the outhouse. We peeked into the beaver dam. We swept and wiped every surface. We washed the windows, real squeaky, real glass. We unpacked. We planned.

We had spent only half our investment earnings on the property and had enough from Wilber's work to spend some time getting settled before he had to work again. Our furniture was limited: an antique dry sink Kenny had scavenged from an old building in Driggs, a table from Hansi's patio, the cook stove and pot belly from Tiger. We would have to build, buy, and find the rest. We made lists. The swale in the corner was first, indicating a foundation problem. Wilber was ready to dig in, literally, seeing our fix-it project as our first opportunity to engage with the community. Rental equipment, tools, parts, and log-built expertise would have to be found in town. Meeting and working with the locals—hardworking, born-in-the-backwoods types—would be our first step toward success out here.

I got to work setting up my treadle, making curtains, and planning the kitchen. Wyatt got to work making a mess. In the land of permafrost, the springtime ground had thawed to a mud that covered him head-to-toe. Happy and free, he ran uphill and down on his own private playground, naked but for mud boots and a cowboy hat. With sticks (guns), rocks (hand grenades), and cardboard (shields), he ruled his domain. It was cute, but confusing to our pacifist sensibilities. He had never seen television and was born in the dawn of gender-neutral toys. It was our first lesson, as parents, in Nurture versus Nature.

We often rode with Wilber into town. We wanted to be together, and I didn't want to miss anything new—it was *all* so new.
We followed him through hardware and lumber shops; he tagged
along through grocery and fabric stores. Eventually, we found the
co-op where local back-to-the-land types gathered. We met some
neat folks who were full of ideas for hand-hewn projects and log
construction. Many lived north and east of town, and were true native Canadians. We found a community, and right off the bat. Our
situation was turning out better than we'd dreamed.

We learned to live by Canadian customs. I actually found it
quaint, more than annoying, that the banks and many businesses
closed every Monday. Another surprise: Many taverns in Canada
were segregated, not by race but by gender. One afternoon, we de-
toured into 150 Mile House for a draught on our way home from
errands. Doors were marked "Ladies" and "Men," but we didn't believe it could really mean anything. So Wilber, Wyatt, and I strolled
through the same door into a large dark beer hall, chock-a-block
with billiard tables. By the time our eyes adjusted, we realized that
all the men in the room were staring at us, along with a few ladies
from the adjoining room. Adjoining—but not equal—rooms in a
bar. We found it hilarious, another quaint quirk of our new home,
and so turned on our heels and respectfully returned via our desig-
nated doors. Everybody smiled and all was well.

The giant jacks and mauls were delivered, and the massive foundation project began on a bright spring day. First, we had to dig.
We found co-op pals who would toil in exchange for food, and the
work-party began. Of course, Wyatt had his shovel and would not
be left out. We found him a pile of dirt to move back and forth
across the yard. Unfortunately when the jacking started, the house
shifted and most of the chinking fell out. I guess we'd expected that
eventuality, but it was an improvement we hadn't planned on making right away. Welcome to home ownership. Back in Colorado,
when a cabin deteriorated past the point where we could rehabili-
tate it with our patchwork repairs, we'd pack up and find a new one.
Not here. We were making an investment, and that felt good.

After the jacking had gone on for a while, I walked in the front door and had the immediate sensation of vertigo. With the corners square, the perspective of the house had changed. It was so dramatic I almost fell over—the sinking we'd become accustomed to had been that serious.

I made a hearty lunch, veggie soup, cheese, homemade rolls, and cookies, and we broke bread on a plywood sheet on sawhorses. Everyone pulled up a stump to celebrate the house-raising—our new friends Petra and Paul and their son Ian, the Murphy family, and Tim. They were all delightful. Petra, Paul, and Ian lived in town near the library, and soon their place became our home away from home. The Murphys, Bill and Dorothy, were in their fifties and lived with their daughter Rose and Rose's husband Steve, clear out on the Horsefly. They had carved their home out of Bill's father's land, and they sold the fruits of their garden to the co-op and other grocery stores. We couldn't wait to get to know all the rest of the outliers hidden in these woods. Tim was a wild card, strong and devilishly handsome with long and knotted black hair. He lived around, and was full of schemes and plans he'd picked up in his wanderings. When we needed a drawing or a sketch of an idea, Tim was the artist. He seemed brilliant—we all thought maybe he'd been an engineering student who'd taken a bad LSD trip, but nobody knew, and his past was definitely off limits for public speculation.

It was a good group. We dug and jacked, formed and set for days. Finally, with rebar in place, we were ready to mix and pour the cement. Lucky for us, it had been a warm, dry, and early spring. By mid-May we'd set the log corner back where it belonged. Then the chinking began. The method was crude, its ingredients consisting of clay and lime mud mixed with straw, and many hands. While chinking was an added expense and a definite time-killer, it would have to be done eventually.

While Wilber and the crew, including Wyatt, kept busy digging and filling, I had been free to plan the garden and prospective greenhouse (the next major project). The central garden was to be in the paddock behind the shed, a flat, square plot close to the water. With garden books, catalogues, and sketch book in hand, I spent many hours sitting in the paddock choosing and organizing my favorite vegetables, herbs, and flowers.

When he returned the jacks to the rental shop, Wilber came home with a monster rototiller. I was ready. I'd raked and cleared the paddock of horseshoes, shoeing nails, bits of twine, fencing, and anything else that might make a tiller jump and buck. I attacked it over and over with the giant teeth of the earth-tearing machine. I broke ground with gusto, mixing in the years of horse, and who-knows-whose, manure and old hay and grain. The deeper I went, the darker and moister the earth was. It was a ripe and rich spot. The turned earth was alive with worms, snails, and centipedes, and Wyatt took to collecting bugs in an old can. He was charmed by their wiggly and resilient behavior. Even when I'd chop them in two with the tiller, they squirmed and slid just like the whole ones.

Wilber and I had read and reread Rodale's organic gardening books, written in the 1950s and full of tales of ordinary, post-war gardeners creating extraordinary backyard farms, and proclaiming longevity as one of many benefits. Victory gardens! By the end of May, mine was in sight. I had mounded the dirt into eight beds, each two feet by three feet, and left a big, round center for herbs and flowers. The French Intensive Biodynamic method requires beds with close, alternating rows of broad or tall vegetables. I'd plant lettuce-onions-beets, carrots-spinach-pole beans. That way they'd all have room, and the shade of the leaves would keep down the weeds. Following the gardening techniques we used in Bridgeport, marigolds would be planted with tomatoes, lettuce with beets, potatoes with nasturtiums and beans, and on and on. They helped each other repel bugs and feed the soil. We had never planned, prepped, planted, and produced our very our food from scratch before. Now we were finally poised to find out how it worked, and to work it. We began the planting process. The water in the creek flowed well in spring, and Wilber made a yoke for carrying two five-gallon buckets of it to the house and garden. When the seeds were in, the holey-coffee-can-on-a-broomstick dipped in the bucket made a slow but consistent watering system.

While we waited for our crops, we returned to the foraging we'd practiced in the fields and hills of Swan Valley. Chamomile popped up in the driveway. Pigweed and dandelion greens were picked young for sweetness. Yellow dandelion and pink clover made us reminisce about Tiger, and our first taste of nature. And we discovered and added the larger, richer high-latitude, low-altitude wild foods to our menu. Watercress and mint lined the banks of Knife Creek. Sheep sorrel and fiddlehead ferns were sweet and tender when young. Mushrooms grew in the dark of the forest, but we avoided them until we had local knowledge in hand. Cow parsnip and nettle made hearty soup.

So many surprises awaited us at Knife Creek, good and bad. The chinking and straightening of the cabin were bigger chores—in time and money—than we'd expected, but the garden and the hope our neighbors instilled regarding its potential for propagation were beyond our wildest dreams. We could and would really grow what we needed here. Self-sufficiency was within our grasp. We were thrilled and highly invested in the process. So, on the morning I went to water the garden and found my inch-tall crops nibbled to the nub, I went a little crazy. Carrots, lettuces, beets, onions, and turnips had been ready for thinning. The sprouts would have made tender delicious salads. These were not hobby crops; these were our sustenance. I realized immediately that the culprits were those damned gray starlings. I'd heard they'd come over from Asia years ago and were practically a plague, and I'd seen them. I decided that if I killed a few and hung them up by their little feet from the garden fence, their friends would get the hint. So I did just that.

Wilber laughed at my plan but seeing my resolve, he set me up with the shotgun. I hadn't handled a gun since I'd shot skeet with my father at the Aubichwi Gun Club in Connecticut, but I was determined not to be outdone or undone by those noisy flying pests. I knew they'd be back. There were a few beet greens left. So I waited by the garden's gate, gun across my knees. When the flock flew through my sights, dozens of 'em, I shot, randomly and eagerly. Three birds fell. And three birds were hung up by their little claws. Those crazy marauders never attacked my garden again.

While we worked, we slept on the floor and cooked on the Coleman. We had the wood-fired potbelly and cook stoves from Tiger, favored relics of the old days. The potbelly got right to work, and we were advised to stock coal for the winter. Though we still had bad memories of coal-smoky days from the chicken coop, we were considering all ideas in anticipation of the bitter northern clime. The wood cook stove sat in the corner, relegated to art, as we planned for a natural-gas lifestyle.

The kitchen would have to be built from scratch. An old iron sink hung precariously from the wall, and the counter and cabinets were sagging and too small. Wilber was excited to design and build it all new. He'd rip it out and start fresh with the many ideas he'd seen in the Breckenridge condos. Planning the kitchen and piping for gas, a refrigerator, and a cook stove were modernizations neither of us had enjoyed or considered in more than three years. We would have four wall-mounted gaslights on the main floor to brighten our evenings and allow for crafting and reading during the seemingly endless nights to come. It would be so civilized and simple, and safe.

The barn was a mess, but stout, and we hoped to raise a few livestock or fowl in it before too long. In the meantime, we'd found a perfect place for the greenhouse, up on the hill behind the house, an ample flat area far enough from the trees to allow good three-season sun exposure. Soon, the garden was planted, the house propped and chinked, the barn and yard cleared, and fresh logs cut from the woods, our woods, for the greenhouse. Wilber bought a logger's thirty-six-inch chain saw and made quick work of felling and peeling the trees. At eighteen feet long, our logs would add up to a full-length greenhouse in no time. Twelve logs were soon prepped and laid to cure in the long northern days; Wilber made us a four-poster bed out of the remnants. We'd stack the logs, dovetail-style, then frame a roof and cover it with more visqueen. Tomatoes, peppers, melons, and even a little cannabis would grow well under cover, protected from cool nights.

By the summer solstice, when my parents planned a visit, the sun was setting as late as ten-thirty. A blackout curtain sewn and draped over Wyatt's window at seven-thirty on summer eves told his little brain what the bright sun seemed to contradict. One afternoon, when the curtain had lulled him into naptime, my parents drove down the hill in their brand new red BMW. They made quite the entrance. It was the first time my father had visited us since he'd rushed through Bridgeport when Wyatt was born.

They were all smiles. They'd had a pleasant drive up, an adventure in new territory. They'd always loved Canada, vast and unpopulated. They'd honeymooned in 1950 on the longest undammed river in the Northeast in Canada, and found it so charming. Their town, Driggs, was growing, but they'd never have considered leaving the good old U.S. of A. They were up for the visit, and after we watched Kenny check the car for dings and dirt, we greeted them warmly.

"Do you know how many twenty-year-olds own thirteen-acre farms and log cabins?" my dad whispered as we toured the spread. At first I thought he was impressed, but then I heard what he was saying: "You've not yet paid your dues, and you don't deserve this bit of heaven." My mother-and-wife ladder had been thrown to the ground once again. He never failed, but I soldiered on. This was my home, and he was my guest. He could follow our lead for once, and get to work on the greenhouse. We had plenty for them to do, and work, we knew, was the best way to keep idle minds from generating friction.

Kenny was Wilber's crew and Noonie was Wyatt's pal, and I ran the mess. Meals were straightforward, sprouts only from the garden, grains, and cheese. My parents slept at the hotel in 150 Mile House, a convenient roadhouse with food and bar.

It was a busy few days and we pulled it off, I thought. Wilber had a good, solid plan, all the parts and a knack for the vision.

Kenny was a good grunt and respected Wilber's turf. Noonie trot-ted along behind a diaperless Wyatt, in potty-training mode, as he proudly showed off his acreage. He even took her across the road and into the swamp. Her L.L. Bean boots got a good mudding, which made Wyatt laugh, which made Noonie laugh. He loved an audience, and she was his ultimate fan. I was busy with the garden, and with oiling the new pine floor that replaced bad linoleum. Unbeknownst to us, Wilber and Kenny were quietly inciting each other's male posturing crap. My hope that hard work and gentle-manly regard would facilitate bonding had been naïve, apparently. Stubborn and uncompassionate, my father had begun something he couldn't undo, and Wilber's sensitivities laid him bare. The men in my life, old and new, would not behave. Wyatt was the only one who could really get away with misbehaving.

When my mom's soft voice announced they would cut the visit short, I could hear and see her disappointment mingling with her compliance. Twelve hours later, they were gone.

Chapter Twenty-Two

In the satisfaction of building our very own homestead, we had finally begun to answer, viscerally, the question we'd all been haunted with: Why weren't communes standing the test of time? What was up with the dissolution of the shared life, so dreamt of, the quest of our generation? Wherever and whenever we'd lived the communal life, it seemed human nature, i.e. the ego, had eventually provided a bummer of a deal-breaker. The love and joy we had savored in the commune setting had always been a blend of ideas, attitudes, and goals. Inevitably, few did the work of many, all were not equal, and resentments brewed. As Margaret had said, "What was mine was theirs and what was theirs was mine, but they had nothing." Eventually, sad or refreshing, change had meant distance. At Tiger, our tight—and small—community had initially repelled the intruders who threatened our delicate balance. We had worked and played as one. But inevitably change had come. In Bridgeport, more than anything, Ron's weakness had been the chink in our collective security. In Alma, we'd each grown into our own domain and thrived. If the country had been fertile and temperate, we'd probably be there still. But the human need to sustain oneself had meant a yearning for a wee bit of land to own. In the American/Canadian dream, capitalism outlived communism. It loomed, humbling but true.

We loved Knife Creek and celebrated our luck at having found it. Owning our land seemed to be the fix we'd been waiting for. At night, when it was clear, and so very quiet, we could tune in the short-wave radio. We felt we were on top of the world, reaching our ears out across borders and oceans, girdling the globe. Spinning the dial and eavesdropping on humanity gave us a thrill in our remoteness. With Wilber's German and my limited French, and all the languages I'd heard around the world, we could trace most sounds to a continent or country. Though we often heard excited and loud voices in unrecognizable tongues, over scratchy and fading frequencies, we challenged each other to connect the mystery to a geographic location. Sometimes we'd find *CBS Radio Mystery Theater* and hook in to a drama or maybe a comedy show. And there was always music. When we just wanted entertainment, the AM and FM stations came in clear with news and popular songs. We could easily stay current with the world we'd left behind, if we wanted to.

We were far more intrigued by the history of our own region and the local doings. We knew Sheila was right: These days there was nothing but woods and water from our spread east to the Rockies, west to the Coastal Range. We would devour the stories of the native peoples: how they lived with and on the land, stalking the elusive caribou, fishing the interconnected waterways, surviving the winters. Their legends took flight in our imaginations. However, the history we heard was European, as usual. The Gold Rush of 1858 had swelled the Fraser River region and yielded one of British Columbia's most furious population booms. By year-end, more than twenty-five thousand Americans had flooded, unchecked, up the river into the colony, declared British Columbia by Queen Victoria. The discovery of unusually rich gold in gravel east from the Fraser at Quesnel sent gold seekers into the Cariboo. In the spring of 1862, five thousand more speculators arrived. The hillsides were denuded, earthworks littered the land, and towns sprang up everywhere. It resounded of the damage we'd seen in Colorado. Though the images of gold-seeking pioneers rushing here in the 1860s were exciting, we liked our untouched and crowded forest.

What we found in Williams Lake was an activity fed by the second cash grab in North America, still ongoing: clear-cutting for timber. The Cariboo was home to several mills, its highways and gravel roads crowded with giant rigs hauling ancient trees to be molded into lumber. It was big business, and when Wilber went looking for a job to pay the bills, the sawmill offered an easy and adequate paycheck. Determined to swallow pride and philosophy to feed his family, he took a job at the Simpson Mill as a chipper attendant. He would watch the rejected logs fall into the chute, rumble along a deep conveyor belt, and slip into the chipper, where they were ground to bits for particle board and other waste products. His responsibility was to see that the logs didn't get snarled or jammed. If any metal (watch or pocket knife) fell into the conveyor, a sensor by the chipper chute would stop the belt, and that would have to be cleared, too. He could call overhead and tell the guys to hold up while he got on or near the belt to fix a problem, then signal when all was clear. It was a job for an uneducated man, but Wilber saw himself as above no one, equal to all. He would begin right away.

Our most important projects had been completed. The greenhouse was framed and planted, awaiting late summer for its visqueen cover. Wilber had framed a clever kitchen, and our gas fixtures were set. Four frosted glass lights hung on the log walls, and the small but magically frosty fridge sat next to the small and efficient cook stove. The natural gas tank stood next to the house, an eyesore that gave us untold comfort. During long, light summer nights, he and I would work on the cabinetry. The pine floor looked great and was already aging finely.

The garden was our pride and joy. Willow arches hung with peas and beans, herbs and flowers bloomed, and veggie crops for the root cellar grew well on long, hot summer days.

In the evenings, after Wyatt was asleep, Wilber and I would curl up in our only two chairs and either spin the radio dial or discuss the day, which mostly focused on the progress of the house and of our son. We had cherished our two months of working together to fine-tune our home and land, a gift that had provided us with a necessary measure of re-bonding.

"You should have seen Wyatt, handing me nails for the root cellar door," Wilber would start. "More Daddy? More Daddy?"

"That must have been right before he stood at the kitchen door and shouted 'Damrich, Mommy, DAMRICH!!'" I'd fill in. "He sure loves his PB&J."

"How'd he get so damned cute?" The question made us both laugh. We knew that he was so cute because we let him explore his world a little on the wild side. His confidence was unfettered by our demands, his days were his own, wandering from parent to parent always welcome and encouraged.

"He was in the shed after his nap, pulling tools out of your case." I had watched from the kitchen.

"Is that what happened? I thought I'd forgotten to put them back. That little shit!" Wilber laughed. "And there he is sleeping peacefully upstairs as if he'd done nothing at all. We should go up and spank him right now."

"Let's go!" I'd agree and we'd creep up the stairs. In the filtered light of the yet-to-be darkened night, we could see our almost-two-year-old, sleeping like an angel. We'd grin widely at each other. He had sung and bounced himself to sleep, as he did every night, while we listened from below. And as usual, he lay in his blanket sleeper in the pose in which he'd finally given out: arms and legs akimbo, hanging loose through his crib bars, messy blond head smashed into the headboard, and neck crooked. We'd pick him up and hug him tight, lay him back down straight and tuck him in. That simple nightly routine was probably the best measure of the success we'd reaped in our lives thus far.

In our journey together, I had proven myself an able and willing crew. I'd crafted opinions and made decisions. Without a commune's concert of voices, it was easier for me to make up my mind. As a partner, I was dependable and focused, and I still cherished Wilber for his experience and clear decision-making. I didn't complain, much, and when I did, Wilber tried to fix whatever wasn't working. Here, in this place, this man, this child, I believed I'd found everything I'd sought. In the peace of the woods, I had harmony. In Wilber's care, I belonged. In Wyatt's needs and sweet love, I mattered. Yet in all this contentment, something was missing, and sometimes in the quiet the disquiet amplified. What was it that I longed for?

"I wish I had a..." I'd drift in frustration; stuck on a feeling I could not verbalize.

"What is it, Poms? What do you want?" he'd implore half-heartedly, knowing by now that I wouldn't be able to name my missing piece.

"I don't know, it just seems like I need something," I would continue, getting no closer.

"Would a new coat, s'more yarn or fabric, a day in town make you happy?" He was determined to help me find whatever I needed, but my undefined longing and puzzled, sad expression threw him.

"No, no, I'm fine. Forget it," I would recoil, but I couldn't forget. The longing revisited me for many years, until I realized that it was inner peace I missed. Physically settled, materially fulfilled, loved and needed, I had never paid attention to and always hated the question "What do you want?" I didn't know.

My inner self was uncharted territory, a place we had not been welcome to visit in my family. While my father had encouraged outbursts of hostile feelings, tender emotions made him squirm. We were not supposed to share depth. Those nasty warm-fuzzies or hurty-feelings prompted lines like "Don't get any on me!" and a certain humiliation reminded us to hide our desires. Wilber seemed to know, always, what would enrich his day, fulfill his dream, cause him pain or make him smile.

One longing I knew I had was for another baby. I, alone this time, planned a pregnancy. I had decided that when Wyatt was two-and-a-half, a future playmate should be born. It would widen his world, round out our family, and bring new life to our Canadian future. It was a great idea. And Wilber agreed. Within the first week of August, I was pregnant. I knew it immediately, as with Wyatt. Wilber and I sensed it in the passion of a summer night.

On the work front, being the new guy at the mill, Wilber was ordered to take over the swing shift. To be fair, he'd been given two options: Go to work from eight p.m. to three a.m., or quit. We enjoyed the money and its regularity, especially as we continued to prepare for the coming winter, which we knew would be colder and darker than our Colorado season. The comforts of home, and my pregnancy, were paramount and money was important to our thriving experiment in self-sufficiency. We knew we were working for The Man again, but our goals were within reach. We could count the months until we'd feed ourselves, barter, and need little in the way of the establishment's cash. On the bright side, Wilber would have his days. He could sleep from four to eleven in the morning, then play, work on the place, and have dinner together, before he headed back to town at seven-thirty. He'd be home for daylight and Wyatt's waking hours, leaving for work only after tucking him into bed.

In the silent night, in the absence of vehicle or neighbors, I began turning to the radio for company, to fill the void. About this time, Richard Nixon was resigning in Washington. I had to avoid news from the States, to keep the calm. We were not paying attention, but the world was. We heard about Nixon at the co-op, at Overwaitea Supermarket, at the mill, and at our postal box at 150

Mile House, V0K 2G0. Some told it with glee—U.S. imperialists brought to their knees by humiliation. Some whispered it so as not to embarrass us. And some thought it funny. We, frankly, didn't give a shit. He wasn't our president; we only thought of him as a weak, ugly, evil politician who'd been unable to do the right thing. His face, a caricature of itself, was enough to make us gag. When he was succeeded by Gerald Ford, we were further disgusted. Mentally, we retreated deeper into the British Columbian woods.

August 1974

Dear Folks—

Sorry I couldn't be more conversational the other day, but it was hot & muggy and I was bone weary from another errand day around town. Hope you squared away any confusion about the tricycle, I just wanted to make sure. Wyatt is going to go crazy when he gets his 3 wheeler and I'm anxiously awaiting the day. Friday we go shopping for one.

Nonnie is doing a lot of canning right now and we are busy filling up the shelves in the root cellar. They seem to load up as soon as I put them in. Very nice to see. We have lots of wheat, rice, beans, soy sauce, honey (100 lbs.), peanut butter, tomatoes, peaches, apricots, cherries now & soon we'll have apples, carrots, onions, too.

Wyatt's room is soon to have a new window and ceiling and I have drawn plans for a workshop I would like to start up this fall. Of course there's firewood and the job to fill lots of time, but with a solid shop, I could fix more cabinets without bothering Nonnie's space.

I guess fall time gets hectic when you realize all those projects dreamed up in spring that never came to fruition. Well, next year is another start and hopefully that which we've done this year won't have to be redone next. The garden took lots of work, but with a pumping system in next year much of that work will be reduced. Just more weeding with a bigger garden.

So, we are busy, but not as frantic as we once were. We all take a little more time to sit and talk. It's so easy to involve yourself in duties that forgetting your family is the result. We try to avoid getting so exhausted from a day's labor that we don't have time for one another. Tasks might not happen so quickly but at least our little nucleus can stay together.

I got all your letters yesterday. Dad it must be frightening to retire from all that activity and attention but it's obviously time. You sound mighty depressed, but there are still lots of activities to fill up your day. You have to quit worrying about money. All your belly aching about money is foolish. You've worked all these years and you have enough of a nest egg to retire gracefully without worry.

I mean, it's fun to worry—you've been worrying for as long as I can remember—but all the money you make now you'd never be able to spend anyway. Please try to relax and concentrate on your diet. Your eating habits are suicidal and maybe your sicknesses help keep you in the center of attention, but certainly they don't make anyone happy.

If my presence in Colorado would help you I surely would be there, but after all these years I understand that our propinquity leads to conflict. It always has simply because our rules are different and we see life a little differently. We've tried to discuss those issues, but you never listen, so what's the use. Pop, you're a talker, not a listener. I'm sorry that my move to B.C. is so hard on you, but you must realize (you won't of course) that our move here wasn't a personal affront.

Canada is opportunity for us and a chance to move ahead. At the moment all land prices have dropped and even if we wanted to sell, we couldn't. I always thought land appreciated 10% automatically, but it doesn't. I guess it's subject to the whims of the marketplace like everything else. Well, land is one thing you can't make more of so I'm not worried, but we still have to "bridge the gap" right now. That means lots of labor, "free work," and hours. If we ever sell I'm going to get a good price because our work will have made it so. Exhortations for our return to Colo. can't happen now because we are in the midst of a project and quitting doesn't make sense.

If there is anyway we can come down for Christmas holidays we'd love to see you. The money isn't as big a worry as the unpredictable weather and driving conditions. Maybe around spring you can drive north. I'm sure you'll see why we like it so much when you decide to visit. Our place is really fun and good for kids.

Another kid really hasn't pervaded my consciousness. Maybe because Nonnie isn't big yet or because I haven't considered another baby, but it seems very remote right now. I'm not as excited anyway, but I'm sure things will change this spring. We've decided to have a girl this time, but won't be upset with a boy. A healthy one is what we're really after. We know that it won't be nearly as confusing as the last birth because we are a bit more settled. Boy it's gonna be hectic though. I smile when I think of it.

Well, that's all I've got to say... please try to think a little more positively about your health. I remember your psychosomatic pill popping years when you had medication for everything. And I can't help but wonder if you aren't willing a little of this sickness on yourself. You don't have to be so sick. You don't have to be so fat! TAKE CONTROL ... of your health; if you don't, no one can.

Wyatt skinned his toe and you should hear him complain... "Mommy foot hurts" all day long. After awhile, we'd really think he had a hurt foot—hell, you'd think he really thought he had a hurt foot. Then he thinks we think he thinks he has a hurt foot. And it's nothing at all.

Write again,
Love, Frank

CHAPTER TWENTY-THREE

In mid-August, our dear old Storyland friends Bertie Ray and Roger Sherman showed up on the doorstep. They'd driven north with a burning curiosity: What was this place we'd disappeared to? We were thrilled to have them. Wilber had just begun his swing shift, and company at night was a gift to Wyatt and me. With their help, the niggling house projects took shape during Wilber's waking hours. We'd swim off the sweat and dust in Lac La Heche before sharing dinner and sending Wilber off to the mill. All the while, Bertie and Roger told great stories.

They had been stopped at the border, heading into Canada. Two hippies in an old dry-walling van, according to Bertie's tale, they looked like easy pickings and maybe some entertainment to the border guards.

"So, ya smoke marijuana, eh?" the officer asked, a reasonable question.

"Well, sure…" said Roger, not the best answer if you have someplace to go. Bertie was livid, but Roger was an honest man. Had the question been "Do you have any marijuana?" the answer would have been a decisive "No way!" So because they were honest hippies, they were forced out of the van, which was then joyfully torn to bits by the guards. When they were finished, their shit was scattered across the parking lot, for them to repack and get the hell on their way. We all had a good laugh, and Roger learned a lesson in lying.

With Wilber gone at night, I had a chance to catch up on Alma and Breckenridge gossip. We stayed up late, what with my begging for stories about all my friends. Joe would soon be off to India, again, he and John still frustrated, without old ladies. Stuart and Susan were planning a trip to check out Alaska. Stuart's brother Scott had moved there and loved it. We knew Roger and Cheryl had moved to Haines, Alaska, where Roger was fishing and Cheryl had a teaching job. They were practically our neighbors! Sandra & Mico, Sue & Michael, Patty Day and Planet were still in Alma. Bien had finally come out of his closet, to no one's surprise, and moved to San Francisco. He had always been one of my closest pals, and I was glad for him.

One night, as we wound down our stories and laughing, we heard a loud noise outside. Big Bert went to check it out, and I realized how glad I was that they were there. He found nothing, but the conversation turned serious.

"What would you do, Nonnie, alone here in the night, without a phone, truck, or anything?" Roger asked. Wilber and I had never really discussed it. "I mean, what if a bear, and they grow 'em big up here, or a fucking Charlie Manson, came to the door? What would you do?"

"Jeez." I stumbled a little. "I dunno… run upstairs, I guess…?"

We looked around the cabin for weapons and hiding places. Bert spied our thirty-six-inch chainsaw, brought inside for cleaning and oiling.

"Here's what ya do, see?" He was charged up. "If a giant bear comes up to the door, standing and throwing his body at it, trying to get at ya, grab that chainsaw!!" At which he did just that, and pretended to crank it up. "See, ya fire it up, vroom, vroom, and then ya plunge it through the door, like this," and he ran at the door, hitting it dead center. "It'll go right through and into that fucking bear!!" He was foaming at the mouth a little, digging his brilliant plan. Roger and I were hysterical and had fallen out of our chairs laughing.

"Then what," I'm laughing and trying to get up, "assuming I've been able to lift, start, and move with that huge saw. Now the giant bear is either splayed out over my doorstep, or he's just MORE pissed and bleeding when he mauls me!!"

We had a grand time, telling tales and catching up. Wilber and I were sad to see them go. More than once on those dark nights, that scene passed, not casually, through my mind. I supposed the technique would work on a bear, but I worried more about psychos.

A week or so after they left, we were surprised by a visit from Jane and Paul—more Storyland pals. Summer was a great time to explore the far North. They were pregnant, and following in our footsteps, searching permanency and a good growing climate. They settled in at Knife Creek, sometimes literally at our feet (we had only two chairs), and listened to the lessons of our endeavors. Talk of gardens, logs, fertilizer, crops, friends, work, and emigration filled our days. Oh, how they envied Knife Creek and our pastoral setting. With water and good earth, we had sprouted on and now harvested our own land. We ate out of our garden and greenhouse at every meal. The cold-frame was about ready for visqueen, the tomatoes, pepper, and pot growing slower than we'd hoped, but next year… The process was ongoing, and Jane and Paul would be wise to get started.

They stayed through the Canadian Labour Day weekend, and

with a few full days off, Wilber decided it was time to check in on our friends out on Horsefly Lake. East of 150 Mile House, the five of us drove for hours through unchanging forest, broken only by the occasional logging road cutoff to the left or right. Stopping a couple of times to pick 'n' eat bright Saskatoon berries, we wound our way toward Horsefly. We thought we could all learn from the Murphys and their inter-generational past, present, and future. They were, more than anyone we knew, truly living off the land. We would surprise them no doubt, being there was no way of calling ahead, but we now knew how Canadians always welcomed with a hot cup o' tea, biscuits, and a meal.

Nothing could have prepared us for the oasis we found at what felt like the end of the road. Carved out of darkness, formed of fallen oak, the Murphy's spread was rife with lessons and alternatives, from the traditional pioneer house of the original settlers to the fresh-hewn creations of their offspring. And they were glad and proud to share these lessons, along with a spot o' tea. We ducked in, out, and around the living and working spaces, so well thought-out and built. We discussed the techniques, Wilber and Paul like boys in Shop-turned-Art class, Jane and I like girls in a brilliant HomeEc class. Their solar, water, heating, and kitchen systems were an entire *Whole Earth Catalog* on display. The pages we had dog-eared were here, in practice. The *Handmade Houses* book my parents had given Wilber the past Christmas could have been photographed right here. The author's words resounded: "For remember, they can't disconnect you from the utilities you're not installing—you being an ecology freak, a joyous monk, or an ornery young codger like me. And remember, too, property is sacred… and that's what counts, of that I'm certain."

Rose was a glass artist. Her windows, created from a combination of throwaway and handmade glass and found objects, were things of exceptional beauty in these dark woods. Just a glint of sunshine had the power to transform a room, and a mood. Likewise, Bill's fine hand at carving had turned common house parts into thought-provoking symbols. The spiral-laid, salvaged-wood floor in the entry, the hand-hammered tin on the backsplash, the hidden loft with tooled-leather handrail, and the tree house made completely of scraps were joyful and dramatic. Dorothy's ceramic tinkering contributed colorful tiles, bowls, and frames. Skylights were used liberally to make the most of the filtered sun. We rued the many stops we'd made for berry picking along the way, as the day was short and we had so much to see.

Night descended early in the deep woods, and we were soon into the dinner hour. Bill and Dorothy insisted we join them for a meal, expectedly of their land, of their hands. Rose and her old man, Steve, were in charge of the animals: many chickens, two pigs, and the mandatory goats—the best bet for milk and meat. The enormous garden, far removed from the barn and unpredictable goats, was closer to the lake, filling a vast, south-facing opening. Dinner was a luscious buffet of goat stew, with root veggies and fresh bread, of course, in Rose's cottage. We said a late and fond farewell and extended the Canadian invitation, "Come see us anytime!"

It was back to menial labor for Wilber. The beauty we'd seen at Horsefly gave him hope and courage to keep him going through his miserable and stupid job. The light was within the tunnel, and we would create our version of Horsefly on Knife Creek. On Tuesday morning, after more excited planning and promises, when the banks and shops opened again, Jane and Paul lit out to the south on their quest. We wished them all the luck and karma we'd enjoyed. With renewed determination, we spent the day counting our blessings and resuming our routine. At dusk, Wilber trudged off to the mill.

But he didn't come home at 4 a.m., and I was disoriented, until I woke at 6 a.m. to the sound of a truck pulling down the drive. Where had he been? Why so late? Lifting Wyatt from his crib, I pulled back the curtain and saw Bob Richter, the foreman from Simpson Mill, parking the company truck in our drive, hesitating at the bottom of the hill. Slowly he opened his door and looked around, got out, and closed the door.

We'd met Bob and his wife Debbie at the company picnic, and their house had become another friendly comfort stop on our town days. They had a little girl Wyatt's age, Susie, a playful and endearing child. But when Bob came out with Wilber one day after work to see the place, I sensed his discomfort. I remembered pulling a carrot from our garden, wiping off the clumps of dirt, and offering it to him.

"Can you wash it? My mom always said, 'A bit of dirt won't hurt you.' But do I have to eat a lifetime supply all at once?" he'd said with a smile and chuckle.

People our age in Williams Lake who had grown up in cabins without modern conveniences such as television or even indoor plumbing thought our way of life isolated and dull. They were completely confounded by the notion that anyone would *choose* to live this way. So, I thought, why was Bob here now?

Wyatt and I met him on the porch, both still in our nightclothes. He took off his cap and held it nervously in both hands.

"Hey, Bob, what's up? Where's Wilber?" I looked nervously past him, as his mission began to take form.

"Oh, Nonnie, I'm so sorry," he stammered bad. "There's been an accident."

"Is he dead?" The gut-reflex question was all I could muster.

"No, no, no, but it's bad. You two come with me, now." Bob was kind and in charge.

The minutes that followed were a panicked blur. I remember thinking, "It's September 4th." I got dressed and helped Wyatt pull on yesterday's clothes off the floor. We climbed into Bob's truck. I held Wyatt tight on my lap, burying my face in his warm neck.

"We'll stop by my house. Debbie will watch Wyatt while we go to the hospital. That okay with you, li'l cowboy?" Bob had thought this out, already talked to Debbie? Wyatt nodded. I hoped he thought this was just one of our fun town trips. "You can have breakfast with Susie."

The trees of Knife Creek Road were already behind us when I looked up. Inside the cab it was silent. I heard the wheels turning and Wyatt's heart beat. I thought about the tiny heart beating within me, and its extra beat gave me strength. The valley colors reminiscent of our first visit here and the promise of autumn; the vibrant summer going dormant to reappear dependably next year. Bob drove slowly, without urgency, and it occurred that he was being safe, protecting us. But in a minute, we were in front of his house and he was walking Wyatt to the door. I saw Debbie for a moment at the door, her face gray and weepy, reaching for Wyatt. I knew my little boy would be greeted by the comfort of Debbie's bottomless cookie jar, Sears's tea set, and slippery Naugahyde.

As soon as Bob climbed back in and took off for the short drive to the regional hospital, he began to speak—I hadn't asked for details, and he had held off until Wyatt was out of the truck. Now he was talking fast. I tried to listen carefully, but his first lines threw me.

"It was about two-thirty this morning, the end of his shift. He climbed onto the conveyor, cleared a jam, and gave the guys the okay. Then, we're not sure why, he climbed back in. That's when a twenty-five-meter log fell… on his head… knocked him out… on the conveyor … " Bob stopped. I turned to see him, his face cold and stiff, staring straight ahead. "We don't know the damage."

"Damage?" I thought, *"Brain damage?"* Couldn't he just be cut, bruised, a little broken? Everything was fuzzy. I didn't understand. *The end of his shift.* Just minutes later and he would have been traveling home to us? Suddenly, we were there, at the hospital.

Bob led me through gray halls, up elevators, more halls, nurses, gurneys, and doctors. Dr. Witcom was the father of a co-op buddy, Marshall. He stood before me now, and he said the same things Bob had.

"We don't know the extent, he's had a pretty bad blow." He took my hand. A bad blow, sounded like a two-by-four glanced off his shoulder. I reeled.

"Where is he?" I murmured. Enough talk, I had to see him for myself. Dr. Witcom and Bob were hesitant. *"Please,* where is he?" My face trembled, eyes welling and voice breaking. I wanted Wilber, to see, touch, hold, and be with him. He needed me. Why weren't they rushing me to him?

"Okay, but it's pretty bad, prepare yourself," warned the doctor. I could see the nurses hovering, hear their whispering. Prepare myself? How?

In a minute, I was standing next to my strong husband's hospital bed. His eyes were open, his head bandaged crudely and the purple bruises puddled over his head and neck. I searched his eyes for recognition, those beautiful eyes, now blank. His head looked small... deflated... messed up... blood bloomed through white bandages. Suddenly, he blinked and looked at me. I began to cry, hard. His hand reached out. I looked down and realized that below his neck, he looked normal. Dirty and scuffed but normal, in the clothes he wore to work last night. Tubes rose from his arm, from his chest, to bottles hung from a metal stand. I took his hand, carefully, and he squeezed, weak, but firm.

"Poms? It's okay," he stammered. And the staff rushed in to take him. His eyes pleaded, "Don't worry, I'll be right back." And he was gone.

"For tests," the doctor threw over his shoulder as he left the room. "You can wait in the lounge."

Finding the lounge, a chair, I sat before I could fall. Then I did collapse. I closed my eyes and tried to divine my next step. I had to call Hansi and Fred, call Debbie to check on Wyatt, call my parents. What would I tell them? Technically, Wilber had been in an intense traumatic accident and was "damaged." But "we don't know" would not be an answer or a comfort. When the tests (tests for what?) were complete, we would have more information. Would it be good, or conclusive? I looked around at the aging hospital, decaying not so confidently around me, and began to cry again. I needed my family.

I kept seeing Wilber's deflated head, the blood and his eyes. What was wrong with him? Was he permanently "damaged"? The word began to anger me. Damaged, like in a fire sale? Damaged, like the crumpled car in that accident on the Cariboo Highway?

I got up to find a phone. The nurses looked at me with such pity in their eyes I almost couldn't take it. I made my way to the cafeteria and called my in-laws collect.

I tried to muster a strong voice, but the morning's trauma filled the line all the way to Denver. "Nonnie? What is it?" Fred's voice was flat. "Where's Frankie?" I had never called them, ever, and his response was immediately anxious.

"He's been in an accident… at work." I was crying again.

"What happened? What's wrong with him?" Now I heard Hansi on the extension. "Stop crying and tell us."

"They don't know, I'm sorry," I bleated through my choking throat. "They just took him out for tests, x-rays I guess. I'm waiting for the doctor."

"We need to talk to them, give me his name." Fred was insistent, I felt myself being pushed aside. He would take over from here. I at once felt relieved and threatened. What would Wilber want?

"Dr. Witcom. We don't know him, he's the father of…" but the line went dead.

Minutes dragged and hours blurred. Eventually, Wilber was back in his room, still hooked up, with fresh bandages and spreading bruises. He was on antibiotics, fluids, confined to the narrow bed with rails. Dr. Witcom took me aside, alone and scared. The tests were inconclusive. The log had cracked Wilber's skull. There was bleeding that must be stopped, the crack must be patched, somehow, and his vitals stabilized. He wasn't out of the woods. The doctors seemed confused, nervous, and increasingly unsure.

"Dr. Neumann is on his way here," the doctor told me. Dr. Neumann? Fred? Here? *Why?* I thought. Why? "And we've been in touch with the neurology department at Vancouver General. We'll send test results to them, get their feedback."

"Shouldn't he be sent down there?" I had to ask. It made the most sense to me.

"No, we can handle this," was the reply, then and in the coming days, as the situation worsened. "We'll be following their advice, don't you worry."

Wyatt and I stayed at Bob and Debbie's. Our home—the garden, the projects—were forgotten. The harvest-ready crops withered, the house cold and quiet. Our lives, condensed between the hospital and the Richter's, were on hold as Wilber fought for his. The checks began arriving immediately from Worker's Compensation. Bob had seen to the paperwork. Debbie reminded me to keep paying my bills. She told me the Worker's Compensation Board would be helpful. She was a company gal, and we avoided any discussion of the fact that there might have been negligence in their system. All I felt was helplessness.

The doctors told me stats as they developed, but their progress felt like a feeble, incompetent attempt. With each new day, each visit, Wilber's condition was different. I never knew what to expect. One morning, he would talk and smile with Wyatt; that afternoon, he could be unconscious, sometimes convulsing. Again and again I wondered aloud, why weren't they moving him to the city?

"His condition is too fragile now. Could have done it last week, maybe next week, but not now," the doctors said, and I realized they were stalling. The small-town doctor mentality struck me suddenly. Could they actually be keeping him here to protect their provincial egos, knowing that he'd be better off in Vancouver? Would they risk his life for that kind of personal bullshit? I couldn't believe it, but the more I saw… Our friend Marshall's dad, our doctor, was determined that he was doing the right thing, but Wilber's pallid, sweaty face and darting eyes told a different story. My sense of propriety and inexperience kept me from pushing too hard.

Fred arrived, stayed in a motel near the hospital, and marched the halls.

"My name is Dr. Neumann, who's in charge here?" he bellowed. I was temporarily shifted from next-of-kin, placed squarely in the back seat. He ordered meals for himself from the cafeteria, ordered doctor preference and everybody's attention. He criticized my youthful inexperience and ridiculed Wilber when he awakened.

"Frankie, when are you going to grow up and take responsibility for your life?" he asked his bedridden, semi-conscious, *damaged* son. "What were you thinking, taking a job for idiots and becoming one of them? You shame me!" And the nurses, who were hovering near the door, scattered as he stormed out.

Then his father was gone, thankfully. He had been a burden for Wilber and me. Focused on meeting his own needs, he went home disappointed in the doctors, hospital, and—mostly—in Wilber and me. And he let us know it, a fine how-do-you-do. His character, and the source of pain Wilber held, became clearer to me. I hadn't asked my parents to come. There was little anyone could do. Besides, they were leaving soon for the Far East.

CHAPTER TWENTY-FOUR

Weeks passed and resolve still evaded the doctors. Sadly, in late September, Wilber was discharged to my care. Nothing more they could do. I drove him and Wyatt home, helped him upstairs to bed, and then sat frozen in the cabin wondering what I would do. He was in and out of consciousness.

Late one afternoon, after two weeks of tentative status quo at home, a yellow panel van appeared in our driveway. Peering from behind the upstairs curtain, feeling vulnerable to strangers now that I was the protector, I made out the faded words *Swan Valley* on the side of the van. My heart leapt. "Wilber, Wyatt, we have company!!"

Loud boot steps sounded on the porch. John, Stewart, Tom (also from Madison), Roger, and several others I didn't know appeared, as if divined from heaven. There they were. How did they know? What were they doing, *here?* Faces and souls from our happiest times, they had come to help us through our scariest. Like a crew of woodsmen, they carried axes, chainsaws, winches, and sleeping bags. Wilber made his way as quickly as he could, down the stairs into the arms of his brothers. They all cried in turn and together. I'm sure the sight of him was both comforting and distressing— he was a mere shadow, his body weak and unsteady and his face disfigured.

Over the next five days, the boys worked under Wilber's direction. They cut and chopped, split and stacked cords and cords of wood. They cleaned the barn, sealed the root cellar door, harvested the over-ripe garden beds, secured the watering hole, and laid fresh gravel on the steep driveway. The ladies helped me can more fruit, insulate cracks around windows and doors, set up a clothes-drying line across the kitchen. At night, they helped with dinner and played with Wyatt.

We had left, but our friends had not forgotten us, these visiting angels who readied us for the winter ahead. They knew that Wilber was impaired, but never let him feel unmanly. I was in charge, but they made Wilber feel the boss. By the end of their stay, we felt more prepared and confident than we should have. We were all in tears when they drove away.

Later that week, our only neighbors, a mile across the creek, offered help, their phone, and rides. If an emergency should arise, they'd be at our service, any time of day or night. One afternoon, it did.

Wilber had been having a bad day, in and out of awareness. I was in the garden, salvaging what the birds and frost had not consumed, when I heard Wyatt yelling. I dropped the veggies and ran to him. "Daddy kicking the bed" had awakened him from his nap. I found Wilber in the final throes of a seizure, just slowing to a catatonic state. With the neighbors' help, the paramedics were there within the hour. They lifted him onto a gurney, down the stairs, and into the waiting ambulance. Then, after they'd taken in the sight of me, our naked baby, our hippie hovel, they did their version of due diligence. "Is he on drugs? Could he be having a bad trip?" Quickly, I assessed them, two young local guys, harmless and provincial. I had to focus.

"He's just had a brain injury. Take him to the hospital, and call Dr. Witcom, quickly."

Wyatt and I followed. Again, the doctors took tests and x-rays, sending the results to Vancouver. Suddenly, the head of neurology at Vancouver General, Dr. Turnbull, was on the team. The injury to the brain was more invasive than they first thought. Stronger antibiotics, a skin graft, new options on the table.

Wyatt's second birthday took me by surprise. Living between two worlds, the quiet of the farm and the crazy fear of the intensive care ward, I was disoriented most of the time. Thankfully, Wyatt's need for regular meals and diaper changes brought my feet to the ground. He needed me, too, and I was so glad to celebrate him, the simple joy of a birthday, his health and happiness, for a change. Debbie, ever true and clear, remembered the balloons, candles, and gifts, and made Wyatt's favorite, chocolate cake.

After ten days of observation, Wilber's condition "stabilized," and the hospital called me to take him home.

Take him home? I couldn't believe it. How could he be ready for home again? I was terrified about being the one in charge should there be more seizures or worse. I started making my own phone calls. I had been patient long enough, maybe too long, with their small-minded approach to my husband's life. All our lives, now four of us, hung in the balance. I had to act. I decided there were toes to be stepped on.

I called Dr. Turnbull. Yes, he knew the case. Could I bring him? Yes, bring him. Could he fly? Yes. Fly him down, we'll make room. So, I prepared. I needed someone to watch Wyatt, just for a few days, while I transported Wilber on Air Canada to Vancouver General. Three days, tops. I had met a family at the co-op, new to town looking for a place to live. The Gallants seemed nice enough, had two sweet kids, and made me think of us not so long ago, starting out in a new community. I found and asked them if they'd stay at Knife Creek and watch Wyatt. It would be a win for us both. They agreed.

The next day, October fourteenth, I was helping Wilber up the steps and into the twelve-seater turbo-prop for a quick flight to the city. A taxi, a gurney, a room, and Dr. Turnbull, straightforward and in that order, Wilber was in good hands, and I began to feel hope. The nurses' efficiency and care felt professional and calm. No huddling and whispering, it was wholly unlike the treatment in Williams Lake. They were action- and solution-focused and Wilber and I both sighed a great breath of relief.

"I have to go home and get my son," I told them. "I'll drive back down in a few days." They assured me that Dr. Turnbull would be making this his top case, seeing to my husband's every medical need. Wilber urged me to go.

"Don't worry," he said, repeating his standard line, "I'll be okay."

After two nights in a hospital-recommended guesthouse, I hopped on the BC Rail train back to the Cariboo. Time stood still. It was the first time in six weeks that I'd been without Wilber or Wyatt and unable to do anything for either of them. I'd had no contact with the Gallants. They were at Knife Creek, no phone, but I trusted that all was well. I knew I'd see them as soon as the train, then the taxi, could carry me home. So, I settled into the soft cushions as we chugged comfortably along through the Coastal Range, across the Fraser River, and along the peaceful farms of the interior. I might have taken the opportunity to sleep, recovered the rest that had eluded me in my worried weeks, but mostly I gazed at the world rushing by, seeing for the first time in a long while the bigger picture outside my troubles. In the everyday faces of people waiting at crossings, riding the school bus, working the field, I saw the continuation of lives and futures.

Back at Knife Creek, I found a happy Wyatt, a warm and well-tended house. We were still eating out of the garden, even though it was mid-October and winter cold had settled in the region, a seasonal pattern I made a mental note of for next fall. We shared the space and stories for an evening. I appreciated the help, and the easy trust. The next day, I went into town to call the hospital, taking Wyatt with me. Maybe he could talk to his daddy.

"Hello, this is Mrs. Neumann, calling for my husband, Frank," I said, after dropping enough coins for five minutes into the phone at 150 Mile House. "Can you put me through to his room?"

"Mrs. Neumann, do you mean Dr. Neumann? He's standing right here," said the floor nurse. Dr. Neumann? Confusion and fear overtook me. I reached down for Wyatt's hand.

"Nonnie, where the hell are you?" Fred's voice rattled my nerves. "Our boy's been in surgery. Thank God, Dr. Turnbull called us. Hansi and I flew right up, but you were gone. And there's no way to get in touch with you. The way you choose to live! How could you leave him? *What the hell is going on?*"

"No, no, I was there, I had to come home to get Wyatt. They told me he would be fine." I was gulping my words, trying to get my defense out before he began again. But wait, why should I have to defend myself? "They could have called the Mounties, they would have found me." Everybody in Canada knows that in rural areas, the Royal Canadian Mounted Police would ride out on emergencies. And what about the surgery?

"What happened?" I asked. "Is he okay? Is he out of surgery, did it go well? What did they do?"

"Never mind," he yelled. "Just get down here, you should be with him. He's your husband! He's recovering. Thank God, Hansi and I are here or he'd be all alone."

"I'll be there tomorrow," I assured him. "It's a ten-hour drive, and with Wyatt, it'll take all day. I'll be there tomorrow night. Where are you staying?"

I stopped at the cabin to pack some stuff and see if the Gallants were willing to stay on for a little while as caretakers, maybe pay us a bit of rent, too. Could they call me next week, at the guesthouse in Vancouver, and we could figure out a plan? There was so much I didn't know at that moment. Then I took off, like a crazy woman, to my damaged husband. I don't know how I drove that three-quarter-ton truck along the endless Cariboo Highway, then the Trans Canada and into a strange city without maps or routes, with a bewildered two-year-old roaming the cab. By the time I found the hospital, Wyatt and I could only get to the floor and peek in the window of the intensive care unit. Wilber was hooked up again, and he had a bandage on his poor, damaged head. The room was darkened, he was asleep. One nurse took Wyatt into the lounge while another told me about the surgery.

"Dr. Turnbull did what he could." The words haunt me still. "I was in the operating room," she continued. Thinking of her there, this kind and caring nurse, with Wilber in his vulnerability gave me such comfort. Her sweet, smart face might have been the last thing he saw before the sedation.

"The doctor was completely surprised to find an abscess the size of a quarter under the skull crack." She made the shape with her hand, touching forefinger to thumb. "It had been there long enough that the infection had migrated into the fissures of the brain." Again she used her hands, by bending her fingers in, to show the depth of the folds. "Now he's on our strongest antibiotic and we're hoping it'll stop the growth. The doctor won't tell you this, but the procedure we performed on your husband is extremely dangerous and rarely successful." She held up her hands again, ten fingers splayed. "Out of ten patients, four die on the table, two become paralyzed, three become brain dead, and one survives to lead a healthy, full life. We hope Frank will be that *one.*" Now her hands took mine and gave them a good, confident squeeze. I broke down, the tension of these weeks really finally catching up. I sat on the floor and cried. I had worked hard, constantly, to see him recover. Now hope was all we had. Wait and hope.

Within a few days, Dede arrived. My parents were still in the Far East, so she had taken their BMW and come to be with me. I was so glad to have her, to dilute the Neumanns' intensity, their blame, sadness, and disgust. She was a joy with Wyatt, patient and calm, going to parks and playgrounds, while I sat in vigil. At night I could go to her in our guesthouse and talk about good things: our farm, our plans, our lives, her life, without the gloom of the hospital.

Wilber improved slowly. The surgery had been invasive, and his memory, hearing, and balance were affected. Time was what he needed, and quiet, and a sanitary environment. We visited daily, staying as long as his energy allowed. I was intensely affected by the other patients in his shared room, and by their attending families. One young man, strapped to his rotating bed, had become paralyzed in a cliff dive in Howe Sound. His face was his only moving part, and his expressions were mostly heart-wrenching, except when his girlfriend came to read to him. Another young guy had been in a motorcycle accident and lost a leg, his parents at his side day and night. I was shocked and humbled by the plight of these young men, and I felt, invincibly, that my young man was not a broken statistic like them. We would come whole onto the other side of this, I was sure.

By early November, Wilber was ready to be released. And he felt ready to get out. His long-held distaste for hospitals had not sweetened any after two months in and out of them. Granted, he was glad to have had his life saved, and knew he had the hospital, doctors, and nurses to thank—which he did—but he was done.

"He can't go back to the log cabin without sanitation facilities," Dr. Turnbull warned me. "His is a very serious condition. The brain is still susceptible to infection." His eyes were kind, not judgmental, and sympathetic without a hint of pity. Professional, dependable, and the king of neurology in Canada, he was the first person I'd trusted during this excruciating ordeal.

"He'll have four courses of antibiotics. That will cover him for forty days. But he must have rest in a clean place. And he can't be doing heavy chores… and neither can you." My pregnancy was showing under the empire-waist of my dress. He knew life in the cabin was too much for me to undertake alone.

"We'll go to my parents. They have plenty of room, and it'll be good for all of us." I made the decision. The Neumanns' house lacked a guest room and dripped with fragile and priceless artifacts that only a toddler would dare touch. Denver doctors were undeniably better than the ones in Driggs (were there any?), but we'd be more comfortable with my family. And now that Sarah was off at college, there were two empty bedrooms. The T Bar Lazy S ranch would suit just for a month.

CHAPTER TWENTY-FIVE

"Why do you have to be such a PRICK?" my father screamed at Wilber across the dinner table. Wilber had been hassling Wyatt about his table manners, struggling to uphold some civility at my parents' table. Kenny was furious at Wilber, still recovering from brain surgery, one week out of the hospital. "Can't you just leave him alone?"

Wilber, not surprisingly, got up from the table and left the room, muttering to himself. My mother's shocked expression mirrored mine. Wyatt started crying, and my mother looked down at her plate. My dad returned to eating, self-righteous and unapologetic. He had been inexcusably impatient and mean to Wilber, not just tonight, but during the week and over the years. His resentment toward Wilber had grown as their personalities continued to joust. But now, when he needed to act the adult, he had let his ego dominate the weaker man, taking advantage instead of taking stock. It was a hopeless situation.

We were just settling in. We'd flown down from Vancouver right after Wilber's release—a flight of prescription, not of choice. We wanted to be going home to our little farm, to be taking back our life. The Gallants had agreed to stay on at Knife Creek, taking our life as their own, the good and bad.

These were days of adjustment and angst for us all. Wilber was realizing his limitations, trying to come to terms with their permanence. Physically, his balance and strength were diminished; his hearing had been knocked for a loop. Mentally, his memory was spotty, his normally brilliant mind slow and tedious. All of which threatened his manhood, self-esteem, and his abilities as father/husband/provider. He was a mess. And, because of the brain trauma, his temper was unpredictable—sweet one minute, cutting the next. I was challenged by this new personality, though I tried to be patient and understanding. Wyatt was confused, and I worked to shield him.

I picked Wyatt up and followed Wilber upstairs to our bedroom. He was packing, wildly throwing clothes in his bag, muttering and spitting mad.

"I'm outta here," he said to himself, then again, loud and clearly for my benefit. "I'll take the next flight outta Jackson to Denver. Who the fuck does he think he is?"

There was nothing I could say to stop him. Kenny was wrong. Wilber was hurt and had every reason to want out of this house. My mom and I had tried to step in numerous times, but our attempts to please only made matters worse. We knew our only power was over Wyatt, to be consistent and safe for him.

I drove Wilber to Jackson. He and my dad didn't speak before he left. Of course, his parents were glad to have him home; he would go to their doctors and they would care for him. They weren't taken aback by our description of the scenario in Driggs. Instead, I felt they were almost glad for it, as it proved once again that my parents were fucked up, and they weren't. Come on home, son, they said. We love you.

We decided that Wyatt and I would stay in Driggs. The added expense of changing and adding flights would bend our already strained finances to breaking. It was only a few more weeks before we could reunite at home, finally back where we belonged. Wilber would heal properly when he was the king of his own castle again. In the meantime, we would each be in the care, and control, of our parents, a hellish place to be whether pregnant and with a toddler or recovering from brain surgery. We tried to live within their dictums. But there, we found a place where failure was assumed.

10th December '74

Hello, folks!

I arrived home about 5:00 pm after a very comfortable un-problematic journey. Got one sandwich to Seattle, so I was very grateful for those tongue delicacies. The cabin is in order, clean, and now with a roaring fire, warm and cozy. It is a change to be out here alone. The aura is quiet and peaceful. This evening Nonnie and Wyatt should arrive and I'm very excited. But away goes the peace.

Only a few little items are missing, nothing disastrous as I had conjured. I have the Gallants address and I'm going to write them one more time in hopes of getting eighty dollars. Frankly speaking, I don't count on a response. After all, if rent is due on 1 Nov. and it's now the middle of December…

I had an enjoyable and relaxing time in Colorado. It was exciting to see you all even though you all could use a diet. The weather up here is unseasonable – high 30's to low 40's and nights in the mid-20's. Just like Colorado! Hope your weather stays mild so it can be an easy winter for everyone.

Enclosed is the $250 loan. I hope it helps put you in the black again — maybe you can even stay there for awhile.

Write soon,
Love, Frank

Wyatt and I flew into Williams Lake, Wyatt an excited little boy eager to see his dad after too many weeks away. We had missed most of a season together. I picked at my cuticles during the flight, a childhood habit reestablished in my father's house. There had been no break for any of us. I worried for all the males in my life, foremost my husband, and for my ability to care for him. With the risk of post-brain-surgery complications and their emergent nature, I dreaded being alone with him, so far from help. The cuticle tearing persisted.

Wilber met us at the plane, looking tired and defeated. Hadn't he relaxed with his parents? Pushing worry aside, I made the best effort to take charge. We were both glad to be back at the farm after weeks in emotional transit. But as we adjusted back into the family unit for the first time since the accident, we were apprehensive, too. Wilber was returning to unfamiliar territory. He was still unsteady; a woodsman confined to stoking the stove while his pregnant wife chopped and hauled the wood and carried the water. His capacity as decision maker, too, was tempered by his erratic confusion and disorientation. He'd have to count on me, to choke back his pride. Wilber had always been a mountain man. Strong, powerful, and proud, those were his identifying features. My heart ached for his disappointments, continually revealing themselves. He could not be, for now anyway, the hero and protector of our lives.

One night soon after our return, in the early dark of December, Wyatt sat on the kitchen counter as I brushed his little teeth. I was telling him a story about teeth, strong, clean, and white. Suddenly, I heard a scampering of claws on the floor. I froze. Wyatt kept squishing toothpaste through his teeth and smiling. I brushed some more and heard more skittering. Something flashed in the corner of my eye, and I turned to see a fat rat propped on the hutch, not three feet away. Not four feet from my baby boy.

"Get away!" I shouted, waving my hand at the disgusting creature, trying not to draw Wyatt's attention or act as terrified as I was feeling. Then the damn rat snarled at me, baring his jagged fangs. I screamed. He ran. Wyatt laughed. I carried him upstairs and put him into bed. I went to our bed to find a dozing Wilber. I sat down, now more than five months pregnant and exhausted.

"There are rats in the house," I whispered, attempting calm. "One of those fuckers just snarled at me. In my own house!"

"Yeah, I thought I heard something the other night." Wilber was half asleep and not concerned as I'd hoped he'd be.

"What should I do?" I wanted action, and my calm was slipping away.

"Well, whattaya want to do?" Wilber's reply confirmed my other fear, that I alone would be making the decisions, taking the actions. I told him that I'd heard stories of rats chewing the fingers off small children. Little Wyatt in his crib was basically bait. My frustration rose, along with my voice. I couldn't live like this, wasn't going to spend the winter worrying about Wyatt's fingers, not to mention the new baby. I was ranting. Wilber suddenly opened his eyes, as if he'd been waiting for me to finish.

"Get the shotgun and shoot the fucker," he said, with his trademark gift for simplicity. "It's under the bed, and the shells are on my dresser. Go for it. I'm just not up for it right now. But you can do it." His confidence sent me packing.

I was a desperate woman, in the family way no less, and that fucking rat was going to be sorry. If I had my way, he'd be sorry only until his lights went out, for good. I got the gun, the shells, and let Wilber load it and show me the trigger. Then I went back downstairs and positioned myself on the counter. The gas and kerosene lights lit the cabin, vaguely, but I knew I'd see the rat and his beady little eyes. I watched and waited.

Not for long. The little varmint appeared as if on command. He scampered across the floor, looked at me, and then headed up the stairs. Oh no, not my baby boy! I screamed, which made him stop on the landing. Ka-BLAMMMMM!! That shotgun went off, kicking me back and splattering the unsuspecting rodent.

"Didn't think I had it in me, eh, you little fucker?!" I said as I passed him, his fat body now covering the logs, a smear of blood and guts. I was pretty damn proud of myself, and knew, after the birds of last summer, that I'd taken care of the rat problem.

"Okay, now you go and clean it up," I told Wilber as I replaced the gun and crawled into the warm bed. I'd put an end to cohabitating with rodents, for now.

For the first time in his life, my Jewish Midwestern husband would have a true New England Christmas, and Wyatt would have his first Christmas to remember as well. I yearned to recreate old traditions, make up new ones, and show them the warmth and love of the season. The holidays of my childhood had never been particularly religious, although our girls' choir always sang at Trinity Church on Christmas Eve. In the afternoon, we'd walk through the snow to attend a festive neighborhood dress-up party. Our neighborhood was full of kids our age and, though there were only five houses nearby, we made the most of it. The parents swilled Brandy Alexanders and we drank eggnog, no rum. But when our parents went to get their coats, for our trip to the evening service, we'd drain their glasses of the creamy brandy and nutmeg.

Now in Knife Creek, we invited our neighbors, whose phone had rescued us months ago, over for a Christmas Eve party. An older couple living alone, they were touched by the holiday sentiment but busy with their own family that evening. So we had our own little party. We decorated the cabin with boughs, ribbons, and a perfect little pine we'd found over by the swamp on a quiet snowy afternoon. We had hot chocolate and gingerbread cookies decorated by Wyatt and me. The tree decorations were all part of the fun. We'd popped and strung popcorn for hours, Wyatt handing us the corn, "one for me, one for you," then draping the delicate strands on the tree. Our construction paper balls and bunches of rose hips tied with yarn added color, and Wilber's ingenious version of the five-or-six-pointed (depending on your perspective) star was perched on top. We lit candles all around and sang carols, which I had to teach everyone first. Over a chair, in lieu of a mantel, Wyatt and I hung the treasured knit stockings my mother had made, one for each child in the family. The green, red, and white yarns on Wyatt's were bright and new, mine slightly faded with age. We added a big wool sock for Wilber. As we snuggled into the warmth of the evening, I told what I could remember of the magical story of baby Jesus. It was the birth of a holiday tradition at Knife Creek, and we toasted the future and our great fortune with a stein of good beer. The sound of a train whistle echoed across the frozen land and completed the wonder of the night.

The good news for our first winter in Canada was that Wilber was home all the time. The checks came from the Worker's Compensation Board like clockwork, and they were sizable. Through the winter, our visits to town became a comforting routine. We looked forward to those jaunts, and when an icy driveway or a blinding storm kept us inside, we would all feel cheated until the weather broke. I had even sewn myself a going-to-town maternity outfit, a pair of pants and a top made of corduroy and seersucker. I was proud of my handiwork and its look of clean sophistication. It gave me a certain respectful look, one that might not draw the locals' stares. I'd always clean Wyatt up for the trip, positioning us as members of the community rather than dirty hippies. We visited Petra, Paul, and Hugo for news and showers, Overwaitea grocery store for fresh oranges or milk, the library for books, and the post office for mail. Doing laundry and seeing the doctor for my prenatal and Wilber's check-ins were cause for other trips to town.

We had plenty of food put up. The hauling of water and chopping of wood, our two daily constants, fell to me. I couldn't let Wilber take the chance of a fall or a strain that might affect his delicately healing brain. Chopping ice for water got tough in January when the temperatures hovered around -30º, and smacked of the brutal days in the chicken coop at Monte Cristo. Once I made a hole big enough for the dipper, it would take a while to fill the five-gallon buckets. I could only carry one at a time now, which threw me off balance, and the addition of the frontal bulge under my overalls made a slip on the worn path that much more likely. Chopping wood for the stove was easier since John and the boys had split the rounds; I was mostly in need of kindling. We had taken the locals' advice and stocked up on the dreaded coal, and it made all the difference to have a fire burning through the night. Even so, the water bucket we used for rinsing out poopy diapers was frozen solid every morning on the potbelly. It was cold and grueling to face these tasks alone and pregnant.

But Wilber continued to be infirmed, resting and recuperating. As he lay in bed, day after day, he became ornery at the frustration of being weak and unable to contribute. His outbursts were frequent and somewhat predictable. I tried to keep Wyatt with him on the good days and with me on the bad. I sometimes had my own tantrums, but I tried to expand my capacity for compassion. For better or worse… And he had almost died, I kept reminding myself. His body and spirit needed time to heal properly.

One day, I lost it on one of our treasured weekly trips to town. I guess I might have seen it coming. This particular trip didn't include a doctor's visit, so I was taking the opportunity to wash my special corduroy pantsuit, wearing my old overalls. In our well-practiced Laundromat routine, I'd always ask Wilber to check and empty his pockets, and he did—until that day. So when I began folding my cherished pantsuit and found it slashed and dotted with blue permanent marker ink, I was livid. It had already been through the dryer, so the stains were set for good. I knew my poor husband was doing his best, but this was too much. In my attempt at respectability, my corduroy outfit had given me such joy and pride. Now, the last symbol of civility was gone. I cried in defeat. It was too late in the pregnancy, and too expensive, to make another, so I vented instead.

My birthday was coming. I would turn twenty-one. We'd have a cake and candles, my entry into adulthood celebrated in the seventh month of my second pregnancy. Now I'd be able to buy a drink at any bar! That seemed fair, but the fact that my parents' twenty-first birthday tradition was extended to my sisters, and not to me, struck me as unfair—Dede and Betsy had each been given $1,000. But when it came my turn, my dad declared, "I'm no longer Nonnie's main man. I don't have to give her a thousand bucks. Wilber can do that if he wants." Really I didn't care, didn't NEED the money, but I thought it was a chicken-shit reason and another slap in the face.

I could tell my mother was not happy with the idea. She had always paid special attention to presents, holidays, and traditions. It was beyond principle to her, she just loved giving. So, a week before my birthday, I was not surprised when the postmistress at 150 Mile House called out to me from the gas station.

"Mrs. Neumann," she shouted, almost bursting, "you have a heap of packages here. Can you pick them up?" We went over and, lo and behold, there were a dozen boxes of varying sizes, all from my mother. We took them home, only to go back the next week to find a dozen more. The postmistress was floored, and I must say so were we.

When the day finally came, Wyatt was as excited as he'd been on his birthday. It never mattered to him that it was someone else's birthday, as long as he got to sing, blow out the candles, and eat cake. Wilber and Wyatt gave me a new cast iron skillet and some local berry jam. But Wyatt was chompin' to open the boxes. He'd waited too long. So we proceeded. My mother, not to be undone by my father, had sent me twenty-one presents. Each was in its own box, so I'd have the pleasure of opening and opening, and opening. We were delighted and enchanted. The presents were unique and expensive, or plain and cheap, each thoughtful and personal. She sent a velvet pillow, a fancy grater, soufflé dishes, a cookbook from a new store, Williams-Sonoma, a family silver serving spoon, beautiful book plates, *A Gift from the Sea* by Anne Lindbergh, down booties, and much more. She had cross-stitched and framed my birth flower, "Snowdrops for Nonnie." And she wrote: "To Nonnie-Poms, our lovely girl on her twenty-first birthday. Some snowdrops to last forever – 'til you're an old lovely lady!" I was so touched, her compassion and care reaching out over the 500 miles between us. My twenty-first birthday had been a unique and memorable day, without need of barhopping or revelry.

It wasn't until late January, at a doctor's follow-up appointment, that we learned the extent of Wilber's injuries, some of which he must have already known. He was deaf in his left ear, had only forty percent hearing in his right, and the damage in his inner ear was causing his unsteady gait. He had no sense of taste and smell. He could tell salty from sweet, but that was it. After I recovered from the shock of the tragic assault on his 29-year-old body, I laughed, and gave him a gentle slap on the arm.

"So, when you hated the taste of my peanut butter and bulgur casserole last week, you actually couldn't taste it? Not one bit?" I asked, still surprised at his only-ever objection to my cooking since the pancake incident. He gave me a guilty grin, and then admitted that just the idea of peanut butter with bulgur had made him queasy.

"OK, it was pretty weird," I said, "but you lied." I gave him a wide berth on all things physical. The fact that he'd never again enjoy or savor the foods he loved, all foods, was a great sadness and discouragement for him.

Later, thinking about the hearing loss, I realized that in the truck, now that I was the driver, his left, or deaf, ear was to me. As we drove, I talked and he nodded, glancing regularly in my direction.

"So you can't hear a word I say in the truck?" I asked.

"Nope, not a word." It was the truth.

"Then why do you nod, all the time, like you're agreeing with me?" I was upset, but quickly realized what was going on.

"Because, Poms, you're always right…." He was very sweet, and very sad, and I hugged him hard at the pain of it. We had to preserve and encourage his remaining hearing. He needed to be listening when our new baby tested her lungs. It would break his heart to miss the cooing and laughter of a tiny voice, as well as Wyatt's tender words and frustrated demands, or even my incessant chatter. We would find out if there was anything we could do.

Wilber had decided, without my consult, that we were definitely NOT going to have our next baby in the hospital. I had to sympathize with his disgust. He had had a pretty miserable time in Cariboo Memorial Hospital for many months last year. But when he told me, late in the pregnancy, that he would drop me off at the entrance but absolutely not enter the hospital, I was shocked and dismayed. This was a birth, after all, not a trauma. I had to think it through carefully because, ultimately, I knew he was serious. If I chose a traditional birth, with the aid and comfort of modern medicine, I would be on my own.

Wyatt's birth had been without complication, save for the misunderstanding between the midwife and me. We had read, and restudied, all the birth books, and I knew Lamaze instinctively. I knew I was fit to deliver simply, and the second birth was bound to be quicker and easier. These things were true. But we were over thirty miles from town, without benefit of phone or power, and we had no midwife. My doctor, Dr. Atwood, was expecting us in the delivery room. He would not be happy about a change in plan. What if we had an emergency, even something simple, like hemorrhaging, and couldn't get to town soon enough? What if the baby, or I, died?

Wilber had, he confided, a strong belief about that. If something went wrong with the birth, the baby, or the afterbirth, it was "meant to be."

"I don't and can't believe that," I admitted. "If the baby dies or is permanently damaged because we neglect the medical facilities so close, I won't be able to live with myself. We aren't pioneers-of-old; we have the benefit of equipment and medicine. What if I'd let what was 'meant to be' rest in your hospital bed, and not taken you to Vancouver? YOU'D be dead!" My point was heard, I think, but Wilber was determined. I would have to choose when the time came.

CHAPTER TWENTY-SIX

Wilber's birthday came amid a shower of gifts and an early spring storm. He was twenty-nine on March eighth, pushing the dreaded thirty. I was celebrating the fact that he was young and alive. But he was feeling old and feeble. He could not be consoled, except by Wyatt and his demands.

"Daddy sing for the cake, come on, it's chocolate!" Wyatt made it festive, singing and dancing around in anticipation of the cake moment. We gave Wilber a new pair of Carharts, a hand-knit hat, and a new spade for working the barnyard. Our next project, after having the baby, would be buying and raising baby pigs, one for the Richters, one for us, to fill the barn. We would need more tools, but the spade was a start.

The willows and aspens had yet to show their springtime glow. The chinook winds of February had made puddles that now glistened with ice. The #10 tomato can under my side of the bed had kept me from urgent and dangerous mid-night trips to the outhouse—I had grown far too unwieldy to totter over slippery snow in the dark. Wilber had had to resume the water gathering, which meant slower trips but a returning sense of pride. Our windows had let go the frost, and the water bucket on top of the potbelly was no longer frozen solid in the morning.

The day dawned bright and cold. It was the Spring Equinox, a hopeful sign, when my contractions began in earnest. I'd been having Braxton-Hicks contractions, or false labor, for a few weeks, but this felt different. Wilber was alerted and we loaded into the truck. Wyatt had his "gun" and jammies, and knew only that he was going to play with Hugo. We didn't talk on the way to town. Silent in thought, Wilber and I considered the day ahead and the options we had long since stopped discussing. In town, we took Wyatt to Petra's for what was for him an exciting play-day.

We called the doctor so that I could describe my symptoms.

"Sounds like the real thing," Dr. Atwood confirmed. "Now you just have to decide what you want to do. I'll be here if you come to town." I had told him, at our last visit, about the possibility that we'd do a home birth, without midwife or help. He had been disappointed and discouraging. Wilber had walked out.

"What do you want to do?" Wilber asked, and I was reminded of the night with the rat.

"Let's go have this baby," I replied. We loaded back in the truck. I still wasn't resigned to Wilber's belief in fate, and I silently resented him for making me choose. There was no safe option. Going to the hospital alone to have our baby would break Wilber's heart, and mine. Going home meant taking a chance with nature, the unpredictable teacher. I was willing to take a chance, I guessed. I hoped for a fast labor, without time in which to doubt my decision. I hoped for a healthy birth and baby.

We arrived home to a splendid afternoon and went for a walk down to the creek. When we were almost to the bank, my water broke and gushed down my legs. We turned and hobbled back inside, where the warmth from the stove and the glow of sunset made me feel hopeful. I went upstairs, where Wilber was covering our foam pad mattress with plastic before replacing the bedding. He was so excited and sweet. I crawled onto the bed as labor began in earnest. Wilber went down to boil water (for what?) and I rested between cramps.

After a few hours of gently progressing contractions, the force and frequency intensified. We decided I was in transition and that the time was coming. Remembering the tipi labor, Wilber massaged warm oil on my perineum. He rubbed my sore back and feet, and he smiled a lot. When he wasn't attending, he was pacing, up and down the stairs and around the room. I was breathing, changing position and cursing. The pain got tough, the pain that builds and builds and promises to tear you limb from limb. I yelled, I begged, and I swore. Wilber tried to comfort me.

"You're doing so good, Poms. So good. It's almost time. Look," he came in close, "here's Teddy, it's just you, me, and Teddy." He put Wyatt's darling bear a little bit too close to my head, and a primal response ensued. "Get that FUCKING BEAR away from me!! Are you fucking kidding me!" A poor stunned Wilber went off to boil more water. He was only trying to help, but I wasn't in the mood for cute.

Fortunately for the baby and for us, I was soon pushing. For the first time I recognized the "urge" that Mary had wanted me to feel, an urge I could not resist. The baby was ready.

"The baby is here," Wilber said. "I see the head!" I was on my back against a pile of pillows, pulling up and against my knees. Bearing down, pushing out, I felt the hemorrhoids coming. I felt the perineum tearing where the episiotomy had been. I didn't care. Pushing out the baby, I was doing it. "She's coming, I see the shoulders." Wilber was holding the head. I pushed out the shoulders, he caught them, and the rest of the tiny body flopped out with a gush of fluid.

"It's a girl!!" he shouted, in tears and laughter. He syringed her nose and mouth, and she let out a hearty squeal. And we laughed and cried together. Relief, joy, triumph, and love… I held her, gazing in awe, while Wilber ran to get the water and towels. Excited to finally get to use his water, he plunged the towels in it and began gently wiping the baby. I looked at the clock: 7:20 p.m., March 20, 1975.

"Cora Lockwood," he whispered. "Right?" He looked up at me.

"That's right. Cora Lockwood Neumann, we love you." I couldn't take my eyes off her. I had wanted a girl to complement my boy, but I had kept that to myself. Now, joy and fascination overwhelmed me.

"Welcome, sweet Cora," he said in the magic of the moment. He never forced the point, but what we had just done, bringing her into the world in the quiet and peace of Knife Creek, *was* magical.

For long minutes, I sat in an aluminum washtub waiting for the placenta to birth. I had been told that it would be pushed out by a series of contractions. I sat with Cora and waited. And waited, eventually feeling silly.

"Hey, I think you're sitting on the placenta," Wilber said, finally noticing a fleshy, bloody sac sitting in the pan. "Yup, let's get you out of there." He lifted me up and laid me on the bed, then tied and cut the cord and we rested at last. The process had been perfect, each stage moving naturally to the next. Now the final cut, and we were done.

Wilber joined me in the bed. Between us, tiny Cora suckled vigorously. Under the glow of a kerosene lamp rather than an iridescent glare, in the absence of an army of snooping staff, we did what mothers and fathers have done for generations, admired and inspected our new child. We counted fingers and toes out loud and with glee, checked her ears, eyes, and hair, and basked in her newly exposed being. She was perfect, ten digits in the right places, dark eyes, lovely ears, and long body. Her tiny nose bumped a bit at the end, like mine. Her olive glow, brown eyes, and dark hair gave her Wilber's Semitic air. Wyatt had been fair and bald. While classically cute Wyatt resembled Coopers and Fergusons worldwide, exotic Cora would carry the beleaguered Neumann genes into the future. I had hoped for a little daddy's girl, and she was all that!

"We'll need to go for stitches," I reminded Wilber, "and I want to have Cora weighed, measured, tested." I had acquiesced to his home birth, now it was time for him to take us to the doctor. He went to warm up the truck. I pulled on underpants with the necessary Kotex, fastening my overalls over a turtleneck while I prepared myself for the judgment of the traditional medical establishment.

When Wilber came to get me, I was ready. But as I walked toward the truck, I felt a flood of blood filling the pad. I worried but didn't want to delay us and so kept it to myself. I held Cora wrapped and covered in the quilted blanket I had sewn, with Noonie's knit blanket and Oma's little hat providing extra layers of warmth. Wilber helped me up, and we set off. But he gunned it to attack the steep hill, and within moments we were sliding sideways, then stuck. We wouldn't make the hill—Wilber needed to chain up. He ushered me out of the truck, across the icy yard and back into the house, where he deposited Cora and me on the chair near the stove.

As I sat and waited, he located and applied the chains. He had to jack up the truck to do it and it took more than a half hour. I thought of what would have happened if we had been in the midst of an emergency. What if Cora had been stuck in the birth canal, if I was hemorrhaging, if Cora was born blue? I sat and rocked and felt the relief of luck and timing, of what was "meant to be." I was overwhelmed by my own strength, by my own weakness, by my choice to risk lives to serve the comfort or pride of my husband. I was angry at his uncompromising "belief." I doubted his theory, that he would have accepted tragedy as fate. Now, as he frantically hurried our escape to medical aid, I sensed his worry. And mine increased as well. I put Cora down, and went to find another Kotex as I felt a surge of discharge.

Soon, we were up the hill, down the road, and at the emergency room door, so familiar to us now. Dr. Atwood was called and arrived quickly. He weighed, measured, and inspected Cora, declaring her "perfect." Then he turned to me.

"Need a few stitches, do we?" He cocked his heavy brow. I undressed and got in a gown, climbing up on his table. For the first time, my feet were in stirrups, my legs and vagina chilled by the emergency room draft.

"This would have been a lot easier for me, you know," he said on inspection, "if I could have shaved and prepped you properly and even cut, but here you've got this messy tear. We'll do what we can." I looked at Wilber, who was gazing at Cora, then at me. He winked. It was all going to be all right.

By the time we were done with the medical assessments and securing a birth certificate, it was ten o'clock, too late to pick up Wyatt. He would be comfortably asleep at Hugo's, and tomorrow was just as good. So we rolled home and treasured our first night alone with baby Cora on her first night of life. We knew Wyatt would adore her, smother and brother her, so it was special to have her all to ourselves. We lay around her and marveled at her flawlessness, nature's work. She nursed well and hungrily. She was mighty strong, though she'd weighed in at only five pounds and measured nineteen inches, tip to toes. Our little peanut, she was.

The next day, we piled into town. Wyatt was busting to see her. We had talked lots about the coming baby. He got so excited as he watched Petra and Paul admiring her. His sister, his baby…

"You want one, you can get one!" he told them and anyone who showed interest. He'd been infatuated with the sound of "twenty," so he went on. "Yup, twenty minutes, twenty dollars, twenty miles to Overwaitea!" Even when we stopped at Overwaitea, and he and Wilber went in for some supplies, he told the checkout girl about his new baby sister.

A few days later, we went to pick Noonie up at the airport. Staying at the 150 Mile House Hotel, she would be close and a wonderful help with Cora and Wyatt. She hadn't seen Wilber since the screwed-up visit to Driggs, but she and he got on well. This would be a good opportunity to rebuild that friendship, unencumbered by Kenny. Again, I was happy to have her. Not only was my mother easily entertained and comforting, she was without attitude. She wanted what I wanted and trusted the choices I'd made, whether obvious or not.

"Overwaitea, twenty bucks!" Wyatt rushed to tell her, when she swooned over Cora. We all laughed and he seemed pretty proud.

Our family was complete and bliss prevailed. With the lunar beginning of spring, we saw the signs, slowly but steady, of its coming. Birds returned to the creek, green grass sprouted along the foundation, and the ground thawed. Permafrost heaves on the road and in the yard looked like earthquake fissures and eruptions. The forest let go its snow. The creek rose and burbled louder than ever. Across the water, my favorite view came alive with the colors of spring: the rosy glow of kinnikinnik bushes, the bright burst of greens, and the slow golden of willow. The weather was gray and chilly, but with all the color, each day promised the approach of the breakout of summer.

Noonie stayed for a week. Easter came and went, with the creation of a bunny-shaped carrot cake, a feast, and a few chocolate eggs. Of course the cake needed candles for Wyatt to blow out. He was becoming a holiday freak, and would grow up, I imagined, loving the traditions without bother for religion, like me. After another successful visit, I drove Noonie to town for a ladies' lunch and a quiet visit before we headed to the airport. She lauded our family and home, with pride and a little sadness that Kenny wouldn't come. Time may heal.

I returned home to find that, in a matter of hours, the aspen seedlings by the creek had completely disappeared. With his compromised hearing, Wilber hadn't heard a thing, so we all went out for a better look. Closer inspection showed they'd been cut to the ground, the teeth marks of beaver on the dozens of stumps and a new dam across the creek our telltale signs. It was beaver time and they were damming. They had done their work cleanly and swiftly, the natural course. Actually, their clearing led to a better view from the outhouse. Fantastic!

Wilber was gaining strength. With his balance stabilizing and his confidence growing, he was ready to reconnect. Six weeks after childbirth, my healing was complete and I welcomed his advances. We hadn't made love since before the accident, almost eight months, and I worried that the lack of closeness was further harming his self-esteem. If Wilber was up for it, I wanted it too. We would have to be gentle and sensitive, slow and sensuous in search of the intimacy we both craved. My memories of long ago summer nights in Tiger made me swoon. So much had changed, for better and worse, and I had missed his tenderness.

Soon, we were ready to consider running the pigsty we'd discussed the previous summer. Bob and Wilber had been looking into it. Buying two baby pigs at $50 each from a local ranch was best. We would raise them, keep 'em clean and healthy, splitting the costs. In summer, we'd butcher them, each family putting 120 pounds of tasty meat in the freezer. A local processor would make us our very own bacon, sausage, salami, roasts, and loins; we thought it a great return. We would feed them, according to Foxfire and the rancher, a combination of grain and milk, and kitchen scraps. Bob and Wilber set about reinforcing the fencing and barn door, walls and stables. The piggies would be able to roam in and out. The corral was covered with hay, to keep down the filth, and Wilber carved a sturdy eating trough.

The piglets were delivered in early May, somewhat cute, pink, and clean. They were already noisy, and I was glad they'd be housed up the hill, away from sleeping or napping children. Wyatt was warned never to go to the pigs alone. When they rooted around his feet that first day, I think he was adequately humbled and scared. We did nothing to dissuade him from his fears. Pigs, in general, were not pets, and could not be trusted. And soon they'd be enormous, bigger and stronger than any of us. They would be capable of knocking Wyatt over and trampling him, without even realizing it.

The feeding system was simple but incredibly demanding. A fifty-five-gallon barrel was cut in half, so that it wouldn't be too deep, and placed on an iron frame Wilber made with his horse-shoeing forge and anvil. Under what was now the cooking pot, we'd build a fire. In the pot, water, milk, wheat berries, oats, and kitchen scraps would cook, until a suitable—and disgusting—mash was concocted. Every morning for three months, that was the routine. We scooped the mash into buckets and hauled it up to the trough. Ours were the best-fed pigs in the province, indeed, and I was their personal chef.

Collecting the ingredients for the daily feast became a full-time job. Since little was wasted in our kitchen, we took to scouring the dumpsters behind Safeway and Overwaitea for produce that was past its prime. Sometimes we'd find full boxes of broccoli, peppers, potatoes, and more, thrown out in perfectly good condition. A lazy stock boy, I assumed. We'd visit the local dairy to collect their expired products: milk, cream, yogurt, and cottage cheese. In an agricultural region, no one doubted that our scavenging was for the sake of livestock. We'd stop at the feed 'n' grain store for wheat, oats, rye, or whatever else they had. The route became a weekly routine.

When we got home, I'd run an initial inspection on rot and expiration dates, picking out the food that was edible for us. We usually had dairy, two days past its prime but still sweet, and produce with the soft spots cut off to supplement our stored foods. Yup, we were eating out of dumpsters, but not directly. We were only making use of that which was too good for the piglets. The bulk was then thrown in the barrel cooker and stirred with a great stick over the fire until bubbly and soft and stinky. We would use the base over and over, adding to it real store-bought pig food, full of nutrients.

Once we got the pig farm up and running, it was time to prep and plant the garden. Wyatt was two and a half and wanted to help with the dirty work. Cora was two months and happy in the Snuggly with me or Wilber as we went about our chores. This year we could start plants in the greenhouse, covered with a layer of heavy plastic. In this way, we helped tease the chill off the early spring dawn. Soil and manure from the corral had been raked off before we added the pigs, and sifted clean for the prized crops of the greenhouse. So, we turned, cleaned, and planted the beds once more. We were glad to see the fruit of last year's labor in the darker and softer dirt. The seeds were laid and I taught Wyatt how to gently replace and press the dirt back over them. He liked the game for fifteen minutes at a time, and then he was off to see what Daddy was up to. This way he played/worked with us both, all his busy daylong. Lunch we shared together, then Wyatt was off with Daddy and Cora for a much needed nap. We got garden, greenhouse, pigs, and children growing robustly and safely. And Wilber was feeling stronger, more centered and more himself, which made us all smile.

Chapter Twenty-Seven

John was dead. Nelly, John Nelson, little John, our loyal friend, best man and gentle soul, was dead. Wilber got the news during one of his Sunday evening calls to his parents, standing in a phone booth in the 150 Mile House parking lot. They had heard it from Joe, but had been unable to reach us until Wilber called them.

Wilber had been planning their visit to Knife Creek, confirming dates and arrangements for his parents and Margaret. They would rent a car, no trouble, at the Williams Lake airport. Freddie already knew his way around. "Don't worry about us." They were anxious to meet and hold Cora, pinch Wyatt, and see for themselves how Frankie was faring. They hadn't seen him since last December and they worried, generally more than they should have but in this case understandably so. Finally, just before he hung up, they told him about John, said that he needed to get in touch with Joe. They knew little of the circumstances—a motorcycle wreck, on the road between Alma and Fairplay, at the end of May.

Indeed, John had crashed his motorcycle on a notorious stretch of road, narrow and winding, with long stretches where a driver could pick up some serious speed. He had been drinking. He had been unhappy, struggling with Wilber and Joe away, without a lady, and trying to cope with the death of his German shepherd, Lady. The funeral had been in Wisconsin; his family had come to Alma to pick up his body. Joe had been in Seattle planning for a move to Alaska, but had gone back to Alma to help the Nelsons. The old friends cried together, bemoaned the loss and waste and what they wished they'd done. John was such a fragile, but sparkly character; now his angst had been buried with him.

Wilber brought me up to speed when he got home and was finally able to break down.

"I feel so old," he cried in my arms. "When your friends start to die, you *really* feel old… so fucking old."

"Oh, darlin'," you're not old, John wasn't old. Twenty-nine is NOT old. It was a horrible accident, not old age." I tried to make him see the random and cruel nature of it, but he could not be consoled. And I realized he *should* not be consoled. I had to let him work through it. I cried beside him, we felt the loss together. For John's family, for little Shanti, for us, for us all, John had been a strong and deeply caring friend. He had led the charge just last fall, for eight friends to show up at Knife Creek and prepare us for the long, hard blow of winter. He had refused to go home until he was sure that Wilber and our family were safe and warm. And he'd spent his time boosting Wilber back into the saddle, gently, but with the knowing confidence only your oldest and dearest pal can muster. No one could have done that for Wilber as well as John, with subtle love and nurturing.

Now we had to do something for John. Wilber talked of going

to Wisconsin. We knew we had neither the money nor the time for him to make such a trip. Besides his health, the new baby, the pigs, the new garden, and his parents due any day, he just couldn't leave. Timing is never good with death. John's family would understand. Too bad Joe hadn't been able to go either. Couldn't we write his family a letter and send them some photos from John's trip here? Wouldn't they love that? Wilber set about writing a lovely essay, an epitaph, and right then, while John and his love were fresh. I penned my condolences and feelings of loss in a postscript.

As I went about caring for Wyatt and Cora, I found myself beginning to think about all the turmoil in the outside world. I rarely had the time to dwell beyond the basic focus of our existence, as we toiled to have the life we wanted. Even as our lives hung in the balance of Wilber's recovery, I realized that war, famine, disease, and violence had somehow passed us by. I felt incredibly lucky watching over my growing brood. I thought about John, never really knowing his son, Shanti, estranged from Maxine. I thought about the unloved people and was overwhelmed by my luck. The care and sense of significance that I'd missed out on growing up I'd found in the family of my making. I had set off from my lonesome life in search of a better one, scanning my horizon for compassion, seeking to belong in the wilderness of America. I had chosen well.

Wilber's parents arrived before we'd had a chance to process John's death, and we were still raw when they drove in. Margaret was ironic and warm as ever, and she set the tone for a casual visit. Wyatt marched her over hill and dale, showing off his spread and making her laugh. We toured the lakes and had dinner in town, but mostly we played and cooed and hung around the farm. They were out of their element and I worried that Marjorie Morningstar might rear her pretty princess head, but politeness reigned. Hansi kept Fred from his nasty commentary and Margaret kept Hansi from a running critique on child rearing. It was a predictably short trip; they had to get back. There was Margaret's work, and, anyway, they had had enough of our deprivation. I think what they saw—our work on the farm, our garden and pigs, our darling, healthy (though noticeably filthy) children, and Wilber's increasing strength—gave them the comfort they'd come looking for.

Next up was Joe. Before his move to Alaska, he drove up to see our situation for himself. He was a loyal pal, like John, subtly assessing Wilber and our nest, and a sweet uncle to Wyatt and Cora, with whom he forged a lifelong bond. When he took Wilber on a fishing gambit, his new fetish, Wyatt begged to go, but I insisted he stay behind and help me make cupcakes instead. They were only off to Quesnel Lake for a few days, but the scene was of young boys and adventure, waders and hats, poles and bait over broad shoulders, packing the truck. Wilber and Joe needed man time, to sort out the conditions of their now dwindling tribe. I knew they would grieve for John while baring and buoying their own hopes.

I could tell Joe was concerned; the change in Wilber was visible. His compromised ego could be heard in his plans and dreams, which now included putting the farm on the market and moving. Unbeknown to his parents, we'd hatched a plan to relocate to Vancouver so Wilber could pursue training in a safer field. I even thought of taking some courses. University of British Columbia had married-student housing, on campus and cheap. We'd done some research, and the modern conveniences, with Wilber's limitations, were of growing interest to me.

The news from home via Joe was good. The hippies of Breckenridge were making their way into conventional society. Soon they'd all be buying and settling, like us, grabbing their piece of the peace. Joe was taking on investing, with a course and certification as a stockbroker. He would be living a comfortable lifestyle in Juneau. Susan and Stuart had set up some sort of a pyramid scheme in Anchorage and were flourishing. Bien was a valued and well-compensated personal shopper to the stars in San Francisco, where Martin, Tommy, and others had migrated. Betsy and Plum had moved on to New York City, working the finer restaurants as a bartender/waitress team. How they all loved and flourished in the cities was a mystery to us, but to each his own Eden.

It was sad to see Joe go, of course. It had been great to have a comfortable long-time friend, and another male around. Over our year in the Cariboo, we had become friendly with many Canadians in our area, hippies and townies, but had never found the kinship of our old friends back home. The culture of Canada was plain and simple, a little like that of the U.S. in the fifties. The conservative consumerism of the area was neither commendable nor condemnable; it was just not our style. And there was a certain, and not always favorable, attitude toward America and her people. Most loved to hate us, and *our* flagrant consumerism. The funny thing to us was that with the Canadian dollar inflated, Canadians were flocking over the border to buy more with their money. Frankly, I thought they hated how much they loved us…

On the first of July, the Stampede was upon Williams Lake again and the air of competition and horseshit filled the town. That year, we went to see it, indulging the ever-enthusiastic Wyatt. The rodeo was new to us, rough and aggressive. We sat in the stands, tiny cowgirl Cora in second-hand gingham and lace, Wyatt in bandanna, boots, and straw hat. We saw firsthand the thrills of Bareback Riding, the hysteria of the Barrel Racing and Pony Chariot Races, and the cowboy's skillful repertoire of Bull Riding, Tie-Down Roping, Cutting Horse, and Mountain Race events. The brutality of it made Wyatt squeal, but Wilber was disturbed and I thought of our upcoming pig slaughter. We ate hot dogs, bought banners, and savored the local color. Wyatt brought home a fascination for horses. He talked horses day and night, striding around in his hat and pantomiming gunfights and outlaws with great flair.

When crazy Tim had a horse needing pasture and approached us, we were happy to offer our yard for the great steed. Early one morning a trailer pulled up and out came a stunning bay horse. Wyatt and Wilber were thrilled by the idea of an animal other than the pigs, one with which they could actually play. Though all we ever did with the horse was to hobble and feed it, the pleasure of the beast was not lost on my cowboys. We watched him graze, and we loved the nuzzle of a great and beautiful beast.

The garden flourished that summer. Wilber was home all the

time. Disability paid the way and no one—doctors or foremen—talked to him of going back to the mill. The veggies and flowers in the garden were lush and gorgeous. Water flowed from the creek to the crops, still carried on our shoulders. The greenhouse was burgeoning with the produce of southern climes. Spicy peppers and luscious tomatoes ripened, while the cannabis we'd planted and nurtured begged pruning. They were stunning plants, thick and brilliant green, and the pinched leaves, dried, rolled, and smoked, gave us a taste of the super-pot we would soon harvest. The workshop was completed in Wilber's thorough craftsman style. With a froe made on his forge and cedar from our woods, he split shakes for the workshop roof. He took great pride in the work, but the finality was bittersweet: He was sprucing up the place to put it on the market.

Hoping to spare ourselves the broker's fee, we put an ad in the local papers, and a sign at the roadhouse: Thirteen acres, Two-story Log House, Barn, Greenhouse, and Year-round Creek. Asking only a few thousand more than we'd paid, we hoped to find a family who would love and care for it as we had.

The Websters were a young Canadian couple with a boy not yet two and one on the way. David and Giselle offered us a fair price and, with a little lawyer work, our dream farm would be ready for possession in late August. It broke our hearts to recall the excitement of our Knife Creek discovery, the hope of emigration, the new start. We had just gotten settled when the accident took our vision and blurred it, only to blind it completely with the acceptance of Wilber's inability to continue. We cried after the transaction, but we resolved to focus on another farm in the near future.

We'd be moving to Vancouver in September, to the UBC campus and to Wilber's completion of a teaching certificate. I was glad and proud of his goal to improve his earning power, but mostly to use his brilliant brain and inspire others through education. His new dream, of teaching history to teenagers, seemed to me a gift to the world—or at least to the community of Lillooet, the town we had plucked off a map. I had ridden through it on the train, on my way back from depositing Wilber at Vancouver General. Through the tears of fear in my eyes, I had made note of the town and surrounding mountains and wondered if it could be a future home. Located farther south along the Fraser River, it was a tiny village, casually growing on the healthy run-off of the Coastal Range. Wilber had yet to see it, but he dreamed of it too. And we were in desperate need of a new dream.

In the meantime, visitors kept coming. Apparently in the long, hot days of the northern summer, southerners swarmed like black flies to the remote beauty. We were happy for it.

The past April, we'd gotten a letter from Betsy in New York City. She and Plum were living on the Upper West Side. She wanted to come out, meet Cora, and see the farm and family. She could take the Canadian Pacific across Canada, then the bus to Williams Lake. She could be here by August 8th. Would that work? Through many months, letters, and calls, we made the plan. Visiting from the city, she would be a little freaked out by our lifestyle, a step back in time for her, but she'd dig it. There would be much for her to do, and we'd see a bit of the province while she was here. She didn't know that we'd sold the farm.

Chapter Twenty-Eight

Betsy's visit brought a simultaneous breath of fresh air and familiarity at a time of change and movement. Wilber loved her and her enthusiasm, remembering the way she enlivened Tiger with laughter and her willing wanderer spirit. She reminded us of the easy friendship of our brothers and sisters back in Colorado. I welcomed her, my long-separated sister, best friend, and confidante. With the kids, she was a Mary Poppins without the petticoats and umbrella. Wyatt's every whim was her inspiration, Cora's every whimper her intent. At night, she'd regale us with tales of city conquests, work, and entertainments. She seemed at the end of her urban exploration, finding the pace tiring and draining. We urged her to move back west, to find her own community of peace. There was no shortage of like-minded folks in her future.

She was impressed by our purity of lifestyle. Since our first communal kitchen, Wilber had insisted on healthy foods—no sugar, refined flour, prepackaged foods of any kind. It was another nod to his parents' poor habits, their sausages, cakes, and unhealthy weights. We would all be active and fit and not feed ourselves the poisons of modern society. I cooked from *Diet for a Small Planet,* when I used recipes, and still made the Tassajara bread. Homemade granola, crackers, yogurt, and sprouts—I loved creating our own staples. Wyatt was keenly aware of the restrictions; it only took one trip through Overwaitea to showcase what he was missing. Bright, child-seducing packages contained irresistible cookies and candies. He knew it.

After hearing Wyatt's mantra—"Wanna baby? Go to Overwaitea, twenty bucks!"—Betsy wanted to check it out. We had plenty to do in town, so we planned a trip. In the store, Wyatt in the cart guided us through the well-known aisles. It was a hot summer day, and Betsy naturally gravitated toward the frozen food chest. She bent over and picked up a container. Wyatt's little eyes widened, his mouth fell open, momentarily speechless. ICE CREAM?

"How about some chocolate ripple, or an ice cream sandwich for the ride home?" she asked. I looked at my little boy. He raised his pointy little finger to the item in question, his face red and eyes alert.

"Uh-oh!" he warned. His training spoke, his finger waggled. "Daddy weell keell you!!" Betsy stopped, looked at us, one to the other, and eased the container back to its icy depth. We all laughed, Betsy more surprised than I, and hugged Wyatt, Daddy's little champion.

Back at the ranch, it was indeed time for Daddy to kill something—the pigs. But after the rodeo we feared Wyatt would see the slaughter as sport, shooting and hanging the giant animal. To him, how could it be so different from the calves of the corral? So Betsy spirited him away on a walk/adventure while Wilber tended to the dirty deed.

"One minute in milk heaven, the next in piggy heaven," Wilber had said of the killing process. He and Bob had led the now giant pigs to the shed with a pan of milk, and when their heads were down, blam, blam! They went from animals to meat in moments. Once the butchering was done, we packed the steaks, roasts, and chops neatly in white wrappers to be frozen in our freezer, kept at Bob and Debbie's in town. The rest went to the butcher for sausage and bacon.

August 1975

Dear folks:

> *This note will be the last that I write for a few weeks as we start moving. To where we aren't certain – only somewhere in or near Vancouver. Today it's raining – has been a cool and wet summer save for those two hot weeks in early July. Very bummed out with the weather. Betsy arrived a few days back and tomorrow she, Cora and Nonnie will take a motor holiday into the Okanogan. Wyatt has a bit of the croup so will stay here with me. We can play a lot and hang out in the bachelor pad.*

> *Today I killed Porky and his two halves are hanging outside (cool weather is good for something!) so the meat can "set" for one day at least. Nonnie and I will butcher him tomorrow and take him to the freezer we have stashed in Wms. Lake before they head out. Seems incredible that that task is done, not much left to do save for pack up and harvest the vegetables.*

> *Then I will be off to the lower mainland to find a place to move us. Hopefully, we'll find a nice place near Richmond but with the housing shortage as acute as it is we'll settle for what we get. I'm hopeful and think we'll land a nice 2 bedroom bungalow somewhere.*

> *Anyway, I'll write again from a new location next month. Hope one of you will be able to come up on Oct. 8th for someone's birthday. Please remember never to promise Wyatt anything*

without producing. He pesters us constantly about cowboy boots. He never forgets. Tomorrow I'll try to call Margaret in Vancouver. Too bad she could not come for a visit but that's the breaks.

Take care

Love, Frank

Betsy and I were free to take the truck to the Okanogan for the peach and apricot harvest. We bundled Wyatt (despite his croup, he wanted to come) and Cora into the cab of the pickup, a tent, bags, and cook stove in the topper, and off we went. Down the Cariboo Highway, we drove through land I hadn't seen for over a year. In August it was brown, glowing with sagebrush and the Ochre Hills. Turning left on the Trans Canada Highway, we headed to Kamloops, then south to Kelowna and the verdant valley of the Okanogan River. The many reports of abundant orchards, terraced grapevines, berry brambles, and commercial crops held true. We rolled in, aching with excitement, yearning for the succulent stone fruit, berries, and warm climate veggies. Everywhere we looked, golden orbs of peaches, apricots, nectarines, and greenish pears weighted branches of huge old trees, set in rows as far as our eyes could see. Kids-in-a-candy-store never had it so good!

Work and accommodations came easy. For a week, we camped in one orchard or another, picking fruit in trade for fruit. Pick twenty boxes; get one. From sun up, we stood on ladders, plucking ripe peaches into bags, into boxes, onto tractors until we tired. Almost-three-year-old Wyatt entertained five-month-old Cora for the duration, with occasional distractions from our fellow workers or us. The kids were so good, happy to be warm and peach-fed, and, to Wyatt, sleeping in a tent was an adventurous game. At day's end, we'd walk or drive to an irrigation ditch or the lake for a long, cool soak.

When it was time to go home, Betsy and I learned, to our delight and a little apprehension, that we had earned seven hundred pounds of fruit. The boxes filled the bed of our hard-worn Chevy.

We were blown away. Not only would we have to hurry home to unload, sort, and clean all the fruit, we would then have to pit, cut, and can it all in simple syrup. I had the jars, honey, canning kettle, and—thank goodness—Betsy was staying on for another week. Time was against us as the fruit continued to ripen and soften in cardboard boxes. We headed out.

Halfway home, we pulled off the road to change drivers before we hit the fast four-lane Trans Canada. We were on a viaduct, crossing the Okanogan Valley toward Kamloops, on a good, straight stretch of road. But as Betsy eased the truck over, we realized that the shoulder was too soft. Sinking into the loose gravel, I looked out the passenger window, down a sheer twenty feet to a dry creek bed. The truck slid, the weight of the fruit pulling us onto the precipice. Quickly realizing our dire situation, she stopped and put on the brake. Inching our way out the driver's door, we gingerly transported the kids to a safe distance from the teetering vehicle.

"Jeez, we could lose the whole thing, fruit and truck," I wailed. We stood and worried, imagining our rolling pickup making quick peach/apricot sauce out of our bounty. We had only gas money left, nothing extra—ever—for emergencies. But I realized a tow truck was our only option. We would never drive that truck out of that spot. I ran to the nearest service station.

Panting, I told the attendant of our plight. Casually peering out his window, he agreed. We were in big trouble! He was calling the tow truck.

"Fifty dollar minimum," he warned, possibly sensing my poverty over desperation.

"Okay," I hollered over my shoulder as I ran back to Betsy and the kids. By the time I reached them, I saw two immense logging rigs, empty and piggybacked, pulled over. Betsy had approached one and was nodding vigorously.

"They're gonna pull us out," she laughed as she ran to me, Cora swinging from her hip, Wyatt holding back, craning to see the "BIG twucks!" One had begun strapping our rear bumper, while the other was pulling ahead. Two burly lumbermen, tough and caring, the stuff that built Canada, were working efficiently and fast. Traffic slowed around what appeared to be a tragedy in the making. It was hot and sticky, we were filthy and tired, and we felt completely rescued by these guys before anything even started to move. I could feel my tension ease, or maybe it was a cool breeze off the creek bottom, as the other truck hooked my front bumper. Wyatt was mesmerized.

"Now, one o' you get in and drive forward, real slow," the lumberjack ordered, and I obeyed. I had felt the damsel in distress, now prepared to trust strangers with our precious cargo. I got in, cranked 'er up, and awaited their signal. The first truck jerked forward, and my over-weighted rig lurched onto the road. The second truck followed, urging me into traffic. I soon had four wheels on pavement. They had made it effortless, and free. As they hopped out to unhook, I went toward them offering something, but they both shook their heads.

"Happy to help, ma'am," they offered, but when they finally glanced up from their work, I saw kind and tired eyes. They were happy to help and I wondered if their work was so unrewarding that this had been a bright heroic spot in their day. I gave them peaches in return. Much obliged. I gathered the kids and Betsy quickly; we had to get out of there before the tow truck, with its obligatory fifty-buck minimum, arrived. As we skedaddled across the valley, I saw the towing rig rise in my rearview mirror, and I put my foot on it. We did not need to have that conversation.

By dusk, we were pulling into Knife Creek, glad to be home and ready for the reunion. Piling into the house, we were stopped short by a scene of random chaos. Dishes scattered, chairs in disarray, a sense of disruption, followed by a deafening stillness.

"Daddy! Daddy!" Wyatt called as he burst through the door. Looking around, he turned to me, "Where *is* Daddy?" he asked as he headed up the stairs. We all followed, closely and fearfully.

What we found in the bedroom was confusing and disorienting. Wilber was splayed across the bed, blankets and sheets twisted around him and onto the floor. The windows were closed to the

August heat, and an unidentifiable smell hung in stagnant air. Clothes and shoes, books and cards were strewn around our small bedroom. Wilber appeared to be out cold, and Wyatt raced to wake him.

When he came to, his shock was apparent and greater than ours, and his explanations only added to my growing concern. He rambled about visitors, people coming to see us but not staying. He was sure it had rained hard (though the earth was bone dry), and he'd been unable to work on the packing. The horse had been loose (it was still hobbled in the yard), and he'd wandered far trying to claim it. He said he'd found mushrooms in the woods and picked them for his dinner. He'd cooked and eaten them, maybe he shouldn't have. He'd had a bad reaction. That was it, all he could remember. He'd drifted in and out of his head for the past few days.

How many days? What color mushrooms? What people? I sat on the bed and gently prodded him for answers. He showed no recollection of detail or sense of time. Had we already been to the Okanogan? And home so quickly?

He looked terrible. His hair and beard were matted and caked with food, throw-up, or sweat, I couldn't tell. His shirt was frayed, like he'd tried to tear it from his body. His recently clear and resolute look was weak and pale. He was tired, after sleeping for days, and his head was not right.

I was beyond worry, but I was also trying to humor him, agreeing with his diagnosis in order to avoid wounding his pride. What had happened? I thought about it briefly: the statistics, the "one-in-ten," the risk, his brilliant brain and stoic strength. Then, in my own state of denial or distraction, I let it go. What I didn't know then was that he'd been having seizures, that the scar tissue was causing a dangerous synapse on his brain. And what I couldn't have known was that there wasn't a damn thing we could do about it. But he may have understood the misfiring of his brain; his denial was stronger than mine.

There was much to do before we headed down the mainland in two weeks. Betsy and I cleaned and straightened the house and set about cleaning and canning the fruit. A week went by quickly and before we peeled and quartered the last apricots, Betsy had a train to catch, back to New York. I drove her to the station and we cried as she boarded the last train of the day. Then I gave her a big-sister grin and blew kisses until the train was out of sight. I wished I'd had a giant Canadian flag to wave. I loved the way my mother always took the Stars and Stripes off its bracket and spun it like a cheerleader whenever we left Twin Creek. The drama of tradition was never wasted on me. I stood for a lonely moment on the platform before remembering the enormous tasks ahead of me, and turning toward the truck and home.

For the first time in a long time, I took note of the passing sights on my ride home. Taking my time down the Cariboo Highway, I saw it again as I had just two years before, warm, golden, and welcoming. It had been a gift, this place, a settling and an education. Alone in the truck, I let the lingering summer warmth relax me. In the unusual quiet, my typically task-focused brain was flooded with a fleeting vision of my life and future. I realized how hard I had pushed the borders of my knowledge and strength. Passively gathering the skills to survive, I had led our family through a tough and long year. Emotionally, physically, mentally, I had aided my husband in his recovery, keeping track of the finances and chores so he could focus on healing. I had planted and harvested another season's garden, raised two pigs and two kids, and had been healthy and satisfied in the doing.

Emotions rushed in to fill the silence: fear, sadness, doubt, insecurity, anger, and grief. I mourned the loss, perhaps temporary, of our dreams. I cried in fury at the unbidden horrors we'd endured. I doubted my strength to continue. I choked on the possibility that my husband, my best friend, my rock, my love might be spiraling toward a crisis beyond my help. Was he already beyond my help? I could only stand in the river and guide his raft, calm the waters and avoid visible hazards. There was much unseen and unknown, in his subtle deterioration. I would fight for my family of four. In the calm of the familiar drive, I felt the woman I had become resolve to make the best of whatever lay ahead.

Soon we would be packed up and heading to Vancouver, and I had to admit I was more than a little exhilarated by the idea of electricity and indoor plumbing. For the first time in ages, I would be able to use a flushing toilet that wasn't in a hospital room. I could wash dishes with hot water from a tap, dirty water disappearing down a drain, and I could bathe the kids—and us—in a stationary bathtub. I imagined rubber toys and bubbles. The thought of stepping out of a hot bath into a warm room with fluffy towels gave me goose bumps. Lighting a dark room with the flick of a switch, warming at the touch of a thermostat, and push-button cooking were all privileges I would never take for granted again. And dialing a phone to talk to sisters, friends, and parents! I was pretty psyched to enjoy these luxuries, since I knew that in a short time, we'd return to where we belonged, and longed for—the backcountry. I knew we would again have the wilderness out our door, the satisfaction of heavy chores to keep us warm, and an outhouse of convenience. That's what we loved, how we wanted to live. But the well-trained consumer in me couldn't resist feeling relief at the thought of a costly but effortless lifestyle. It was like heading off on a luxurious holiday.

I turned down Knife Creek Road and bounced along, swerving around the expected potholes, riding between the tracks laid by logging trucks. Not for the first time in a year, sadness overcame me. The dreams of our family were not gone or abandoned, but this scenario and our proximity to independence had been so promising. Now we were turning our backs on all of it for a while. Would it be so easy to return? Life, as we'd seen, was unpredictable and, if we weren't diligent, perhaps our vision would vanish like a vapor in a breeze.

Back at the ranch, Wyatt and Cora were asleep. Wilber was packing the last boxes in the shed; long-abandoned horse-shoeing implements, forge, anvil, and all, would have to be stored until he was fit again. I wrapped my arms around his sagging shoulders and squeezed with all my might. His carpenter's tools, no longer needed for his livelihood, would help us build our own house one day. Each was painted with a red "W," visible but chipped. When he'd painted the letter on his tools back in Tiger, I'd said "Oh, that's W for Wilber?" But he upended the hammer shank. "No, it's M for Mine!!" His humor, so witty and sweet, had waned with the accident and now he set about his task with grim resolve. He was not looking forward to Vancouver. The move was his acceptance of his limitations, letting go his freedom and giving in to The Man, yet again. He worried more than me that we would ever reclaim our dream and saw no joy in indoor plumbing and electric lights. He would not go quietly or happily toward convention.

The new owners were pressing for the place. We would have to be out on schedule, and though they were young like us, they were aggressive. Of course, they were stepping into the paradise we had created. Our sad departure was their joyful arrival. David Webster's business was log-home building—the new log lodges we saw sprouting on newly tilled forest. His plan was to build new on the property. Would he be demolishing our little cabin? We didn't ask or want to know.

We needed a trailer for all the stuff we'd accumulated. The truck with topper could no longer hold the lives of four. The rocking chair from the miner's cabin in Colorado, the wood stoves, tools, my treadle sewing machine and the crib, handmade dressers, and toys of a young family filled the trailer and followed us out. We had to leave the hand-hewn log bed Wilber had built in our bedroom, where Cora was conceived and born. On the headboard, Wilber had carved a crude heart, a simple embellishment of our minimalist life. To disassemble it and drag it into our city life seemed wrong, but so did leaving it for strangers. Such would be the struggles of our coming year, full of decisions that pitted our hearts against our heads.

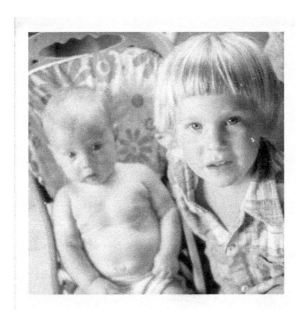

CHAPTER TWENTY-NINE

In quiet contemplation, we drove south. Leaving the Cariboo, wild country we'd just begun to explore, we craned our necks to catch views of lakes, hills, and towns rolling by. Cora slept on the floor or nursed in gulping hunger. Wyatt perched—toot-toot—in his seat between Mommy and Daddy, moving toward an adventure. It was his favorite place to be.

I could see that Wilber was brooding. Far from a journey of discovery and enchantment, to him this was an admission of failure. I worried for him, for us. The roadside was unremarkable, dusty, and depressing until we reached Clinton, where the waters ran from the Cariboo Range and greened the land. At Cache Creek we joined the Trans Canada and soon rode along the Thompson River. The valley opened then shut again where the Thompson met the Fraser River at Lytton. Continuing south, we dropped deeper into the canyon between the Coast Mountains to the west and the Cascade Range to the east. At Yale, the canyon opened up and the river widened again, heading toward Hope. Too bad Hope wasn't our destination—there the river turned west into a lush lowland called Fraser Valley, a verdant festival of market farms, dairies, and parks. As we approached the lower mainland, the river lost its wild tumult and succumbed to the demands of civilization. Large housing developments, expansive towns, pulp mills, and other ills took its fresh mountain waters and returned gray and milky effluent to its discharge in the sea.

In Vancouver, we headed to the townhouse assigned to us by the university. After getting through the city, we entered the University Endowment Lands, hectares of forest and trails. We were enchanted and encouraged by the wildness that separated the campus proper from the city tension. Approaching Melfa Court, we passed parks, playgrounds, and yards around neat, two-story houses. Families were taking in the sunny fall Saturday. The colors of elms and oaks and the purpose of the day reminded us of the back-to-school anticipation of our childhoods. We would be okay here, and Wilber would see the brightness of his future, I was sure of it.

Our little townhouse was a duplex, attached by one wall to another two-story house, surrounding a courtyard filled with identical units. The exterior looked tired, the stucco stained with rust and mold, the trim faded and peeling. But the shouts and laughter of children and the large trees encompassing the square were inviting. We parked and abandoned the truck, all trundling in to our new home, running from room to room, kitchen-living-dining-bath. Wyatt was hot on our heels as we climbed the stairs, bedroom-bath-bedroom with large windows and big closets. The whole place was painted with a fresh coat of white; the floors were wood and the fixtures simple. The living room had sliding doors that opened to a small unfenced patio, grass, and trees. We were on the corner and the sky rolled eastward. We breathed in the openness and went to unpack.

On our first morning, the neighbors came a'visiting, a true Canadian welcome. But they were not Canadian at all. They hailed from New Zealand, Australia, Germany, and California, and had been on campus long enough to offer thorough, welcome advice. They told us where to shop, how to get to the best beaches, when the garbage went out, and where the preschool was. It had not occurred to me to send Wyatt to school, but at almost three, according to the other parents, he was prime for the campus nursery. All the preschoolers in the quad would be there, and he'd love it.

So school began immediately for both Wilber and Wyatt. After an extended trip to the supermarket to stock our ample shelves and fridge and a stop at the Student Union for notebooks and texts, we were set to dive in. School clothes would have to wait until the next weekend.

After our standard breakfast of oatmeal and orange juice, we trudged out that Monday morning at eight o'clock to make classes and preschool. Running across the quad, Wyatt slowed as he sidled up to the brightly painted one-room building. He peered in the large windows and blushed at the sight of the other kids. A super-sweet young teacher was greeting them, each by name and with a kind word. I knew the teachers were all child development students and elementary student teachers, cut out for and dedicated to nurturing. My heart filled with memories of my first school days, when I clung to my mother's legs and hid behind her. I pulled Wyatt to my side and gave him a quick and reassuring hug before sending him inside. Cora and I watched as he navigated the crowd. A few of the older kids we'd met encircled him, shepherding him to their favorite toys. I could see that he was at once enamored of the unlimited options and overwhelmed by the strangers. I turned to leave, knowing that he'd be fine, or they'd call me. I did after all have a phone! And we'd see him in a few hours, anyway; his morning session was over at eleven-thirty. He'd be home in time for the comfort of lunch and a nap with his sister.

Back at Melfa Court, I set to home-making. The weekend had been rushed, and our stuff lay piled all about. After I shook off the immensity of the task, I took it on room-by-room. I filled the kitchen with new packages of cereals, flours, sugar (Wilber had finally relaxed his ban), fresh spice jars, and oils. The coal-grimed jars and boxes from the shelves of Knife Creek looked like throwaways, but to me they were mementos that gave character to the store-bought glare. The living room needed a couch, dining table, and more chairs than the rocker and Wilber's college trunk. We would have fun shopping garage sales, I reckoned, all new to us.

Wyatt had had a good day. In fact he didn't want to leave the school and friends at morning's end. He was set. Wilber, on the other hand, liked his teachers, but was already frustrated with the other students (young and unsophisticated) and the curriculum (simple and outdated). As a graduate of one of the United States' finest universities, he had a leg to stand on, but I wished he'd see opportunity instead of limits. He was bristling with annoyance and long-spent patience when he got home, and he snapped at all of us. I tried to calm and encourage him, but after several attempts at optimism my temper came up short, too. It was a tough evening.

The weeks in our new life flew by as we organized the new house, got our bearings in a new city, and settled in. With all the distractions, I didn't notice the deepening deterioration of Wilber's attitude. He was gruff and impatient with Wyatt, dissatisfied with my housekeeping and cooking, and had little time for darling six-month-old Cora, all of which I blamed on his irritation at his forced conformity. While I tried to salvage the year we had planned, Wilber seemed to be sabotaging my goodwill. He was falling apart.

As if on cue, my parents and Dede drove up for a few days. Their time was short, and there was tension between Wilber and Kenny, as always, but perhaps worse. Their presence did little to buoy my husband or support our choices. My dad never accepted the importance of education, took issue with Wilber's plans for his family, and questioned our ability to pay our own way. Though we had never asked for a loan or handout, I could feel his fear at the possibility that we might end up needing him. His worst nightmare!

In their still-shiny BMW, we toured the city, parks, and campus. We picnicked in Stanley Park, admiring athletes and autumn flowers. Though the weather was crystalline blue and gold, my mother noticed a preponderance of ferns and moss, telling of a damp climate. Of course, it made sense—the coast would be rainy. We were on the west side of the Coast Mountains, where Pacific systems would stall and dump moisture for days. We remembered the drippy season in Bridgeport, and I was happy that we wouldn't be managing it in a tipi, glad for the white walls and many windows of our townhouse. After brunch, on our tiny patio, my parents and their impressions were gone. Dede, too.

A letter came from Betsy, reminding us to appreciate what we had.

dearest nonnie poms a roonie,

back in the city and into the routine-work, play, work, play.
plum still doing the bartending thing and cabbing, late hours. me waitressing 2 jobs.

what can I say, you have the life with your kids and wilber, your amazing garden, sweet place, (no more pig though)! I won't soon forget that day, me in the woods trying to keep wyatt away from the carnage!

so glad we had that time on the road and fruit-picking. wyatt kept us laughing and cora so sweet, I miss them and you.

got some neat photos and I'll send copies soon. hope wilber is feeling better and back on the horse (know what I mean??)

well, life is happy and busy here, though I miss your little family and life in the wilds of Canada.

love to you all, especially you my sister dear.

xoxoxoxoxo bep

I began taking classes at the University Extension. Wilber and I were both excited about the weaving class, which included carding, dyeing, spinning, and making a simple loom. Our natural dyes came from the moss nearby, berries around campus, and the onionskins I could now rescue from the disposal. I also signed up for a writing class, creative and easy. I wanted to write poetry, songs, and stories of my colorful life. The classes were at night, and though it was a complete departure for me, going out at night and by myself, I loved it. I began asking around about the GED, the substitute for a high school education. It was simple to get, and with that "diploma" I could enroll at UBC. I had talked to Wilber many nights about going to college. I would have loved to learn to write, paint, weave, but mostly I wanted to be a midwife. I dreamed of serving women who wished for a birth like Cora's. I wanted to be like Mary, the loving midwife of Wyatt's almost home birth. If I could be that gift to mothers and fathers in our new community, I thought I'd feel incredibly fulfilled. Wilber encouraged me. Living on campus, the excitement over learning was infectious. Whispers of my ambition led me onward.

Hansi and Fred didn't come for Wyatt's birthday, which disappointed Wilber, but the cowboy boots arrived, along with a new hat. We had a small party with the Melfa Court kids, all girls. They swooned over our proud and strong three-year-old, stomping around in his boots, hat, and the cowboy shirt I'd made to complete the ensemble. More chocolate cake, this time at home with Daddy and little Cora. Wyatt was happy. We were all getting happy here, I thought.

But in mid-October, I got a call from Wilber's student-teaching advisor. He had been working in a high school, his practicum teaching history to teenagers. She was concerned with what she called "irrational and hostile" outbursts and wondered if there was a problem at home. She said the incidents were unpredictable and infrequent, but she was considering pulling him from the classroom. I knew that would devastate him, and I asked her to let me talk to him first. She would but urged me to be prompt; the students were at risk.

My fair and pensive husband was losing his cool in public? My

avoidance and acceptance of his condition, it turned out, was unloving and had become dangerous. I was not helping by trying to
placate his moods.

"Wilber, Miss Rogers called today," I began that evening, after
I'd put the kids to bed. As usual, my timing was off and he was
trying to relax.

"What the fuck? My teacher called you? What the hell is going
on?" He was angry.

"Nothing…" I tried to stay calm. "She just said she didn't think
you were so happy."

"Really? What the fuck does she care?" He raged instead of
showing his worry.

"She wondered if we'd talk about it. She said you're doing really
well in class, but you've yelled at the kids? Are you okay?" At that I
saw I'd gone too far, pushed the ego.

"No, I can't believe you two have been talking behind my back!"
He was threatened and a little freaked out. "What the fuck?"

"Will you at least think about it?" I prepared to drop it. "Maybe
you'd like a different field or maybe elementary instead of those
pain-in-the-ass high school kids." He stormed up the stairs to bed.
He was white-hot mad, fuming, and I could feel his energy spiraling. I didn't know what to do.

Experiences with my dad had taught me to run away from anger. I'd never learned how to relieve it, in my loved ones or myself.
Sure, it was easy with kids—a hug, a kiss, a soothing word. But
with Wilber I worried a soothing word would sound condescending, and a hug or kiss would feel pettish. What could I do? I wandered the first floor, picking up the phone, contemplating whom
I might call, and putting it down, over and over. It was too late
in NYC to call Betsy. My mother would only say, "Oh, God, oh,
dear" in soothing tones, but unhelpful, and every other friend lived
without phones. This new phone thing was not so great after all. I
opened the fridge and hung on the door. Nothing in there could
fill my aching. I read a little, then crawled up the stairs. I changed
and brushed my teeth quietly, hoping Wilber was sleeping off his

mood. By the time I crawled into bed, our foam pad back on the floor, I felt tense and guilty. I had not handled the situation well, but I couldn't have let it go. I was damned either way.

Chapter Thirty

I awoke in the middle of the night, in the middle of a storm. Something hit me in the head. My legs were being kicked. Blankets and sheets had been torn away. In the dark, in the shaft of yellow light from the street, I could just make out Wilber's movements. He was flailing and flogging, jerking erratically. With a silent yet violent thrust, he made his way to the top of the mattress until his head bashed against the wall. Then there was noise, harsh and hollow. I rolled off the pad and got to my knees. I reached out to him, but his arm, or leg, slapped me away. I dared not leave him to turn on the light, but what could I do in the dark? My actions became automatic. "Hold him down," I was thinking, "Keep him away from the wall."

I couldn't see his eyes rolling, his arm, legs, and torso moving involuntarily, his face contorted in terror in the dark of that moment, but I would imagine them later. Just as suddenly as the episode began, it was over and Wilber lay exhausted and panting on the bed. He made a low rumbling sound, a nonhuman, mournful non-sound, like a great exhaling of energy. As I crouched, panic rolled through me. I got up carefully to turn on the light and went back to his side. He appeared to be unconscious, his body gone from rigid to flaccid in an instant, his skin white and soft. He always slept naked and I could see bruises forming on his arms. The bedding was wet.

I called his name. "Wilber, darlin'?" I whispered, and then spoke a little louder. "Wilber, what's going on?" I pleaded for a response, but he was out. His breathing was regular, his face calm now, like he was resting. I looked him over carefully for any blood or cuts and covered him with a blanket. Then, panic welling and barefoot, I rushed down the stairs, flung open the door, and ran to the neighbors.

Emma and Todd were from Australia, kind and proactive, that much I knew. That, and the fact that she was a registered nurse. I banged on their door, at least the door I hoped was theirs. In my frantic state, all the entrances off the courtyard looked the same. Todd opened the door, Emma following close behind. I muttered confusion and urgency. She put on her shoes and raced past me to the house. Todd followed. In a flash Emma was kneeling next to the mattress, trying to talk to Wilber while feeling his pulse and checking his eyes.

"Tell me exactly what happened," she whispered over her shoulder. She knew the story of the accident, surgery, headaches, and odd behavior from our mothers' coffee klatches.

"Grand mal seizure," she said, confirming my fears. She turned to Todd. "Call the paramedics."

In the aching minutes we waited, she tried to convince me that this was common, controllable, and soon cured. Her voice wavered. She was not convincing me, but I clung to her knowledge and experience. The paramedics arrived in a blare of horns and a glare of lights. They woke the entire courtyard, and I could see neighbors peeking from their doors. Up the stairs and by Wilber's side, they began taking his vitals and trying to wake him, calling on the walkie-talkie for the gurney from the van. With the activity, Wilber broke out of his stupor enough for them to begin a surreal line of questioning: Have you been taking drugs? A little LSD, maybe? Mixing with booze?

Emma, Todd, and I were shocked. Suddenly, I saw these life-saving heroes as judgmental, hippie-hating rednecks. Emma stepped forward and told them, firmly and clearly, about Wilber's history, about Dr. Turnbull, about the seizure.

"Get him to the hospital right away," she cried. "And get the neurosurgeons in to see him. This man is critically ill." I realized then that in addition to being persuasive, Emma was also scared. She stayed with the kids, who hadn't been awakened by the commotion. "Stay as long as you need," she'd said as I slid in next to my unconscious husband in the waiting ambulance.

Within moments we were hurtling down University Boulevard toward the all-too-familiar Vancouver General Hospital. While one paramedic drove, the other joined me in the back, monitoring vitals and calling ahead. I was glad he was in charge, but as I eavesdropped on his calls I never heard a request for a neurosurgeon, or the words brain damage or injury. After ruing those expressions for so long, now I wished to hear them shouted ahead of us. "Brain damage, incoming!!"

Which is why when we finally reached the ER and were whisked through the entrance, I stood and Wilber lay limp on the gurney in the lobby for what seemed like hours. And why, I guessed, when they eventually got him into a curtained exam room, they took their time checking and questioning him. He was unconscious, shouldn't that have told them something? I waited with him, stroking his hand, his brow, his cheek, and talking quietly and haltingly to him, trying to provoke a response. After an hour, I was so distressed by his unchanged and unattended state and my inability to help that I left the curtained cubicle and moved to the waiting room. I sat on a cold plastic chair, amid the sick and injured.

"What are you doing out here? Your husband's all alone, and you leave him?" A nurse was hovering over me suddenly, frantically shouting at me. "He's calling for you, how could you leave him?"

"He's unconscious," I said, fighting back tears of fear and futility.

"Well, he's calling, he needs you." Her tone was judgmental, condescending. "Are you punishing him or something?"

I was furious, freaked out, feeling a hot welling of shame as I rushed back to Wilber, who still lay unconscious, exactly as I'd left him just minutes before. What was going on? Wasn't time being wasted here? WHERE were the FUCKING DOCTORS?

Finally, two legitimate doctors did arrive, and I begged them to call Dr. Turnbull. "He knows this case, he performed the surgery less than year ago." Did they even have my husband's records?

"We can't just call Dr. Turnbull down to ER in the middle of the night. He's a very busy man," was their dead-end reply. No one was calling Dr. Turnbull. Leave it to them, I was told, they were in charge. I recognized the small-time doctors' egos that had gotten us here in the first place. They must have been residents, because their response showed no gumption at all. I knew Ian Turnbull, and, in hindsight, I should have called him myself.

Their interview and assessment of my unconscious, brain-injured, brain-infected, brain-operated husband went as well as they expected. I couldn't bear to watch, so I waited just outside the curtain.

"He appears to be mad about something," was their final diagnosis. No, they had not seen his records. "Did you two have a fight? Is everything okay at home, with the family?"

"We're going to release him," they calmly announced after a minute of "consultation." "Keep an eye on him for any change, but we think he's just tired and out-of-sorts." I was shocked, but frankly feeling too scared and helpless to know what to do. Maybe

Fred was right about my youthful inexperience. I didn't know where to turn.

"What about the grand mal seizure?" I pleaded. "Can't you test for the cause of that?"

"We're not sure it was a seizure. Your account was sketchy, we have no proof."

"But he had major brain surgery just ten months ago. He has brain damage. Please? Can't you at least keep him for observation??" My pleas fell on deaf ears. The "doctors" were on to the next cubicle. I looked at Wilber and realized I didn't even have a car. I had no family to call on, only friends I didn't know, and two small babies. How could they send me home with this now-semi-conscious man? I began to cry. I couldn't handle this, it had been a long night and I was terrified.

"Listen, you both came in the ambulance, right?" One of the doctors poked his head through the curtain. "I get off in a few minutes and I live out toward UBC. How 'bout I give you a ride home?"

"Oh, yeah, that'd be swell." Like he was offering us a great gift. Dismissing Wilber in this state, and now giving us a ride *away* from the one safe place we needed to be.

Again, we were hurdling down University Boulevard in this man's red Camaro, back the way we'd come just hours earlier. The doctor was feebly trying to make small talk. Where were we from, what was Mr. Neumann studying? Wilber hadn't even been able to walk to the parking lot—a wheelchair delivered him to the sports car. He certainly wasn't holding a conversation and my mind was reeling. Dawn was just beginning to light the day. A rosy glow played in the sky behind us. But as we passed through the Endowment Lands and into the housing complex, I felt a dark foreboding. I directed the doctor to our unit.

As he came to a stop next to our truck, Wilber's arm flopped over the back of his seat, reaching for me. His shaking hand grasped mine. Faintly, he squeezed; audibly, I shuddered. Slumped semi-conscious in the bucket seat, his head lolled on Naugahyde.

In his grasp, I felt his tenacious fight flow between our trembling hands, his touch so familiar, yet so desperate and weak. At that moment, the thrashing and kicking began again. His torso pushed stiff against the seat, his legs beat the floorboards, his arms twitched and, with a final press of fingers entwined, his grasp slipped—from me, from life. Hands bashed doors and hardware, feet jerked and contorted against vinyl.

"Oh my God!" the doctor screamed. "That's a grand mal seizure. We've got to get him back to the hospital right away!" It was over as quickly as it began, and Wilber slumped, all that violent energy now sucked back into his damaged body. His hands, bleeding and swollen, would never reach for me again. That loving touch I will forever remember was the last moment my young husband and I shared.

As he put the car in reverse, I felt the maternal pull of the townhouse—the morning, the children, breakfast, school, and the responsibilities of my other reality.

"Wait," I cried, "let me just check on the kids and follow in the truck."

"Right, okay," he stammered, leaning forward to let me out. "We'll be back in the ER. Come quickly."

I raced into the house. Emma looked up from the pad on the living room floor, concern visible on her face. I whispered that I needed to go back. She nodded with a reassuring smile. I could hear Cora waking and ran upstairs to nurse her before Wyatt stirred. For a few minutes I bathed in her gentle innocence, a contrast to the violence in the Camaro. As soon as she had drunk her fill, I handed her, wet diaper and all, to Emma. I needed to follow my husband. All would be fine at home. I left, semi-aware of racing through the dawn, parking in the lot, running to the ER, finding Wilber and the doctors now attentive. They had called Dr. Turnbull, who was waiting in the ICU. No time for I-told-you-so's, soon we were rolling—the gurney, Wilber, a young aid, and me. In the underground tunnels that connected hospital wings, up and down elevators, we hustled my unconscious husband. The aid looked as scared as I was.

During the long journey, one thought gripped my throat: "What if he convulses now? What will this boy and I do to help him?"

It seemed an eternity before we arrived on the Intensive Care floor. It was at once familiar and terrifying, and I wished Wilber would wake up and comfort me. I looked into his face, gray with fatigue and misshapen with brain damage. Dr. Turnbull was there, busy, focused. He rushed Wilber into an IC room. I was alone, and finally Wilber was with experts. Finding the nearest perch, I collapsed in a flood of tears.

In the deepening stillness, I thought back on the events of the past year: the "mushroom" incident at the cabin, the intense headaches, complaints, and irritations of a tough and steady man. I recalled his nurse's words after surgery—they had haunted me then and ever since—"Dr. Turnbull did everything he could." Was the infection still in his brain and festering? Could the damage have spread?

"Mrs. Neumann?" Dr. Turnbull's authoritative stature loomed over my weeping confusion. I looked at him for answers, good and true ones. "It appears there has been swelling in the brain. We're not sure why. The pressure built up on your husband's brain and caused the seizures, a warning sign. We're doing everything we can." Where had I heard that before? I tried to focus and listen carefully.

"There is nothing you can do for him, and I need to get back in to him." He sounded so sure: a diagnosis, a cure, and a team of competent doctors. "You should go home to your kids. They need you now."

I was torn. Who needed me more? What if Wilber woke up and was alone? Wyatt would be in school by now; Cora safely cared for by someone in the quad. What could I do? My judgment faltered, as it had been known to do without Wilber's guidance. I was frozen, unable to move.

After a few hours spent watching his door and the movement of doctors and technicians, each in turn giving me a kindness and advice to go home and rest, I left my vigil. I walked the hall, looking for a phone. A nurse directed me to a private area and I called Fred. After a brief description of the past twelve hours, I held the phone away as panic and anger filled the earpiece, Hansi gasping in the background. "I'll call the doctor right away," was his predictable response. He hung up before I could warn him that the doctor was pretty busy.

Back at my post, the afternoon dragged on and there was no news from inside Wilber's room. Hushed voices and an electric whirring could be heard (I later learned they had cut open his skull). Looks of sympathy came to me from nurses coming and going. Finally, Dr. Turnbull appeared with a final plea.

"This is going to be a long process. You *must* get some rest." His eyes were kind but tired. It had been eight hours, and I sensed the late October early sunset through the long windows in the hall. I could go home and feed the kids, watch a little TV, and rest, maybe even sleep. Dr. Turnbull was right. I was of better use to Wyatt and Cora right now.

"Can I see him before I go?" I asked, innocent of the policies.

"We're working on him now," the doctor said. "It really isn't a good idea." Reluctantly I left the building and drove toward the setting sun, visions of what "working on him" might look like bumping around in my tired brain and heart.

After dinner brought by neighbors, I called the hospital many times, moved our bed to another corner of our room, and changed the sheets. I hoped that a new perspective would erase the nightmare of last night and allow me to rest. I sang my tender darlings to sleep and settled into my bed. Pulling the phone near, I dialed the IC floor one more time and heard the same update: "condition unchanged." Curled around Wilber's pillow, I cried myself to sleep.

Chapter Thirty-One

Disoriented at pre-dawn, I slowly became aware of the phone ringing. Did I have to answer? I shuddered as I picked up, my voice hoarse with sleep.

"Nonnie, Dr. Turnbull called this morning. *Frankie's gone!*" Fred's voice boomed. "Our boy is gone."

The phone fell from my hand.

I bellowed, howling "NO" to a phone gone dead, into his pillow, now cold and wanting. NO. To a life no longer of my making. NO. This couldn't be. NO. He was too young. NO. It's our family. NO. I'm too young. This was wrong, a mistake, a bad dream. My howl came from the love and hope in my soul, but spoke to no one.

I screamed, and called to him. I wrung myself out weeping.

Soon my brain began force-feeding me the realities of my immediate future. My dark room lightened, and with it, Wyatt and Cora called their morning greetings. "G'morning, Mommy and Daddy," Wyatt chirped. Cora trilled a bird-like call, the spirits of the day awakening. I went to them, lifting Cora from the cradle that Wilber had made, pulling Wyatt close. I carried them back into my bed and clung to them. I just wanted to feel their hearts beating and energy pulsing, to lie with them all day, forever maybe, and shut out the noise of reality. But soon Wyatt got antsy, afraid of my intensity or just being three, or both. He jumped up and began to voice the demands that would eventually lead me out of my gloomy hole.

From my cave-like bed, the day pressed in with responsibilities: the kids, the hospital, the families, the body. The body? I needed to go back to the hospital, to see him one last time. I needed to talk to Dr. Turnbull, to find out what happened and to know what the end was like. I needed completeness, something concrete, not just a voice from a thousand miles away. Between fits of sobbing and stone silence, I called the hospital.

Dr. Turnbull had left the hospital and could not be reached. He must have been distressed, losing a patient he'd seen almost from the beginning. Could I see the body? The nurses and attending doctors advised against it. "We had to do a lot of work on Frank's head to relieve the pressure. We were doing just that when he died. You really don't want to see him in this condition." My imagination conjured gruesome scenes of blood and tissue. No, I didn't think I would want to see.

I called my parents. They were stricken and would come right away.

"Oh. I have to tell you," my father added, "Poppy, my dad, your grandfather, died this morning. I just got a call from your Aunt Anne. Heart attack."

"Oh my God. Then you're going to Baltimore," I said, accepting that priority.

"No, I'll be in Vancouver, I can go east later." His words were a relief. "I loved Wilber more than I ever loved my dad. It's okay." I hoped he wouldn't change his mind. As suddenly as I'd become a widow, my dad had reemerged in my psyche as my Main Man. Unsettling and comforting, in turn.

It was time to take Wyatt to school. Breakfast, nursing Cora, dressing, composing myself. Time pressed on. I'd only had a few hours to grieve. The rest would come later. My parents would be there in the afternoon. In the meantime, I had to figure how to put one foot in front of the other.

"Where's Daddy?" Wyatt asked, naturally, on our way across the campus to his little school. His blue eyes looked to me for the truth. At the tender age of three, he was suddenly fatherless. I was now his only parent, his comfort and consistency.

"He's gone away for a little while," I lied, my judgment impaired by insecurities and fear. How could I tell him that his daddy was gone forever? I still didn't believe it myself. I was the child, awaiting the judgment and comfort of my own parents. They would know what to tell him. I didn't want to upset him.

The following days melded into a surreal pattern of meals, phone calls, arrivals, departures, flights, talks, and, of course, diapers, bedtimes, stories, games, and questions. At some point a man appeared at my door with a large check from the Worker's Compensation Board, which I was relieved to see (as all survivors must be). I signed and cashed it right away. Hansi and Fred would not be coming to Vancouver—they were arranging the funeral in Denver. My parents arrived soon, Betsy not far behind. Kenny went to the hospital for Wilber's things, and to make arrangements for the body. Dr. Turnbull had left for the weekend without signing the death certificate, so we would have to wait until Monday for the cremation. We waited, mostly in silence. I remember eerie walks about the campus, the elevator in their hi-rise hotel scaring Cora, surreal dinners in public places, crying through a movie, shopping for something black, all planned as a distraction. My family tried for normalcy.

But there was no distracting us from the fact that life as I knew it was over. Normalcy was gone and would have to be rewritten. Thankfully, for the time being, nature had worked its wiles on me, causing me to shut down in self-protection, to feel numb to the world and to hold my private pain so deep that it couldn't escape. On Monday, Dr. Turnbull finished the paperwork and the body was cremated.

The finality of that hit me as I sat by a window watching the autumn leaves curl and wither to the ground. At precisely 2:00, I knew Wilber's body was being rolled into the chamber, meeting thousands of degrees of flame. I envisioned flames licking at his rough feet and strong toes, his hairy skier legs, his life- and pleasure-giving groin, his slim waist and wide chest, his long arms (like a monkey, he'd said), and his able hands, the hands I had caressed for the last time just the other night. I sobbed in gulps when I imagined the fire at his face, singeing his thick beard, perfect ears, Neumann nose, supple lips, intense but weak brown eyes, plastic cheek, and thick, irresistible hair. It was gruesome and painful, but my mind went there. There was finality to it, and somehow the torturous pain of that reality gave the other, grander pain a momentary rest.

Soon, we were on the plane to Denver and the rest of the family. Unbeknownst to me, my father carried the ashes in a small case, which incurred the suspicions of the airlines. I noted his deft distraction and the whispers with a nod toward me, which must have abated or embarrassed the authorities, because they stepped aside and let us proceed. When we arrived at the Neumanns' home, I recognized and missed the calm my parents and Betsy had brought to Vancouver. The Cherry Creek house was awash with friends I did not know. The entire Jewish community poured into their little house, bringing food and condolences. "No parent should have to bear the pain of burying their child." Hansi and Fred had lost so much, family and possessions to Hitler, parents and friends to illness and old age. But losing a child to a senseless accident, it was unbearable. My sisters and Margaret encircled Wyatt, Cora, and me.

Finally, the funeral at the neighborhood synagogue, which Wilber had never attended, officiated by a rabbi Wilber had never met. His eulogy, vapid and uncomfortable, made that painfully obvious. I clung to Wyatt and Cora. My sisters reached over the pew from behind, squeezing my shoulders. I cried uncontrollably into my mother's arms. When I dared look up and around, the stoic stares of my in-laws made me gush anew. In their shock, I thought, they could not let the emotions come. My heart broke for them.

The cemetery was bleak, a blustering winter chill settling on the opening in the dirt. A brief prayer, then those who wished to filed up to toss a handful of dirt onto the urn. We sat and watched. I had never been to a Jewish funeral, or any funeral, in fact. The mourners were somber and stoic, of course, but not visibly emotional until our friend Joe came forward. Stepping up to the dirt pile, he grabbed a clod and looked at it, then into the hole, then to the sky. Tears streamed down his darkened face. Suddenly overcome with anger, he raised his arm and threw the dirt at the remains of his best friend with all his might. As if to say, "How dare you leave us?" Joe had boldly acted for all of us. Then he crumpled back into his seat.

That single act was a token of the time and caring of Joe in our lives. The last of the University of Wisconsin three, he was blown away to pieces by the loss of both John and Wilber within a single year. But he was still able to shower the kids and me with comfort and care. He was particularly attentive to Wyatt, knowing the importance of keeping him in focus while heartache rose around him. They kicked a ball around the yard and got silly together. I loved him so—we'd shared so much together, especially Wilber and his life. No one in the world knew or appreciated us better than Joe. So when Hansi took me aside and mentioned that Joe might make a good husband to me and a great father to our kids, I could see how well-intentioned her observation was, despite its wrongness. Joe was my friend and my brother, and he would remain so forever.

That afternoon, when we returned to the Neumanns', the arrival of our friends, the dirty hippies from Breckenridge, opened my heart to truly grieve our loss and celebrate Wilber's life. My dad went out and bought cases of beer and we all sat in the backyard and told funny Wilber stories. We spent the afternoon laughing and yelling out Wilberisms. Everyone had a few, and sharing the joy of his life retied and strengthened our bonds, the bonds we knew we'd need. We all agreed that he would have wanted it that way, and that we hoped there'd be laughter at our funerals, someday.

For now we had to adjust to the fact that Wyatt and Cora would never have or know their father. The love of my life, my soul mate and partner, my guide and mentor, was gone. Just gone.... And the rest was up to me to plan and live. He'd left no instructions. For now I'd go back with my parents to their ranch in Idaho, putting the sadness and reality on hold until I could think again. There was plenty of room for our family of three.

We settled in, and I promptly forgot about the townhouse in Vancouver. That strange place where Wilber's shoes sat by the door, where he hadn't stood since that awful night when I upset him with my meddling, where his clothes hung heavy in the closet, sodden with scents and memories of him and us, and his glasses, toiletries, and towel were right where he left them, waiting to be used. I wasn't ready to return to it. That place held nothing good for me.

My mother cared for us. She fed Wyatt and Cora just the right amount of patience and encouragement and gave us routine, healthy meals to nurture our bodies and keep us on track. She was calm and gentle. She had found her second chance. Curling up under the mohair throw, a grandchild hooked in each arm with a stack of our childhood books, or walking slowly wherever Wyatt wanted to lead her, she managed the care of our souls. At eight months, Cora was my baby dear, still nursing and just beginning to find glee in her brother's antics and a good tickle. Wyatt was animated and funny, building his repertoire as entertainer. I took comfort in the family scene, three generations cherishing an unexpected gift of time. The kids needed the attention from my mom and I needed time to begin grieving. My days were sullen and slow. My nights brimmed with tears and dismal glimpses of our future.

From my father I couldn't help but feel that old judgment. To me, my life had looked like the wonderful product of good intentions and educated choices. Since our mutually designed banishment from his home, I had found and achieved a true and free life, full of honest and clear encouragement. I had thrived in my adulthood, chronologically just barely attained. Now I was a homeless, jobless, unemployable widow with two needy kids and a trusty pickup truck. My new situation sounded like a bad country-western song. Knocked off my pedestal of see-I-can-do-it-all-by-myself, the attitude I had left home with was coming back to haunt me. Kenny seemed almost to gloat at my tragedy, but he was damned sure that I wouldn't return to being his burden. He had just gotten his freedom from parenting (he'd been waiting a while) and was clearly not ready or willing to begin again. He was strict with Wyatt, not taking on the father role I'd hoped. Wyatt wanted so badly to be with him, toddling after him everywhere, just the way he'd followed Wilber at Knife Creek. "Kenny, Kenny?" his call echoed through the house. And I heard "Daddy, Daddy?" He was a brave boy.

So when, after just a few weeks, my father cornered me in what they affectionately call the "womb" room, for a "Here's the deal, Nonnie, see…" chat, I was suspicious. The womb room was a cozy den lined with books, electronics, music, television, comfy leather chairs, and just-right lamps. Never having seating for more than two, the womb room excluded anyone unwilling to sit on the floor. He closed both doors, signaling privacy to the household.

"Nonnie, you've been here three weeks," he started, and I knew where he was going. My stomach flipped. "Don't you think it's time to go home to your house in Vancouver and resume your life? You're going to have to do it sooner or later. Don't you think it's time?"

It was time, he claimed, for me to reclaim my life. Nothing to be gained by hanging on here. Of course, I thought, and I saw another mutually designed banishment in the works. I was ready, physically and mentally able. I could function, on the barest of levels. I'd proven I could cook, clean, drive, write letters, and pay bills. But in what condition? I was a robot. Wyatt and Cora were thriving under Noonie's care. Could I alone do that for them? I was terrified. I wasn't ready. My father had twisted and simplified the facts, psychologically badgering me into accepting the consequences of my life before I was prepared. This time I was blinded by grief and struggling to breathe, let alone meet the emotional needs of my two unassuming, loving children. They deserved better.

Did father know best? No, but what was I to do, unwanted and shamed?

CHAPTER THIRTY-TWO

Nov. 26, 1975

Dear Hansi & Fred:

Thank you so much for the books. I've been looking through them and they seem very straightforward and honest. They put a very peaceful tone on death and show a healthy attitude. This is the way I've been dealing with Wyatt. He seems to be adjusting very well, but I'm sure he thinks his daddy is still in Vancouver.

(Emotionally, I do too)

I'll be on my way home soon, to Vancouver, to the beginning of my new life. It'll be a sad life for quite awhile, I'm sure, but it'll get better with time. Joe was up and stayed with us in Driggs for a few days. He is a great, close friend and we shared some happy, beautiful memories of Frankie.

Sunday was a very strange and sad day for me. I can't believe it's been a month (tho' at times it seems like years). I guess I just can't believe it at all. It's so unfair.

I want you both to know that you meant very much to Frankie, he talked about you often with much love and respect. He brought me to love and respect you, also, and of course Wyatt and Cora love you very much. I hope we can continue to be close as it's very important for you, me and the kids. Frankie, may he rest in peace (and I'm sure he is), was a loving father, son and husband, a strong and peaceful man and we love him very much. Even though he's gone, we'll always love him. But he is gone and the most important thing, for him and us, is that we have each other. We must continue on in his love and help each other through these very hard times. Together we must stand.

I hope that you understand that I want to be part of your family (to continue to be). We love you,

Nonnie, Wyatt & Cora

As I drove away from my parents' home that wintry and deeply chilling day, I wept again, now out of fear of the lonely unknown. I needed help, and without close friends in Vancouver, to whom would I turn? I had, since we'd met, relied on Wilber's decision-making, his clarity and knowledge. Now, I could only trust that I'd been a good student and learned honest and loving parenting from him. He had been a strict parent, consistent in his expectations and rewards, the antithesis of my childhood. Could I conquer my own patterns and replace them with his? He had parented Wyatt for three years. I was now responsible for the next fifteen, and I had begun with a lie. I would need to tell Wyatt on the way home that his father was dead, not coming back. The books on death that Hansi sent would help me with the words, but would I know how to handle his emotions? Could I be both mother and father for him, a disciplinarian with a soft shoulder? He needed it and deserved it. All this for a twenty-one-year-old high school dropout. Alone with my thoughts in the truck on that day, I knew I would do it. And I realized: I had already been doing it.

On the long drive home, I decided to give Wyatt the truth that would break my young son's heart. Three-year-olds believe the world revolves around them, that they have super powers. I knew he would think Daddy was gone because he had done something bad. I tried to craft the earth-shattering reality positively, but my own heart struggled to find the silver lining. Gentle words were still painful. "Daddy isn't coming back" made Wyatt squirm and gaze at me in confusion. But death was completely unclear, a concept new to us both. He had no idea what that meant and only time would teach the impact. Our "conversation" was horrible and incomplete. We both felt worse, obviously, and resumed our focus on getting home. I'm sure we both hoped that being where we'd last seen him would bring Daddy closer... and maybe alive.

Arriving back at Melfa Court was another reality altogether. The condo was cold and empty in a scary way. I worked to settle us back in, to warm the chill and resume comforting routines. Wyatt went back to school. His teachers worried as he told anyone who would listen, "So, my dad's dead, did ya know? Yup, it's true." His boyish bravado filled his unprepared emotions. How could he process this? He and Wilber had been inseparable since Cora's birth. His allegiance went naturally and easily to his dad, while my arms were filled with a soft and fragile baby. Who was he supposed to shadow now? In his candid and casual comments to classmates and teachers, he was seeking the answer.

As expected, the Vancouver winter set in with a relentless wind and rain. The neighbors were cautiously friendly. Emma and Todd were the first ones at our door, bringing food and cheer while others filtered by, not knowing what to do. They bore food and were always welcome, their company a gift. Emma and Katie (her husband Eric was in the M.D. program) sometimes stopped for coffee or tea, the great Canadian pastime. The warmth of mother-talk and a cup o' tea made my life bearable. The arms of my kids, ever searching love, wrapped me in a belonging I sought, and their needs dragged me out of bed, and my stupor, every morning.

Christmas was soon upon us, a welcome distraction. It had been in the stores since my return, but I was slow to bring it home. Memories of the last Christmas, Wilber's first, homegrown in our cabin, smoldered in my heart. This season could not be jolly, or bright. Wyatt brought home ideas from his classmates, toys that were a must. Every day a new idea for a game or toy, each grander than the last. I went shopping, careful not to go overboard with my pension money or my wish to make him happy. Blocks, cars, and a train set topped the list. Packages and cards arrived from far and wide. We were deluged with love. We got a tree and decorated it with bright cards and construction paper ornaments. Wyatt and I strung popcorn and cranberries, made cookies, and did our best to celebrate.

Dec. 18, 1975

Dear Fred and Hansi;

> *It was nice talking to you last night. After you called, I called my folks and Betsy called me, so it was a busy night on my phone.*
>
> *I have been trying to keep busy doing errands and making Christmas presents. My days are usually fairly scattered, with kids running in and out, and Wyatt and Cora demanding so much of my time. But my evenings are quite miserable, after the kids are in bed and I sit by myself and think about Frankie. I can't say that I've come to grips with the idea yet, nor will I for quite some time.*
>
> *I miss him on a day-to-day basis, someone to help & enjoy our kids, to give me a smile, encouragement and warm words,*

just to be with. And I miss him when I think towards my future (our future). Can I go on without his silly, warm joking or his cynical seriousness? When I see a beautiful sunset or a silly grin on Cora's face, I feel really sad that Frankie is missing it. What can I say? These thoughts rush through my mind all day long. I keep expecting him to walk in the door.

All this sorrow is something that only time can take away. I just have to wait long enough that I'm finally used to the idea.

Hoping you have an enjoyable holiday in Sun City.

We love you,

the younger Neumanns

On Christmas Eve, anticipating the crushing loneliness, I invited all the families of our quad to our house for a little cheer. I had never had a cocktail party, but I remembered the way my childhood neighborhood would celebrate the excitement of the coming of Santa and Christmas Eve. Dressing up, sharing yummy treats, and toasting the season might bring joy to our lives, if only for an hour or so. I made special cookies for the kids: gingerbread, wedding cakes, and lace. For the parents, I put out crackers and cheese, some grapes, and bottles of wine, red and white. I bought little napkins with holly and berries, like my mom might have, and dressed up my Sears platter with greens from the trees dripping outside. We sang a few carols. The kids danced and reeled. The party was a jolly success. My new friends were amazed that I had pulled it off, that I had had the energy to undertake such a feat. What they didn't know, but may have sensed, was that I had been driven by a selfish desire to make Wyatt and me feel loved and our spirits lifted, on that Christmas night especially. As they filed out, the kids tired early and Santa's work still ahead for the parents, I thanked each one profusely for coming and bringing joy to our home. Their glowing faces disappeared into the night.

The kids went neatly to bed, and I set about doing my Santa thing. Wyatt's train had to be constructed. Noonie-made stockings, this year a new one for Cora, had to be filled. I plopped down by the tree and gazed at my challenges. Facing the simple but significant tasks, the extreme aloneness overwhelmed me. For the first time, but not the last, I recalled the movie *Carousel* and the death of the young, handsome, and swashbuckling husband. His ability to watch over the doings of his wife and lovely daughter had always intrigued me, but as a non-believer in heaven, I had dismissed it as a sweet story. Now, seated on the floor amid my children's future, I imagined Wilber watching me, encouraging me, pushing me forward, reaching out to the children and witnessing our lives forever. I cried again, for the events, everyday and significant, that Wilber might watch while being unable to touch, smell, or feel us, to show us his love and care. He would be unable to participate in any of it, truly share it, but I would always remember that he was a spectator of our lives, and that would give me some comfort. When the kids were old enough, I would share that with them and they would be comforted.

A knock at the door woke me from my lamentations. Maybe one of the partiers had forgotten something? But when I opened the door and found Todd holding out a bottle of wine and a big warm smile, I knew I had been rescued.

"You need help with that train set?" he said as he moved into the living room. I looked up. Wilber had had a hand in this. Todd was gracious, bringing a familiar humor and parental condition to our tragedy. We laughed at ourselves as we attempted the complicated train construction, drinking his bottle of wine and relaxing into the work. When we were finished, and it was suitably late, I thanked him with words insufficient for his time, wine, and friendship, and I thanked Emma for her generosity at sending him over on this special family night. He said his good-byes and let himself out.

I sat in the glow of human kindness, sustaining spirits, and the power of good intentions. Holding a bit of holiday sparkle, I summoned my pioneer spirit and faced my new quest and horizon.

About two months after I returned to Melfa Court, sometime

after my twenty-second birthday, my doorbell rang in the middle of the day, in the middle of the week. I opened the door to find Heather. Heather lived next door, in the adjoining unit, with her husband, Mike, and their daughters, Tracy and Tina—older and younger than Wyatt, and thus not playmates. I knew little of them, actually, and hadn't seen and talked to them since the Christmas Eve party. They were young, and they were big consumers, always hauling in the newest TV, stereo, or toy. I wasn't naturally drawn to them.

Heather was fidgety. "I need to talk to you. Have you got a minute?" Cora was napping. The house was quiet.

"Sure, come on in," I said. "I'll put the kettle on."

"No," she countered, "I need you to come to my house."

"Okay," I said, grabbing my keys. Cora would be fine with me right next door, and now I was getting curious. I followed her into her living room, where she directed me to sit on the overstuffed velour club chair. She perched on the matching sofa, noticeably nervous. I was beginning to worry. What could she possibly have to tell me? I hardly knew the woman.

She turned ashen white, shaking visibly as she began to speak in a voice that was almost trancelike, steady and monotone.

"When I was in high school, my best friend, Cindy, and her boyfriend, Jake, were killed in a car crash. They were the golden couple. It was terrible and shook the whole community. The police report said that he'd been drinking, veered off the road and killed them. The community embraced the story and got angry with him.

"About two days after the funeral, I was alone in my room when my friend Jake appeared at my window. I screamed and closed the curtain. I told myself it must have been a shadow, passing car lights, something. But the next night he appeared again. I saw pleading in his eyes, but I closed the curtain and tried to forget it. This went on every night for a week.

"'What the hell do you want from me?' I finally screamed at the vision, the ghost. I was being haunted and I'd just had enough.

"'Please,' Jake begged, 'please I have to tell you.' That freaked me out and I closed the curtains again."

Her voice was becoming more and more agitated. She went on, running it all together like a paper chain.

"But the visions continued for another week, until finally, I screamed in frustration, 'What is so important?'

"'Please, Heather,' he began, 'you have to tell my family that I was not drunk driving the car that killed Cindy. You have to tell them that a deer jumped in front of us and I swerved to avoid it, crashing into that tree. Please, you have to clear my name, and Cindy's reputation.'"

This was freaking me out. Why was Heather telling me this bizarre story?

"Now, you might not believe this either, but just wait. When you all were away for your husband's funeral... What was his name? Wilber?" I nodded, and trembled. "Anyway, it was about a week after you left, and I was putting Tracy and Tina to bed. You know they sleep in this front bedroom, with the floor-to-ceiling windows in the corner. So, I'm in the room and out of the corner of my eye I see something, I turn around and there's Wilber! Just floating in the window!"

I felt faint, my knees tingled and my brain spun. I tried to focus. I didn't want to miss a word.

"It'd been six years since the thing with Jake and I'd all but forgotten. Anyway, I couldn't believe it was happening again. No way! So I closed the curtain."

No, I thought. NO. Don't close the curtain!

"Next night, same thing. But I knew this routine, knew that I'd never have peace until I let this spirit speak his mind. Obviously he had unfinished business, dying so suddenly like he did. So, I said, 'Okay, what do you want to say?' and here's what he said, just real calm and sure:

"Please tell Poms that I love her, and I love the kids. Tell her to take good care of Wydie and Cora-Mora. They are precious to me. Tell her to make sure she goes to college, and has a good life. And please, tell her

I'm so, so sorry. Please just tell her.'

"That was all he said," she finished, still shaking. "Are you Poms?"

EPILOGUE

Rivulets of golden aspens flowed toward the valley floor, studded with vermilion willows, rustled by the chilling breath of fall in the Northern Rockies. It was the last brilliant hurrah before a harsh white blanketed the scene. From the Montana State University campus, the view of Gallatin Valley ringed with mountains was a comfort, a reminder of why I had settled my heartbroken family in Bozeman. Following Wilber's missives, I had searched for a college town, small enough to be country, large enough to offer variety. A dozen universities from Vancouver to Seattle to Eugene to Pullman to Missoula had been visited and vetted. Then, Bozeman and MSU stole my heart in a flash.

In 1978, the classic community of Gallatin Valley fit our family to a tee. Doors were unlocked, backyards were communal, struggles were shared, and children ruled the 'hood. We loved it. It was just what we needed to rebuild our lives and restore our hearts in safety. I knew that Wilber approved; I believed he had found it for us. After Cora's tranquil homebirth, I'd had a strong desire to train as a midwife, to provide a natural homebirth option to other mothers. Wilber knew and encouraged my goal. Midwife school was the sensible, and legal, route and nursing was the beginning. MSU offered the science and pre-med I needed. Between turn-of-the-century brick edifices, I peddled to class from our sweet Victorian cottage. Wyatt walked to the nearby kindergarten and Cora to neighbor/daycare while I pursued my degree part-time. With our new friends, we skied, hiked, camped, road-tripped, and generally explored our expansive region. In parks and forests, rivers and lakes, with tennis, rafting, swimming, soccer, dance, we were three kids on a lark.

When the crisp days and frosty nights heralded a Halloween spectacle, Superheroes and princesses, donned jackets and boots over capes and gowns. Wyatt and Cora bundled in insulated, handmade Batman and Robin costumes. They had practiced and delighted in dastardly deeds, little Cora yelling, "Holy Halloween Shenanigans, Batman!!" After a costume parade around school, they joined our neighborhood gang of little rascals to trick or treat. I followed, with other parents, giggling in surprise and relishing our kids' illusion of independence. At that moment, the sense of belonging filled our imbalanced spirits and we were glad for it. We needed it.

It was clear that our journey to healing was beginning, and would continue forever. Our path was of our making. Our hearts were seeking. And our love propelled us. With our spirit guide to inspire and protect us, we found life's gifts in mysterious places. Ultimately, we built on Wilber's compassionate strength, and flourished as he had hoped.

CPSIA information can be obtained
at www.ICGtesting.com
Printed in the USA
LVHW08s1611170718
584050LV00001BA/186/P

9 780996 676557